THE Eminence IN Shadow

7

Art **Anri Sakano**
Original Story **Daisuke Aizawa**
Character Design **Touzai**

The Story So Far

Cid doesn't want to be the protagonist or the final boss—he wants to be an "eminence in shadow" manipulating things from behind the scenes. As he reincarnates into another world and enrolls in the Midgar Academy for Dark Knights, he begins stealthily (?) acting out a made-up scenario in which he, as the puppet mastermind Shadow, starts a secret society called the Shadow Garden whose mission is to wipe out an evil cult. But what he doesn't realize is... the wicked Cult of Diablos actually exists!

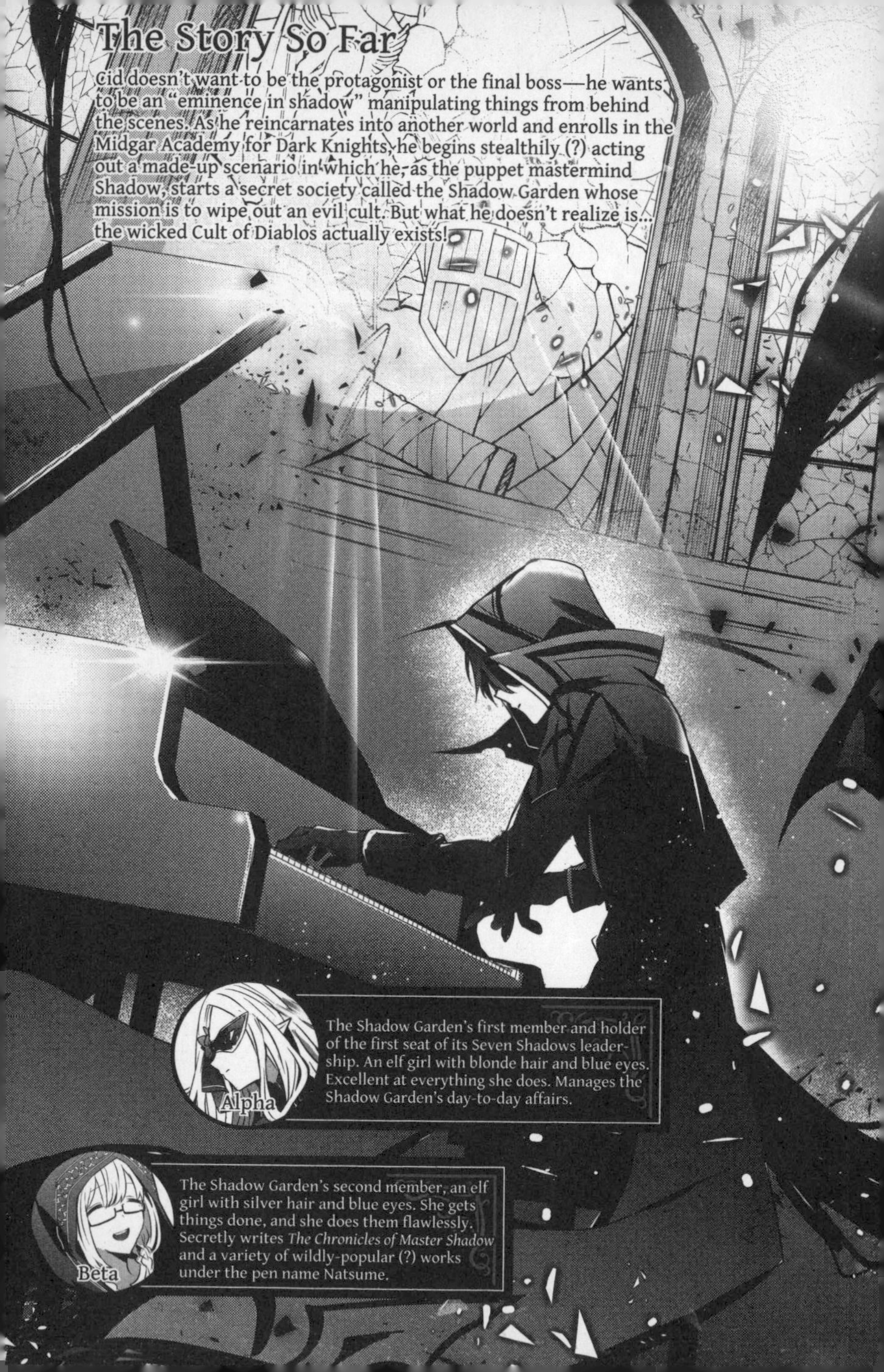

Alpha

The Shadow Garden's first member and holder of the first seat of its Seven Shadows leadership. An elf girl with blonde hair and blue eyes. Excellent at everything she does. Manages the Shadow Garden's day-to-day affairs.

Beta

The Shadow Garden's second member, an elf girl with silver hair and blue eyes. She gets things done, and she does them flawlessly. Secretly writes *The Chronicles of Master Shadow* and a variety of wildly-popular (?) works under the pen name Natsume.

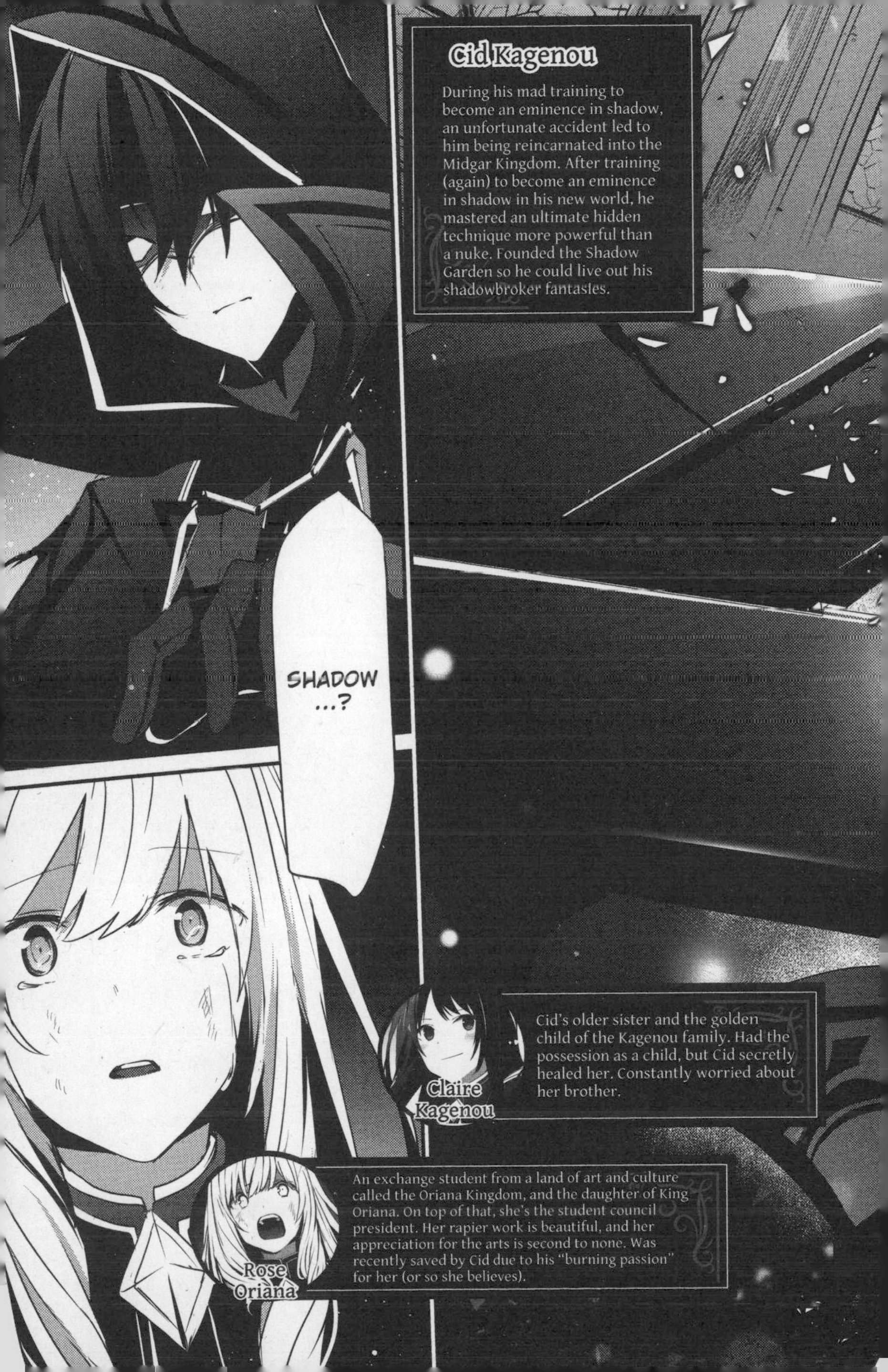
Cid Kagenou
During his mad training to become an eminence in shadow, an unfortunate accident led to him being reincarnated into the Midgar Kingdom. After training (again) to become an eminence in shadow in his new world, he mastered an ultimate hidden technique more powerful than a nuke. Founded the Shadow Garden so he could live out his shadowbroker fantasies.
SHADOW ...?
Claire Kagenou
Cid's older sister and the golden child of the Kagenou family. Had the possession as a child, but Cid secretly healed her. Constantly worried about her brother.
Rose Oriana
An exchange student from a land of art and culture called the Oriana Kingdom, and the daughter of King Oriana. On top of that, she's the student council president. Her rapier work is beautiful, and her appreciation for the arts is second to none. Was recently saved by Cid due to his "burning passion" for her (or so she believes).

[CONTENTS]

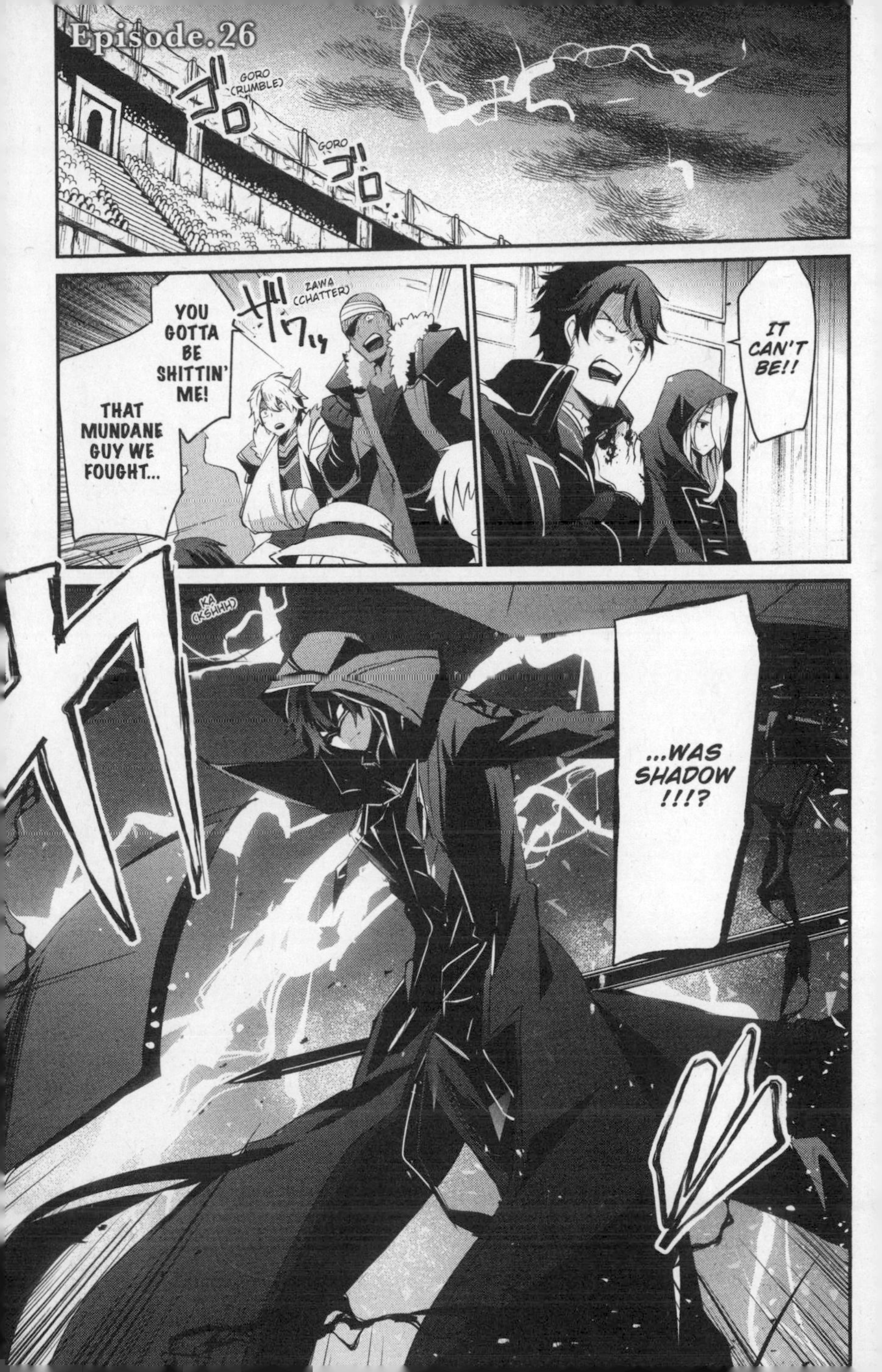
Episode.26
GORO (RUMBLE)
GORO
IT CAN'T BE!!
ZAWA (CHATTER)
YOU GOTTA BE SHITTIN' ME!
THAT MUNDANE GUY WE FOUGHT...
...WAS SHADOW!!!?
KA (KSHHH)

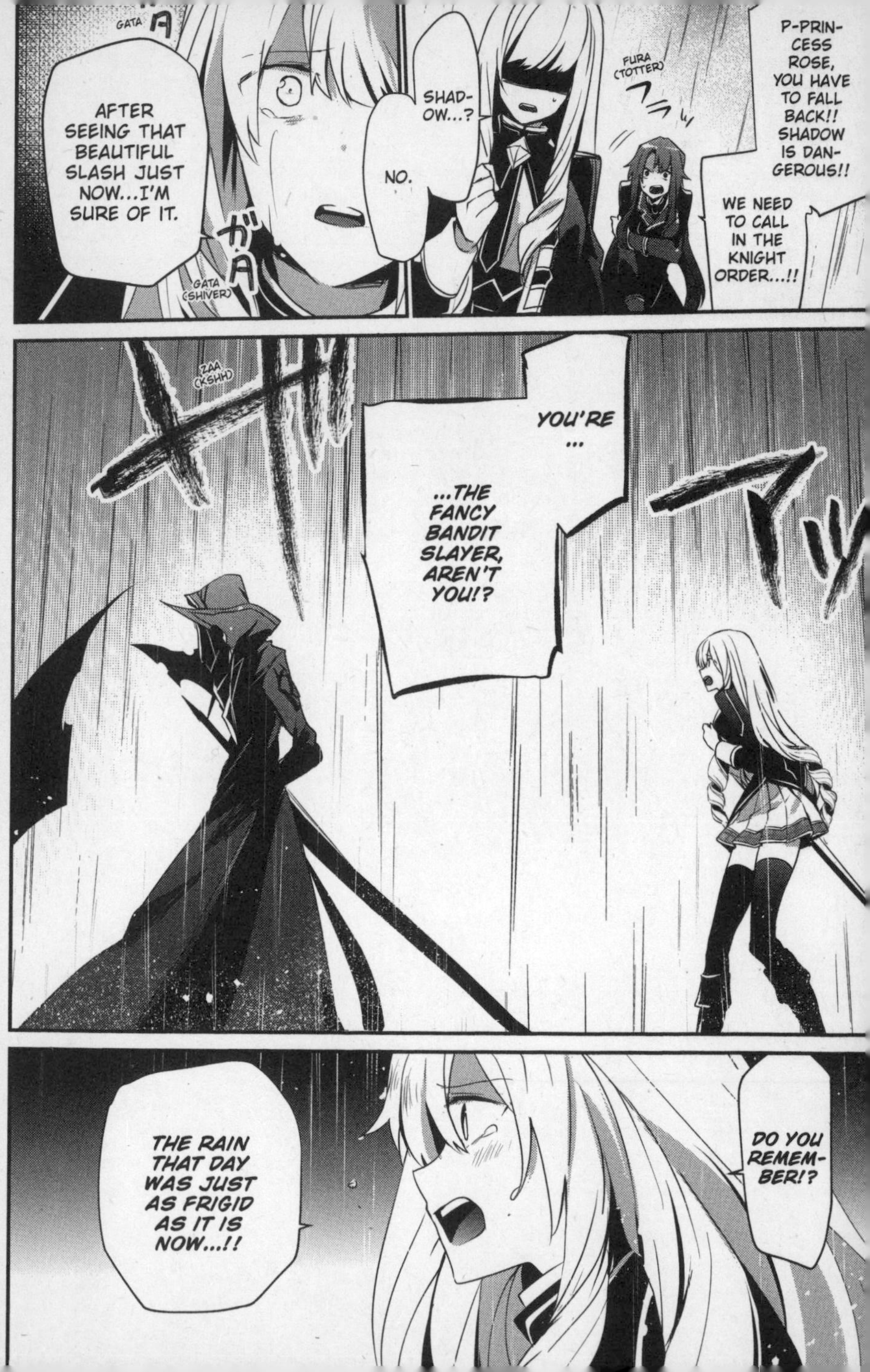
P-PRINCESS ROSE, YOU HAVE TO FALL BACK!! SHADOW IS DANGEROUS!!
WE NEED TO CALL IN THE KNIGHT ORDER...!!
FURA (TOTTER)
SHADOW...?
NO.
GATA
AFTER SEEING THAT BEAUTIFUL SLASH JUST NOW...I'M SURE OF IT.
GATA (SHIVER)
YOU'RE ...
...THE FANCY BANDIT SLAYER, AREN'T YOU!?
ZAA (KSHH)
DO YOU REMEMBER!?
THE RAIN THAT DAY WAS JUST AS FRIGID AS IT IS NOW...!!

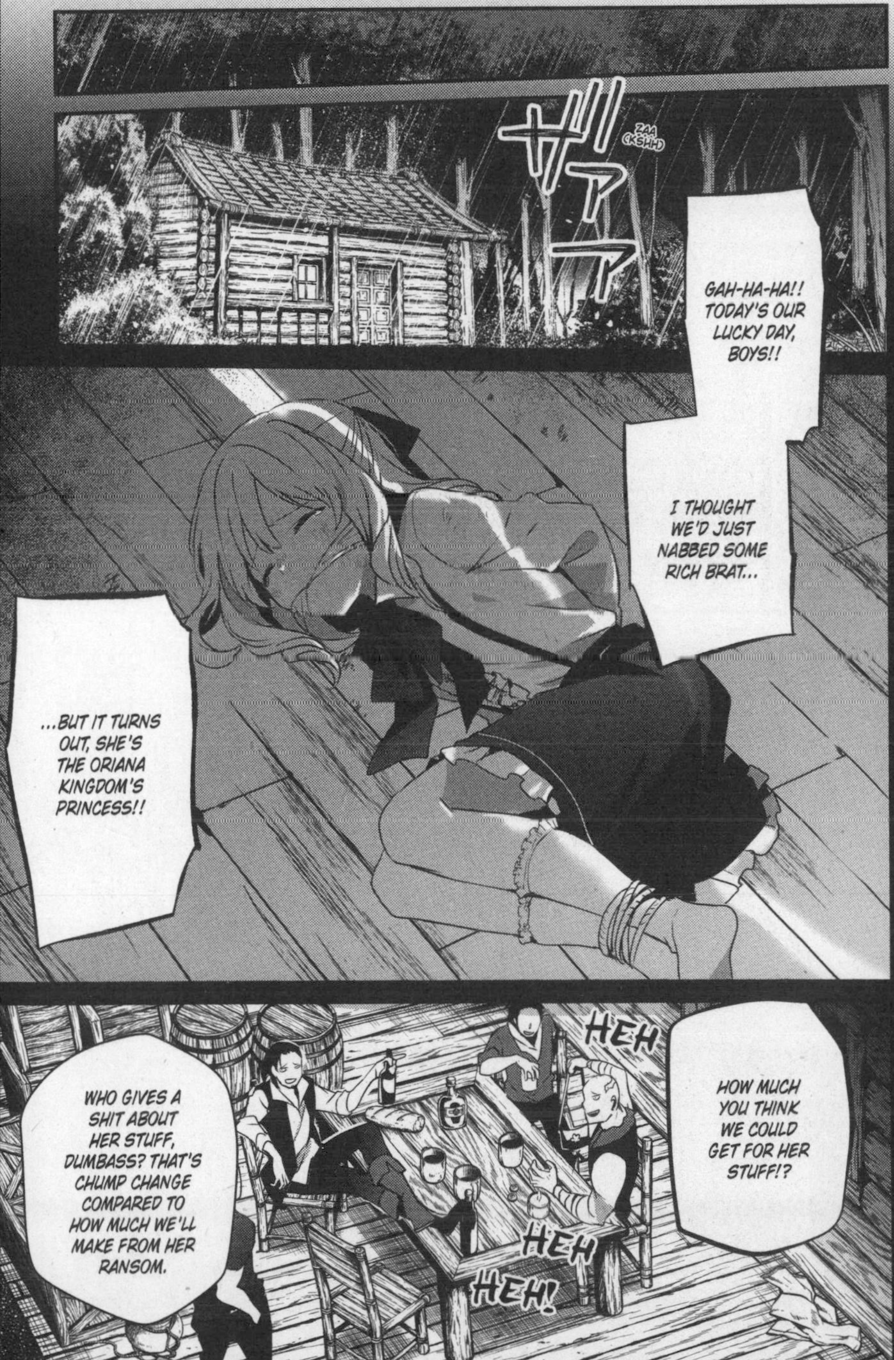
ザァ
ZAA (KSHH)
GAH-HA-HA!! TODAY'S OUR LUCKY DAY, BOYS!!
I THOUGHT WE'D JUST NABBED SOME RICH BRAT...
...BUT IT TURNS OUT, SHE'S THE ORIANA KINGDOM'S PRINCESS!!
HEH
HOW MUCH YOU THINK WE COULD GET FOR HER STUFF!?
WHO GIVES A SHIT ABOUT HER STUFF, DUMBASS? THAT'S CHUMP CHANGE COMPARED TO HOW MUCH WE'LL MAKE FROM HER RANSOM.
HEH
HEH!

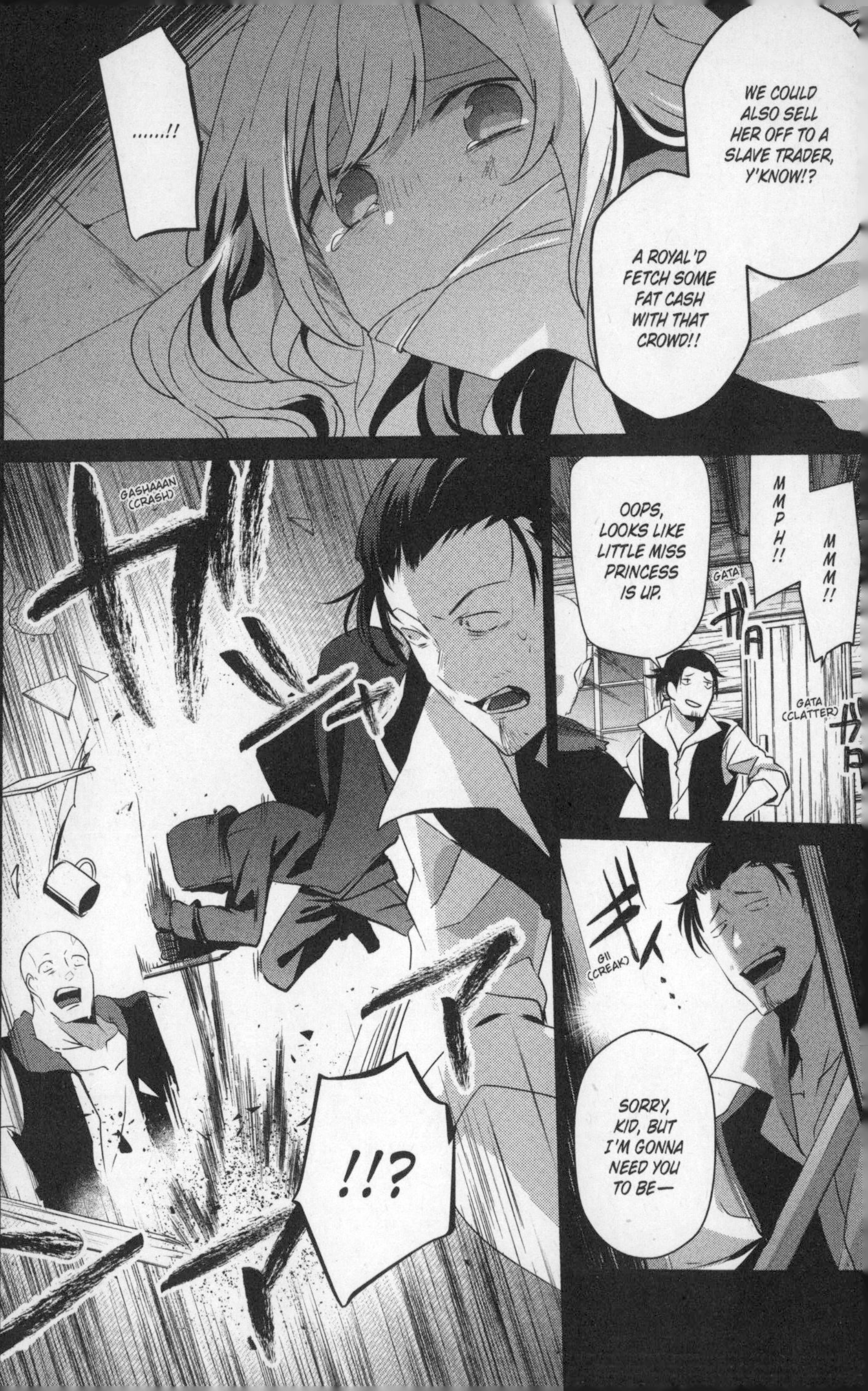
WE COULD ALSO SELL HER OFF TO A SLAVE TRADER, Y'KNOW!?
A ROYAL'D FETCH SOME FAT CASH WITH THAT CROWD!!
......!!
MMM!!
MMPH!!
OOPS, LOOKS LIKE LITTLE MISS PRINCESS IS UP.
GATA
GATA (CLATTER)
GII (CREAK)
SORRY, KID, BUT I'M GONNA NEED YOU TO BE—
GASHAAAN (CRASH)
!!?

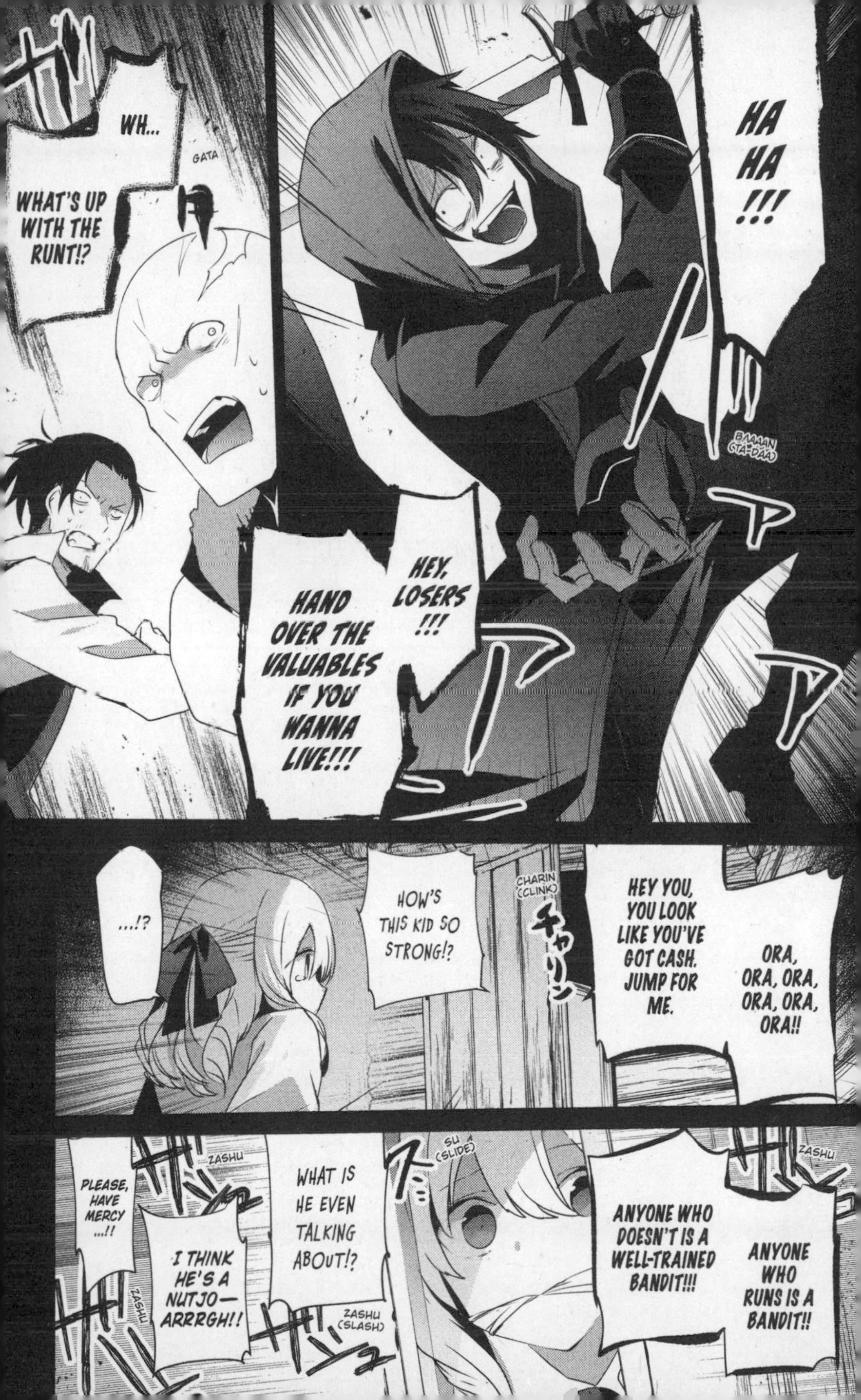
HA HA!!!
BAAAAN (TA-DAA)
HEY, LOSERS!!!
HAND OVER THE VALUABLES IF YOU WANNA LIVE!!!
WH...
GATA
WHAT'S UP WITH THE RUNT!?
ORA, ORA, ORA, ORA, ORA, ORA!!
HEY YOU, YOU LOOK LIKE YOU'VE GOT CASH. JUMP FOR ME.
CHARIN (CLINK)
チャリン
HOW'S THIS KID SO STRONG!?
...!?
ZASHU
ANYONE WHO RUNS IS A BANDIT!!
ANYONE WHO DOESN'T IS A WELL-TRAINED BANDIT!!!
SU (SLIDE)
WHAT IS HE EVEN TALKING ABOUT!?
ZASHU (SLASH)
ZASHU
PLEASE, HAVE MERCY...!!
I THINK HE'S A NUTJO—ARRRGH!!
ZASHU

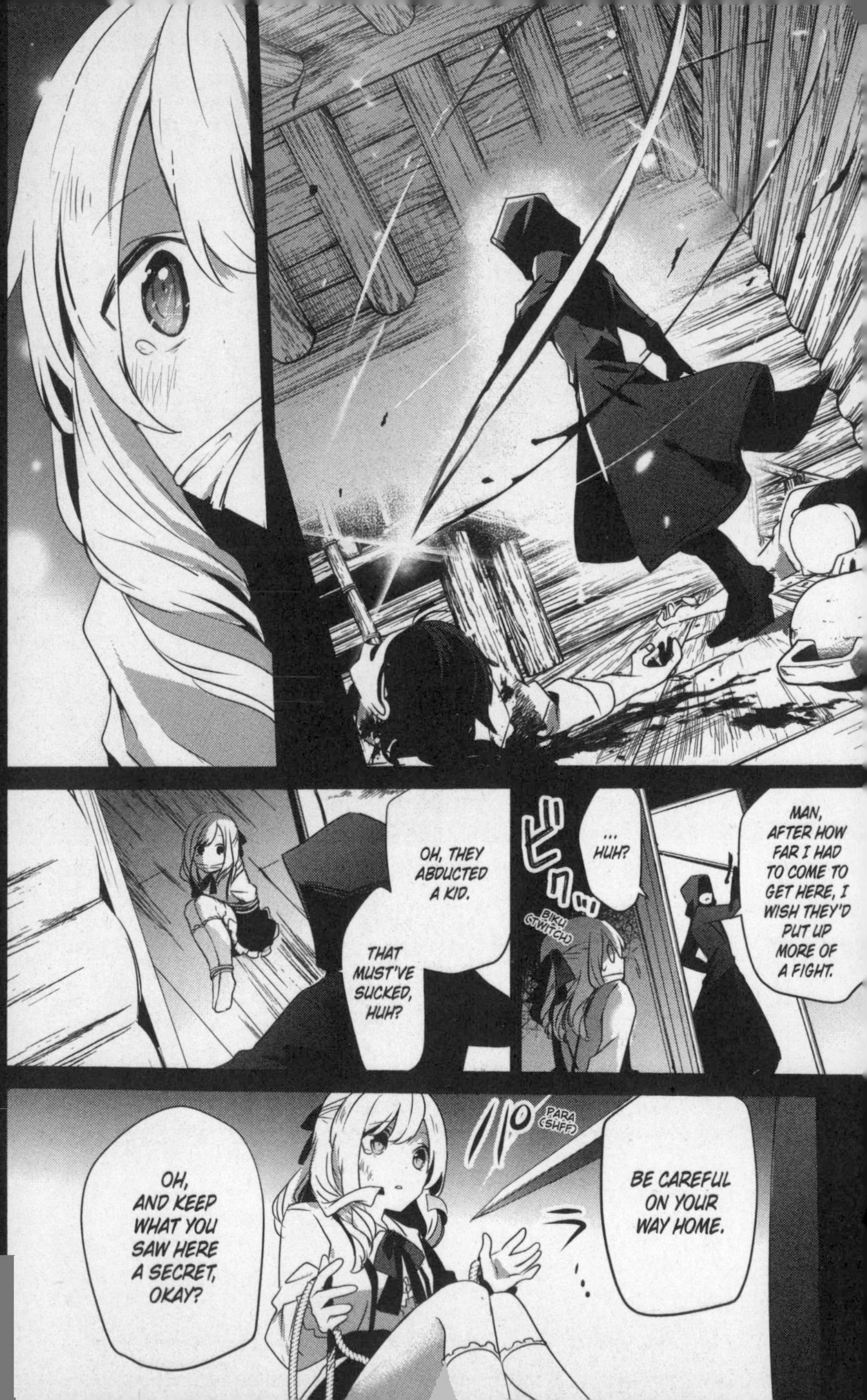
MAN, AFTER HOW FAR I HAD TO COME TO GET HERE, I WISH THEY'D PUT UP MORE OF A FIGHT.
... HUH?
BIKU (TWITCH)
OH, THEY ABDUCTED A KID.
THAT MUST'VE SUCKED, HUH?
PARA (SHFF)
BE CAREFUL ON YOUR WAY HOME.
OH, AND KEEP WHAT YOU SAW HERE A SECRET, OKAY?

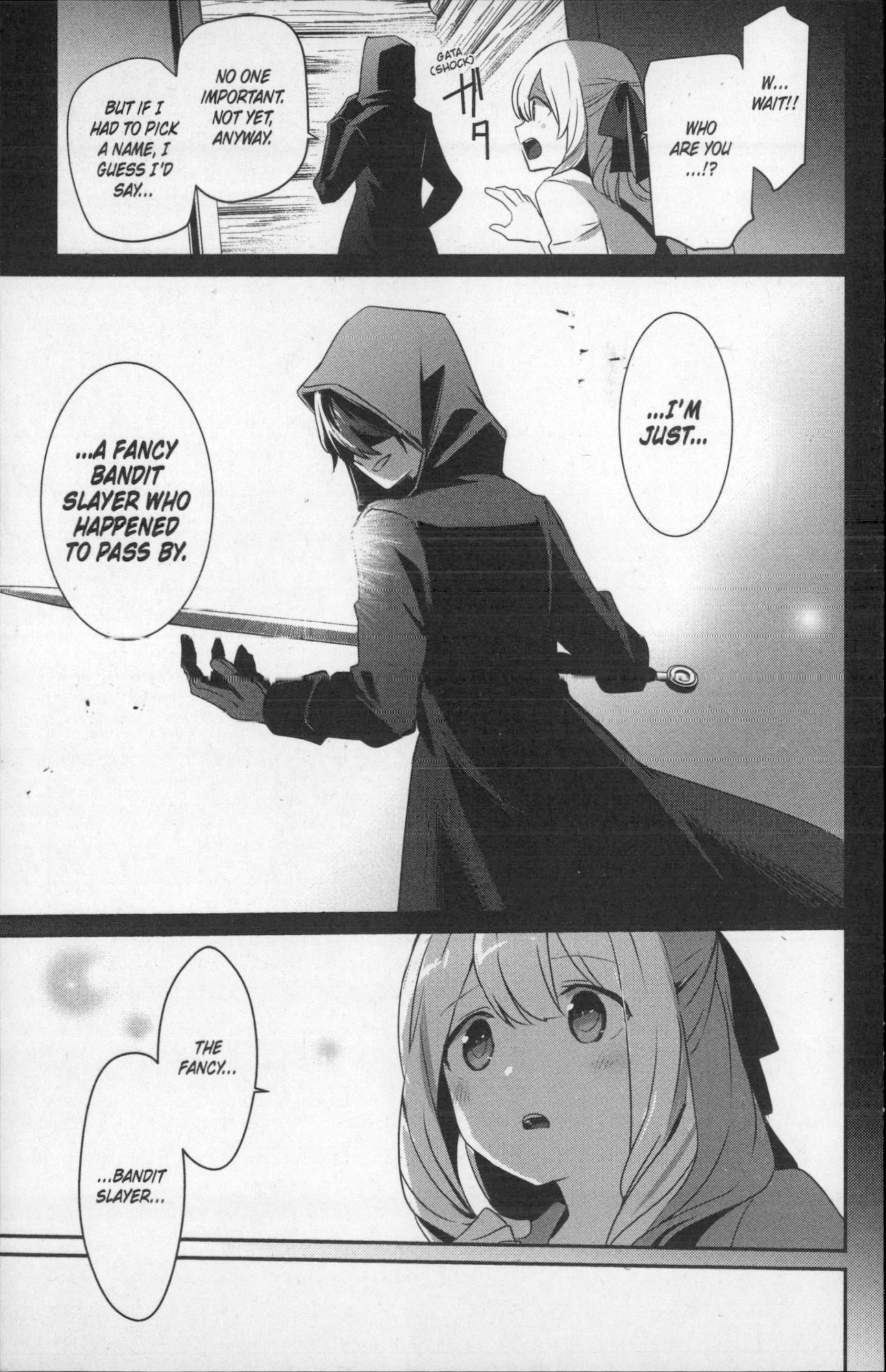
W... WAIT!!
WHO ARE YOU ...!?
GATA (SHOCK)
NO ONE IMPORTANT. NOT YET, ANYWAY.
BUT IF I HAD TO PICK A NAME, I GUESS I'D SAY...
...I'M JUST...
...A FANCY BANDIT SLAYER WHO HAPPENED TO PASS BY.
THE FANCY...
...BANDIT SLAYER...

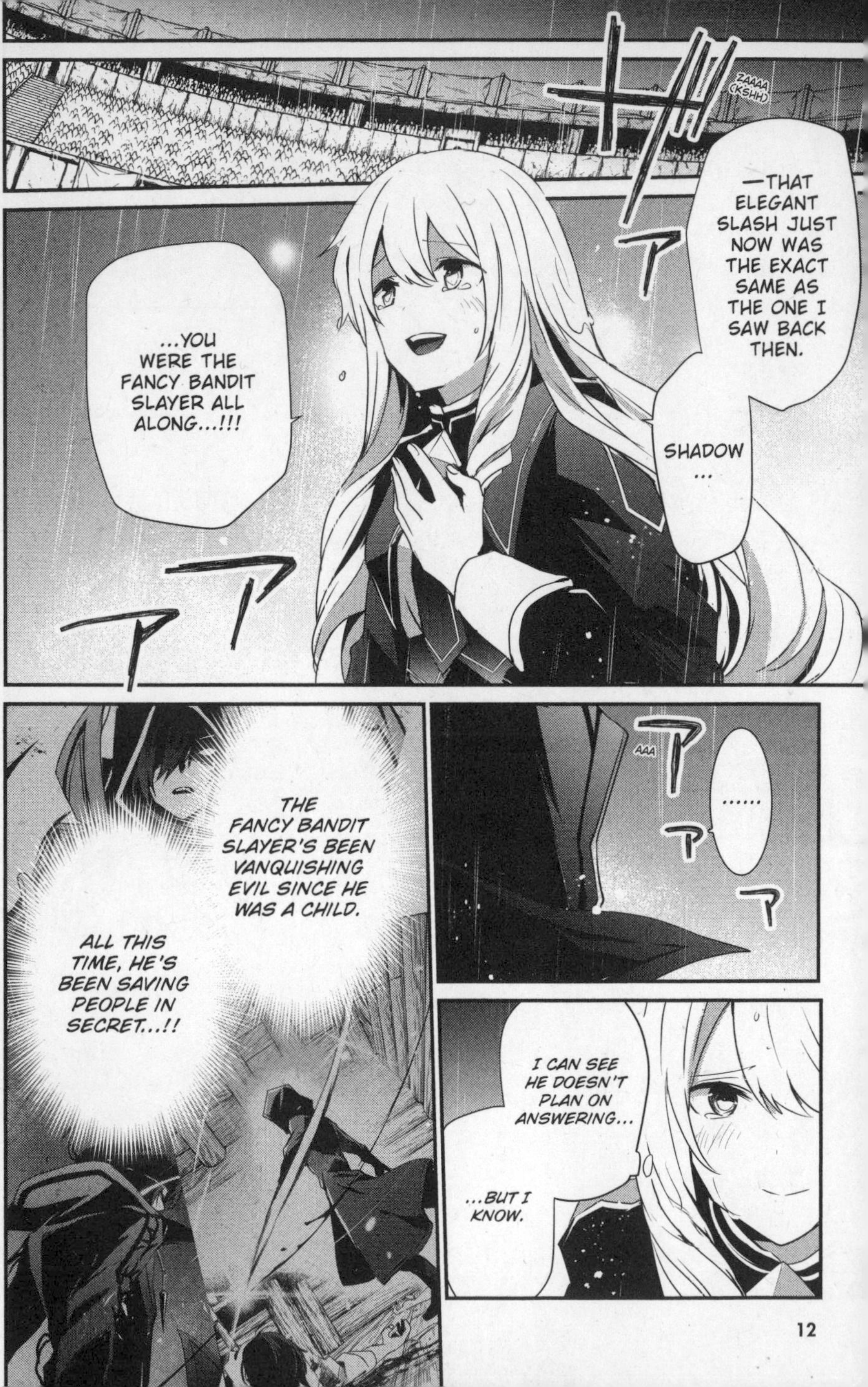
ZAAAA (KSHH)
—THAT ELEGANT SLASH JUST NOW WAS THE EXACT SAME AS THE ONE I SAW BACK THEN.
SHADOW...
...YOU WERE THE FANCY BANDIT SLAYER ALL ALONG...!!!
AAA
......
I CAN SEE HE DOESN'T PLAN ON ANSWERING...
...BUT I KNOW.
THE FANCY BANDIT SLAYER'S BEEN VANQUISHING EVIL SINCE HE WAS A CHILD.
ALL THIS TIME, HE'S BEEN SAVING PEOPLE IN SECRET...!!

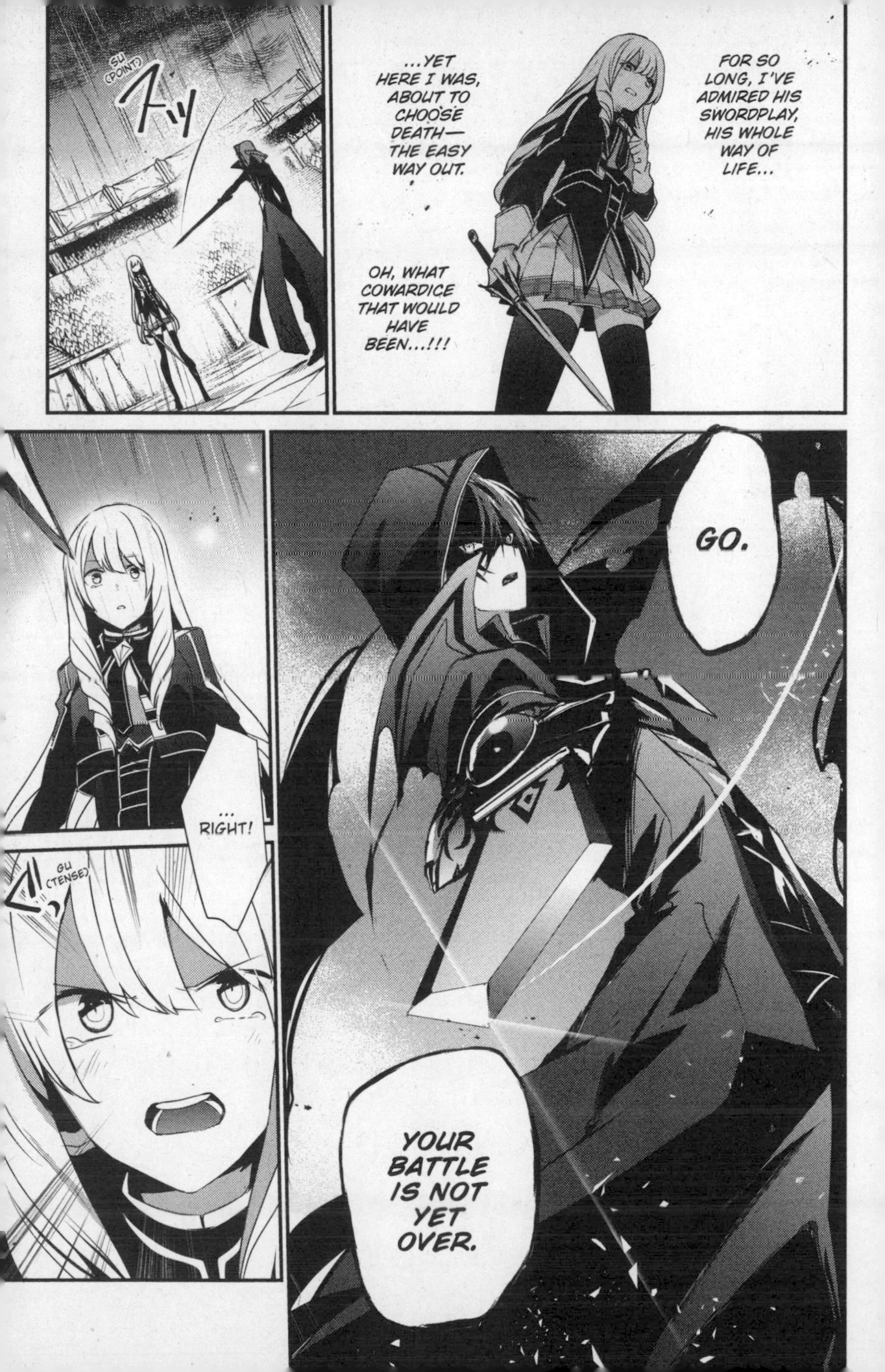

FOR SO LONG, I'VE ADMIRED HIS SWORDPLAY, HIS WHOLE WAY OF LIFE...
...YET HERE I WAS, ABOUT TO CHOOSE DEATH—THE EASY WAY OUT.
OH, WHAT COWARDICE THAT WOULD HAVE BEEN...!!!
SU (POINT)
スッ
GO.
YOUR BATTLE IS NOT YET OVER.
...RIGHT!
GU (TENSE)

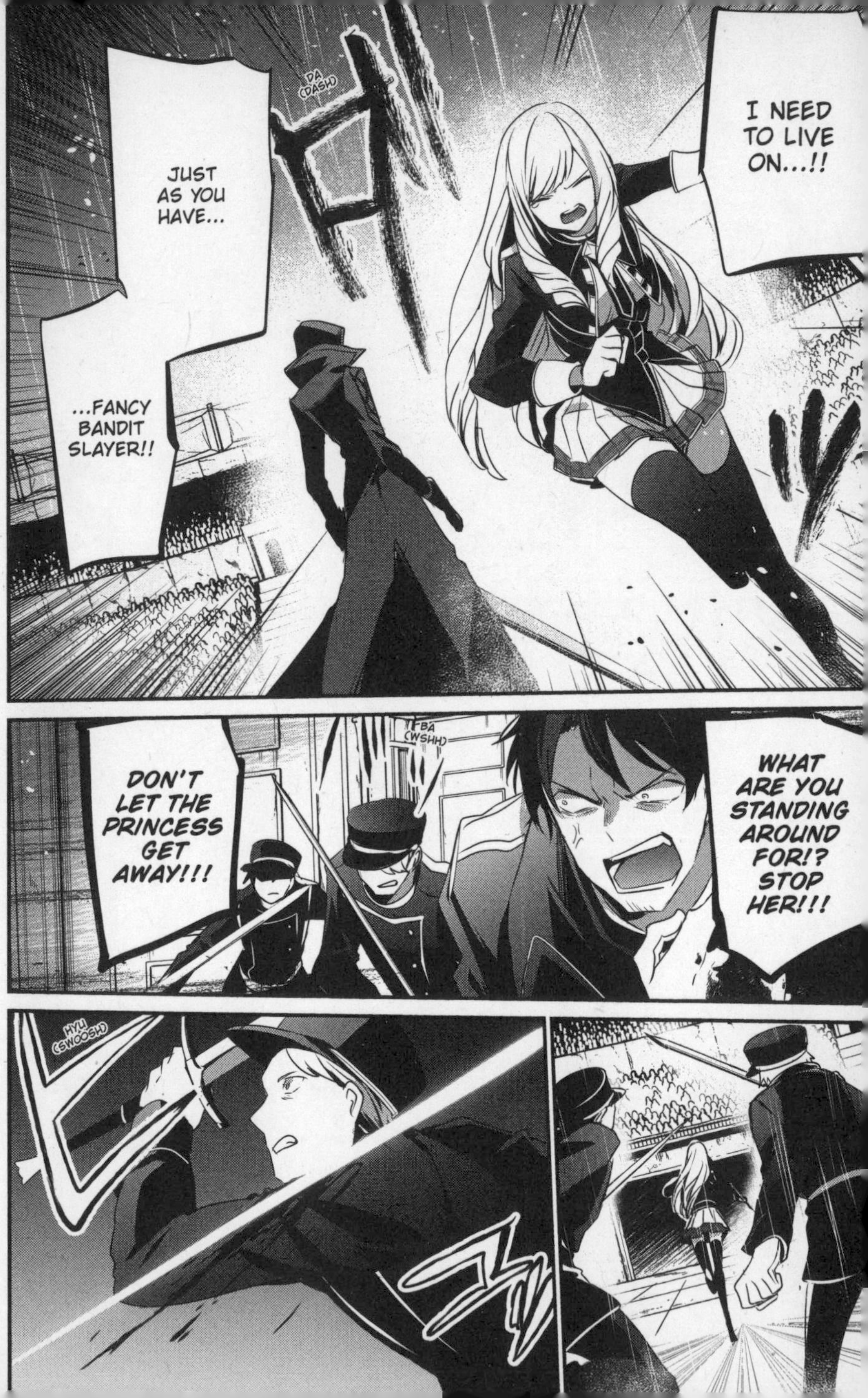
I NEED TO LIVE ON...!!
DA (DASH)
JUST AS YOU HAVE...
...FANCY BANDIT SLAYER!!
WHAT ARE YOU STANDING AROUND FOR!? STOP HER!!!
BA (WSHH)
DON'T LET THE PRINCESS GET AWAY!!!
HYU (SWOOSH)

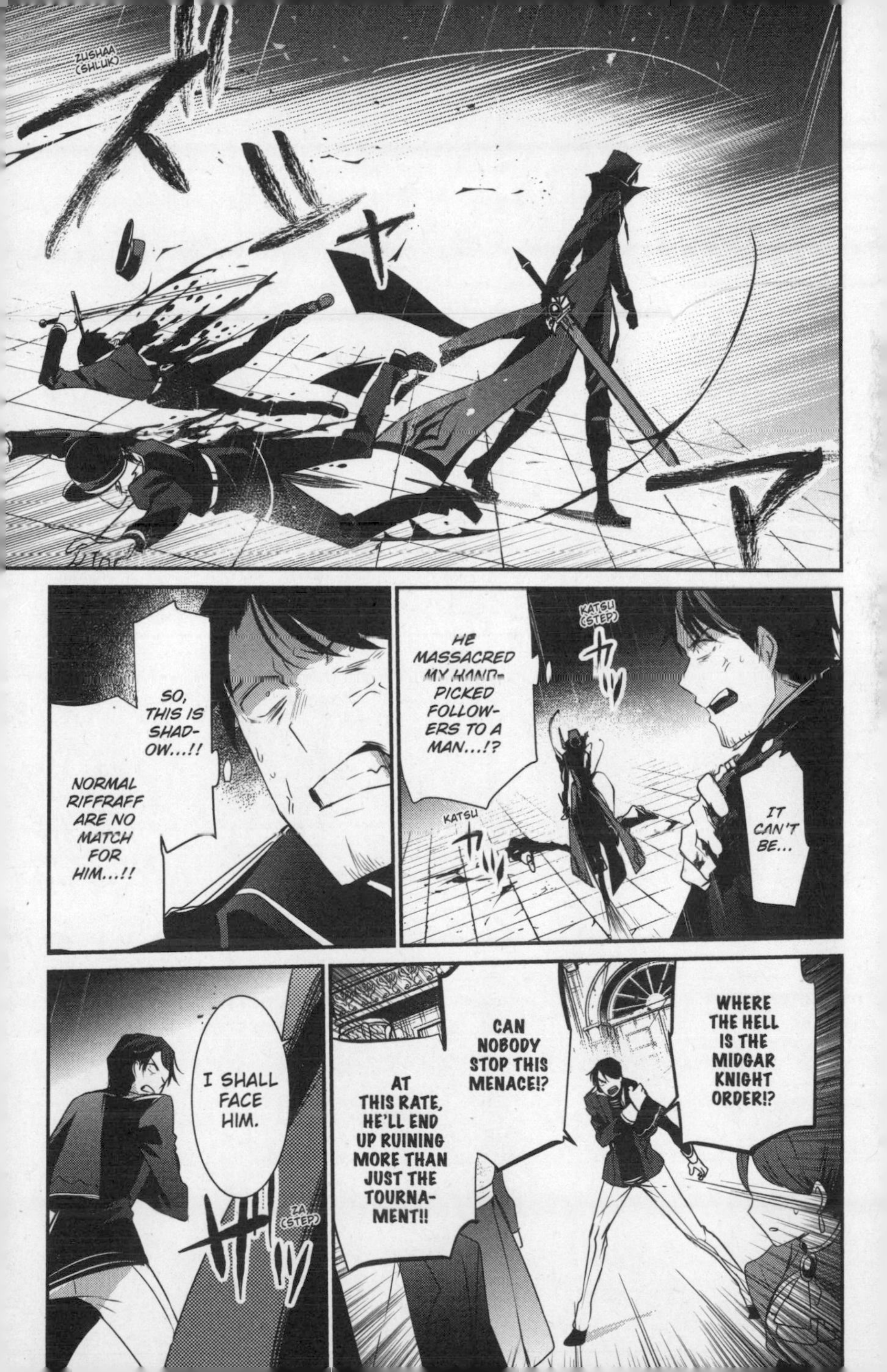
ZUSHAA (SHLUK)
KATSU (STEP)
HE MASSACRED MY HAND-PICKED FOLLOWERS TO A MAN...!?
KATSU
IT CAN'T BE...
SO, THIS IS SHADOW...!!
NORMAL RIFFRAFF ARE NO MATCH FOR HIM...!!
WHERE THE HELL IS THE MIDGAR KNIGHT ORDER!?
CAN NOBODY STOP THIS MENACE!?
AT THIS RATE, HE'LL END UP RUINING MORE THAN JUST THE TOURNAMENT!!
ZA (STEP)
I SHALL FACE HIM.

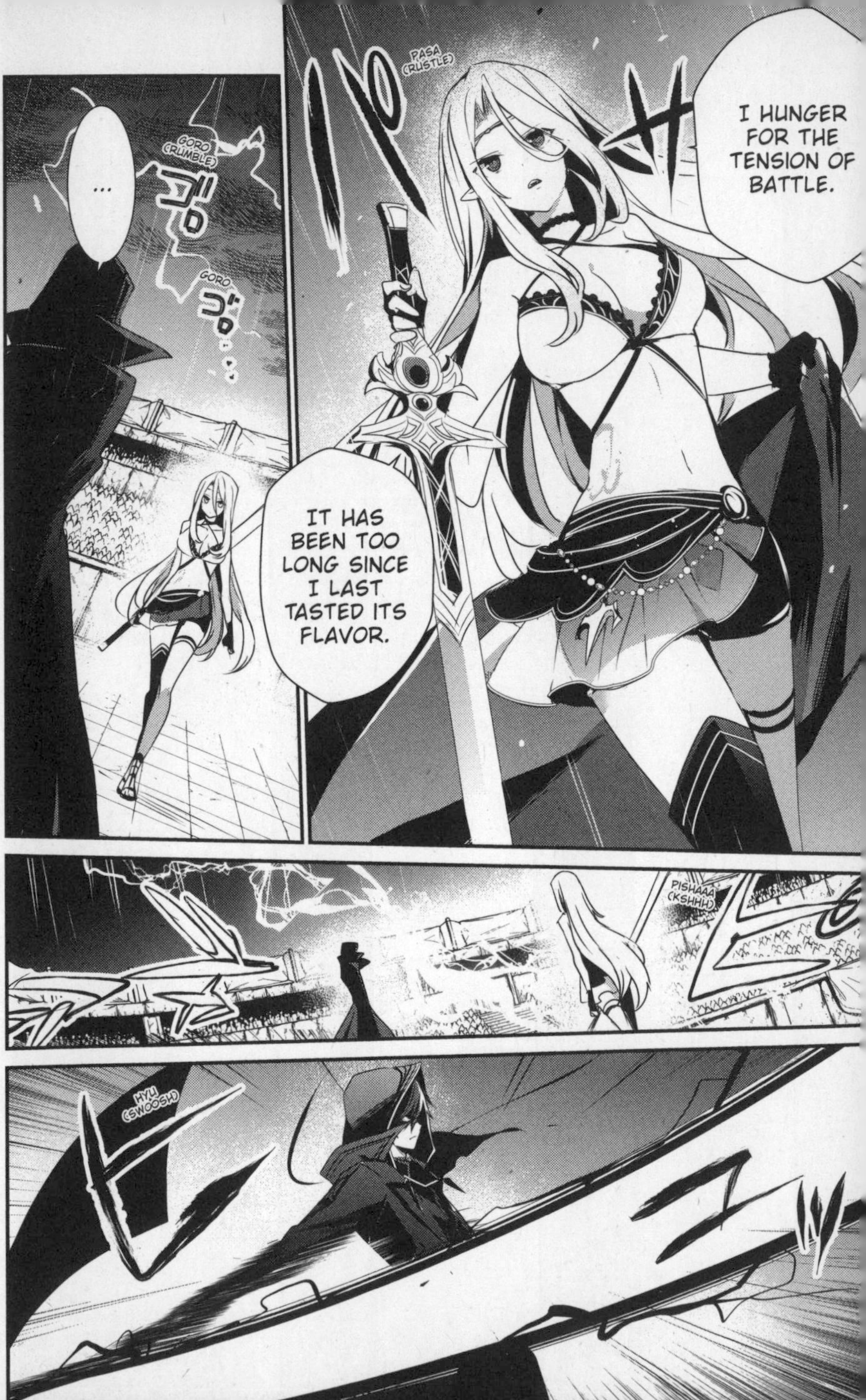
PASA (RUSTLE)
I HUNGER FOR THE TENSION OF BATTLE.
IT HAS BEEN TOO LONG SINCE I LAST TASTED ITS FLAVOR.
GORO (RUMBLE)
GORO
...
PISHAAA (KSHHH)
HYU (SWOOSH)

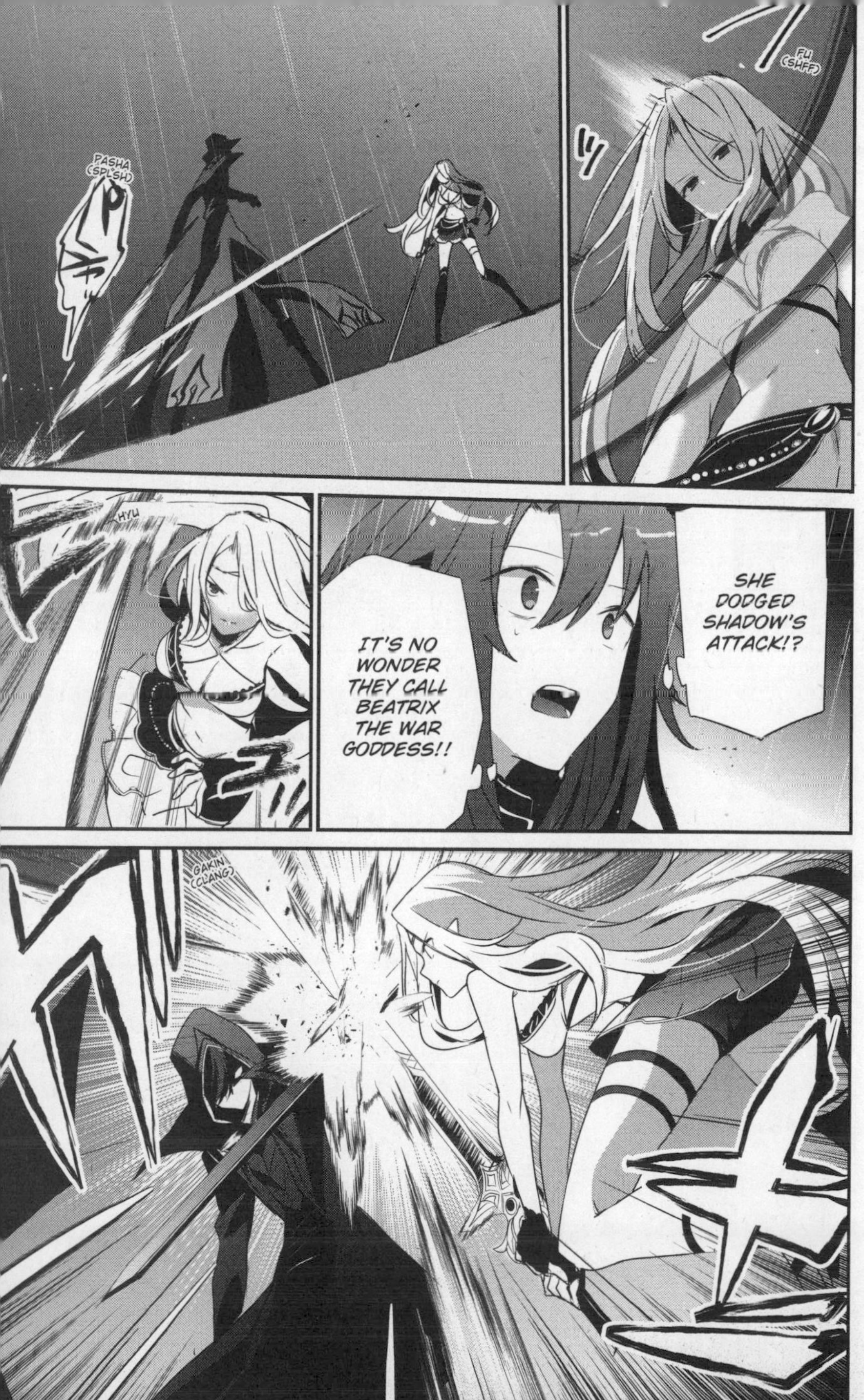
FU (SHFF)
PASHA (SPLSH)
SHE DODGED SHADOW'S ATTACK!?
IT'S NO WONDER THEY CALL BEATRIX THE WAR GODDESS!!
HYU
GAKIN (CLANG)

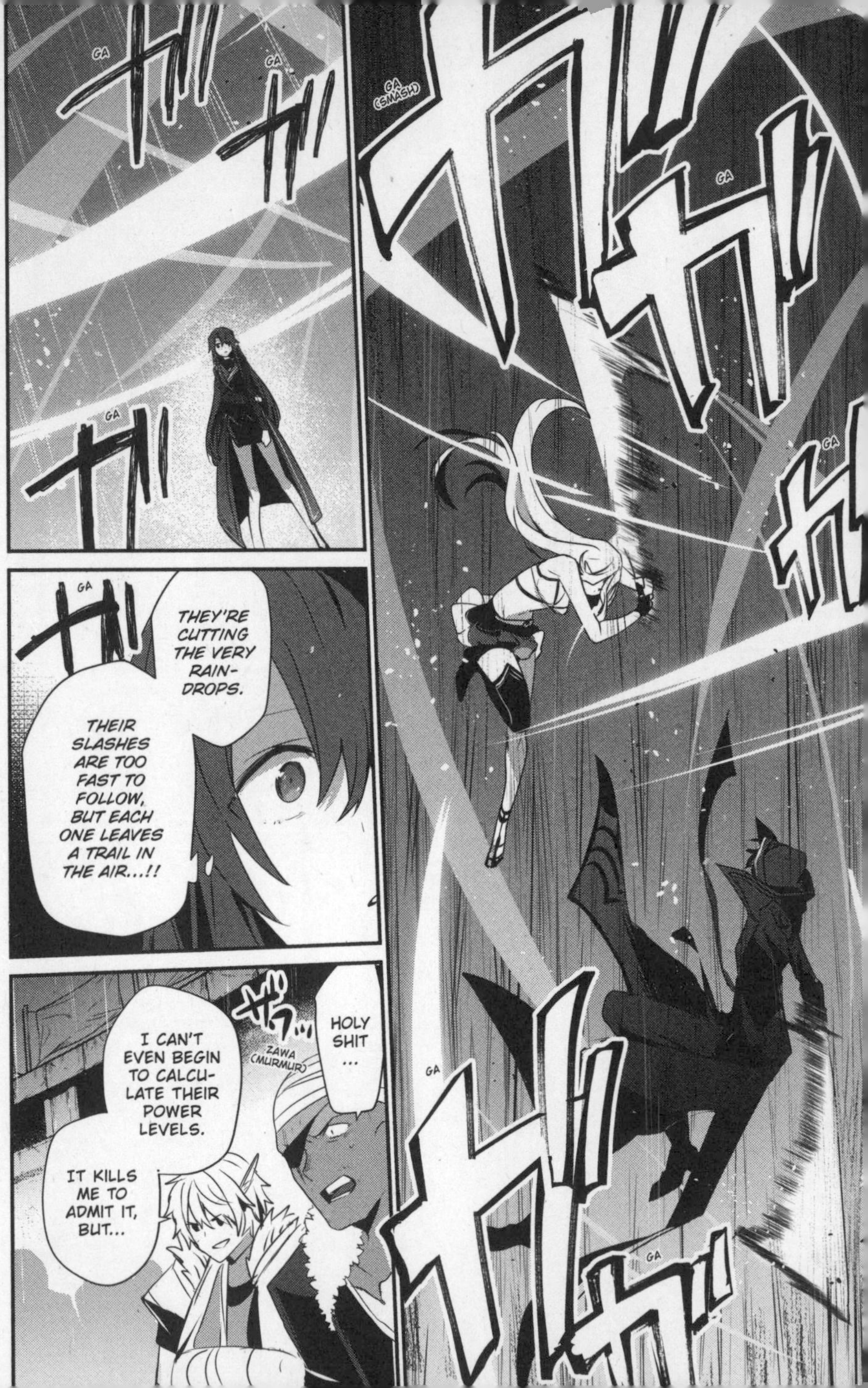
GA
(SMASH)
GA
GA
GA
GA
GA
GA
GA
GA
THEY'RE CUTTING THE VERY RAIN-DROPS.
THEIR SLASHES ARE TOO FAST TO FOLLOW, BUT EACH ONE LEAVES A TRAIL IN THE AIR...!!
HOLY SHIT ...
ZAWA
(MURMUR)
I CAN'T EVEN BEGIN TO CALCU-LATE THEIR POWER LEVELS.
IT KILLS ME TO ADMIT IT, BUT...

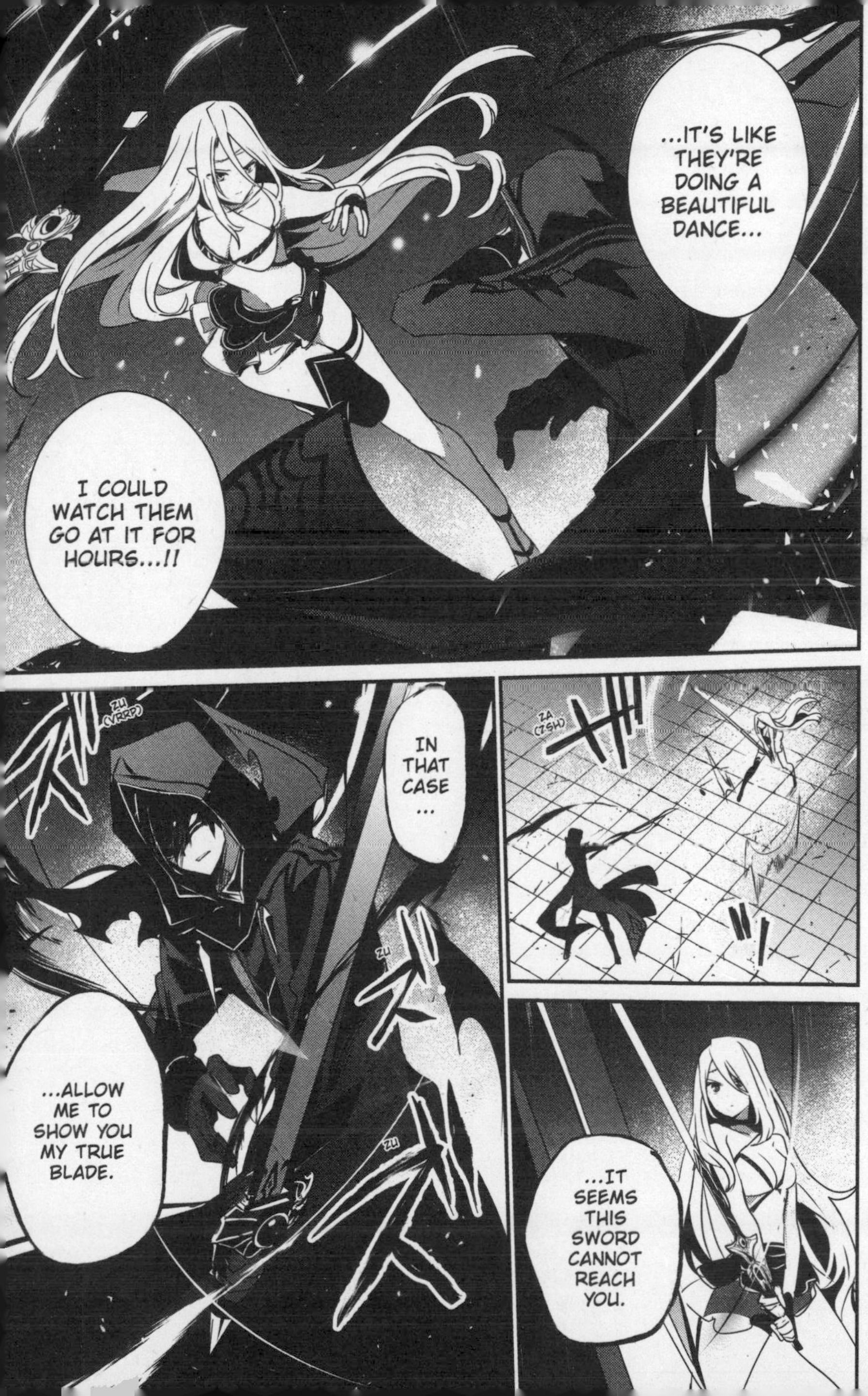
...IT'S LIKE THEY'RE DOING A BEAUTIFUL DANCE...
I COULD WATCH THEM GO AT IT FOR HOURS...!!
ZA (ZSH)
...IT SEEMS THIS SWORD CANNOT REACH YOU.
ZU (VRRP)
IN THAT CASE...
ZU
ZU
...ALLOW ME TO SHOW YOU MY TRUE BLADE.

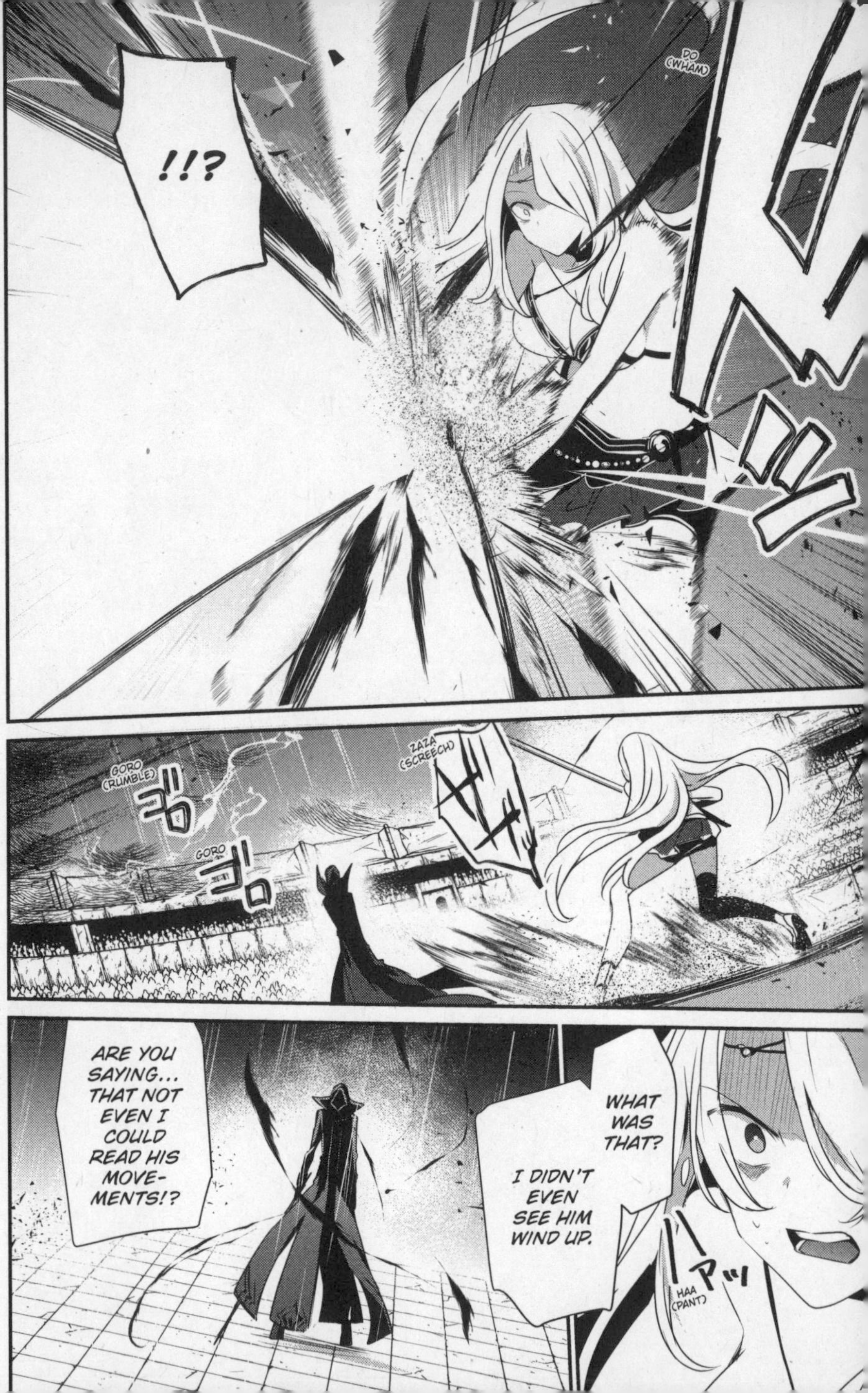
DO (WHAM)
!!?
ZAZA (SCREECH)
GORO (RUMBLE)
GORO
WHAT WAS THAT?
I DIDN'T EVEN SEE HIM WIND UP.
HAA (PANT)
ARE YOU SAYING... THAT NOT EVEN I COULD READ HIS MOVE-MENTS!?

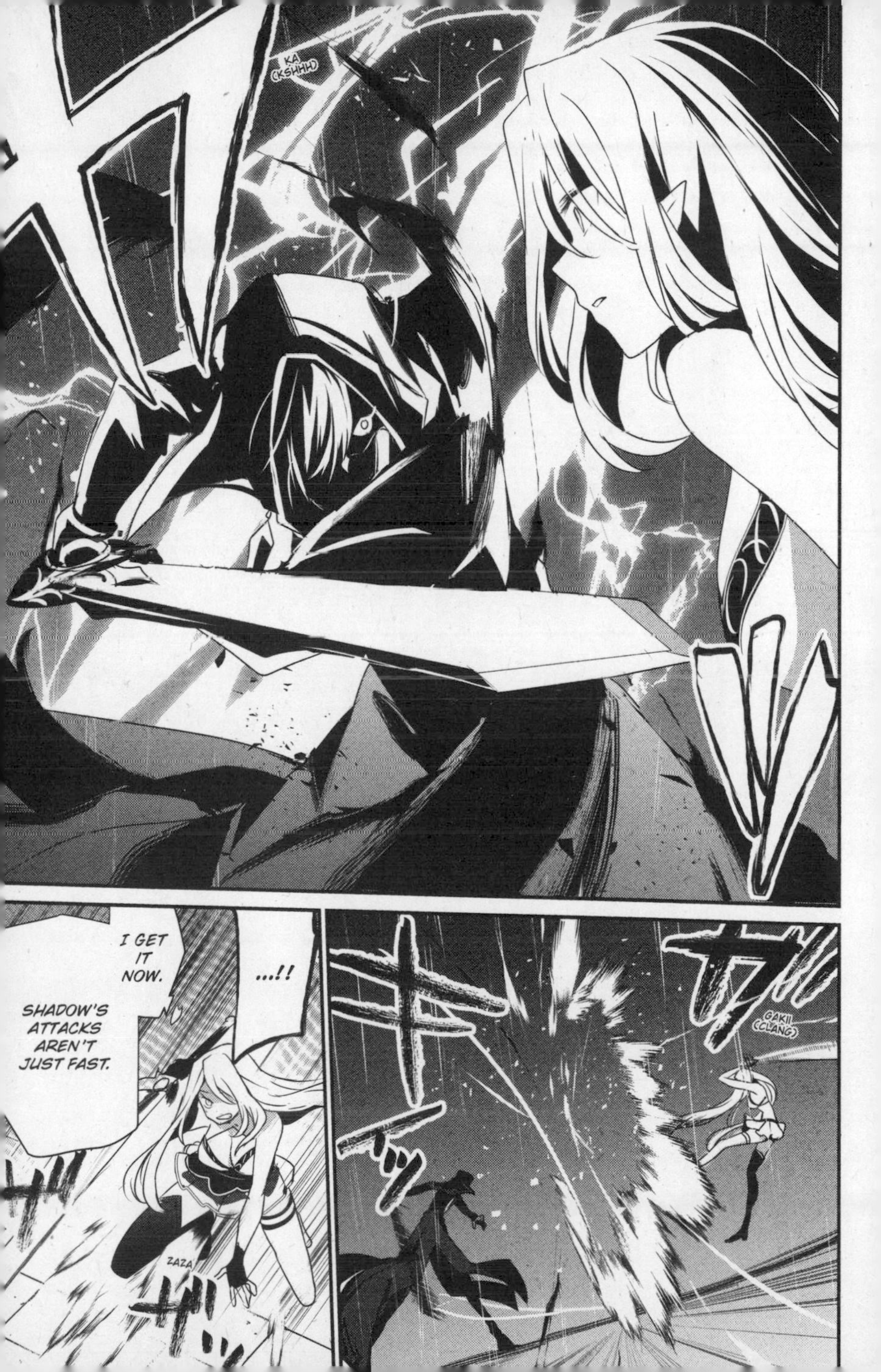
KA (KSHHH)
GAKII (CLANG)
...!!
I GET IT NOW.
SHADOW'S ATTACKS AREN'T JUST FAST.
ZAZA

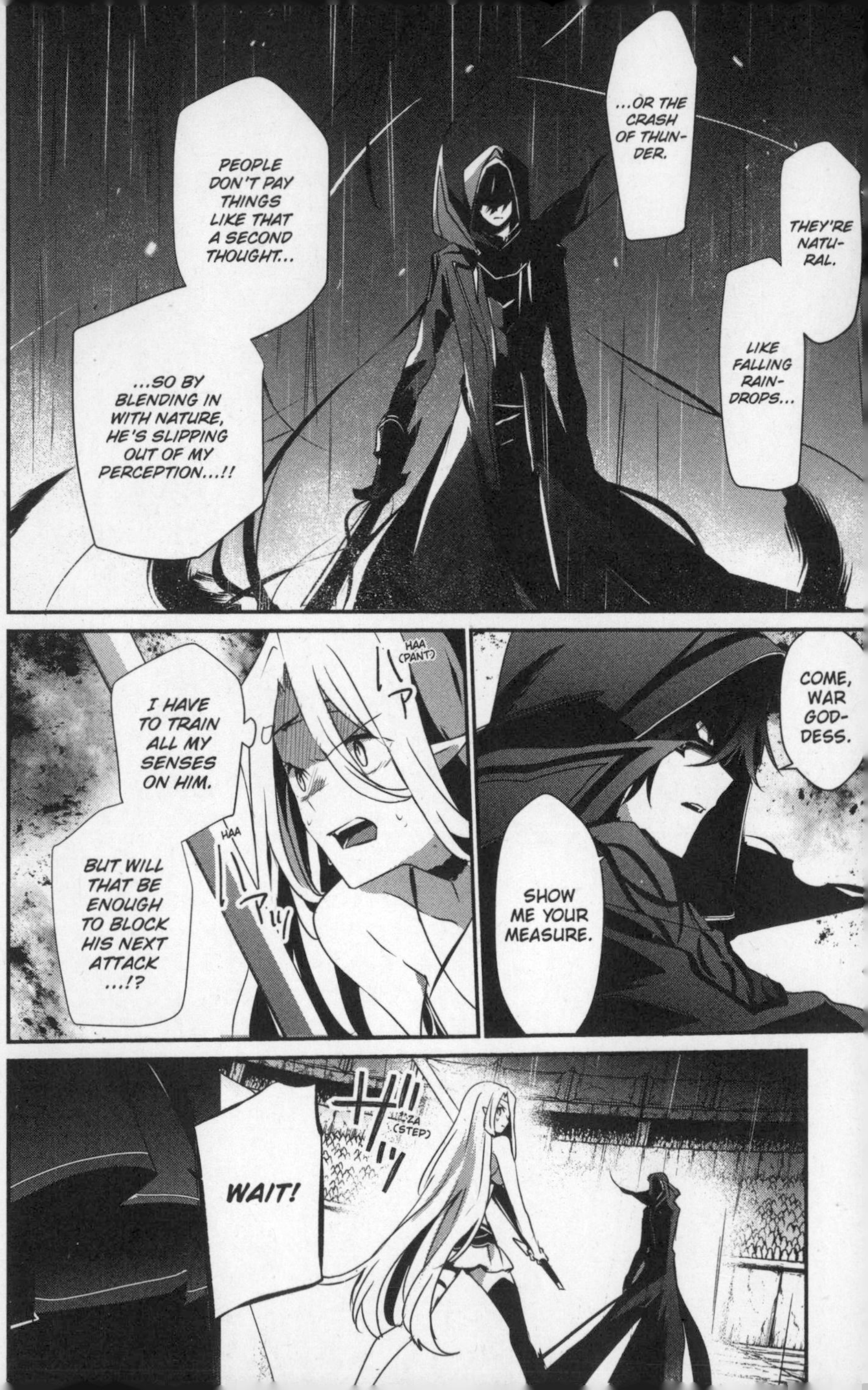
THEY'RE NATU-RAL.
LIKE FALLING RAIN-DROPS...
...OR THE CRASH OF THUN-DER.
PEOPLE DON'T PAY THINGS LIKE THAT A SECOND THOUGHT...
...SO BY BLENDING IN WITH NATURE, HE'S SLIPPING OUT OF MY PERCEPTION...!!
COME, WAR GOD-DESS.
SHOW ME YOUR MEASURE.
HAA (PANT)
I HAVE TO TRAIN ALL MY SENSES ON HIM.
HAA
BUT WILL THAT BE ENOUGH TO BLOCK HIS NEXT ATTACK ...!?
ZA (STEP)
WAIT!

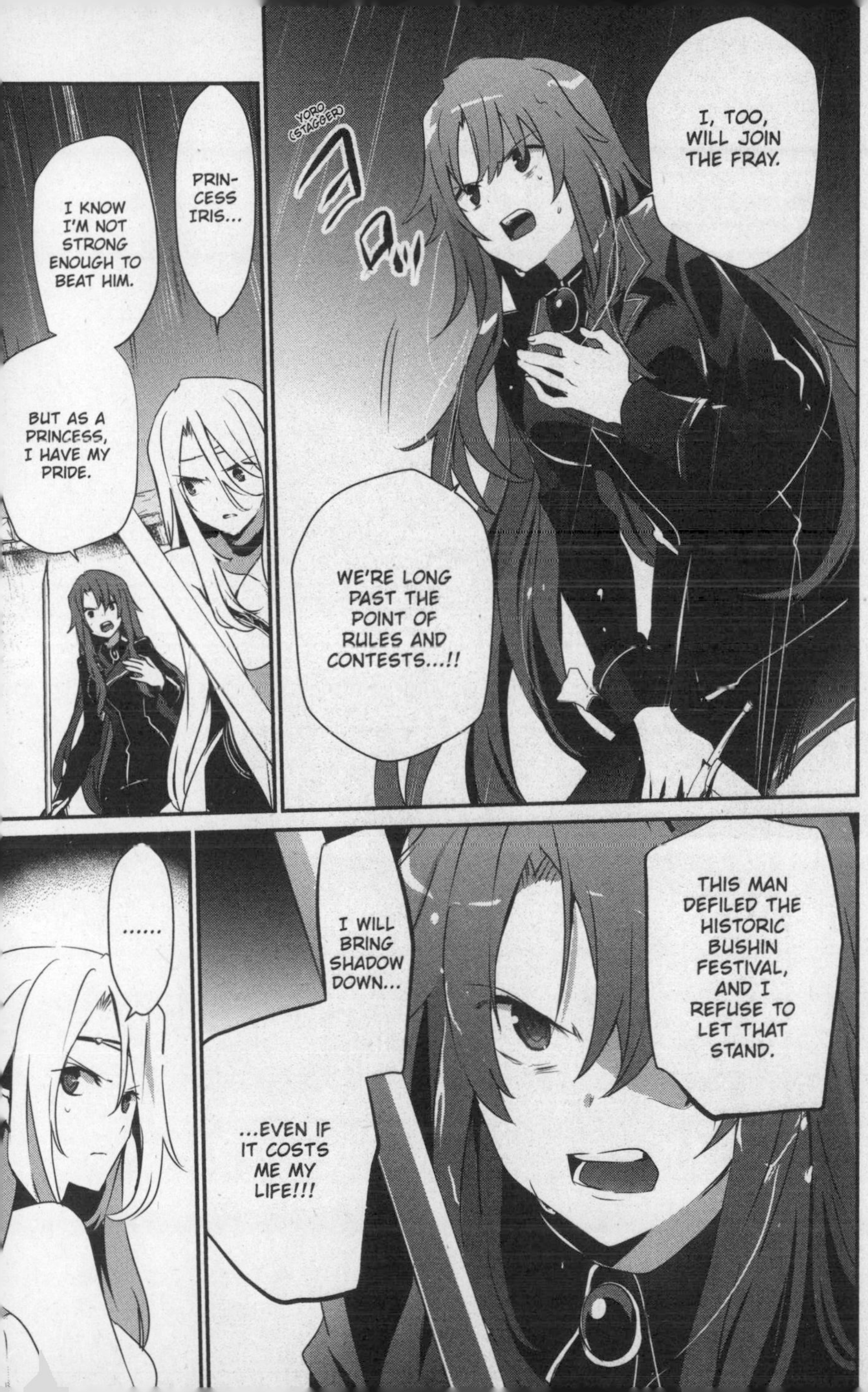
I, TOO, WILL JOIN THE FRAY.
YORO (STAGGER)
WE'RE LONG PAST THE POINT OF RULES AND CONTESTS...!!
PRINCESS IRIS...
I KNOW I'M NOT STRONG ENOUGH TO BEAT HIM.
BUT AS A PRINCESS, I HAVE MY PRIDE.
THIS MAN DEFILED THE HISTORIC BUSHIN FESTIVAL, AND I REFUSE TO LET THAT STAND.
I WILL BRING SHADOW DOWN...
...EVEN IF IT COSTS ME MY LIFE!!!
......

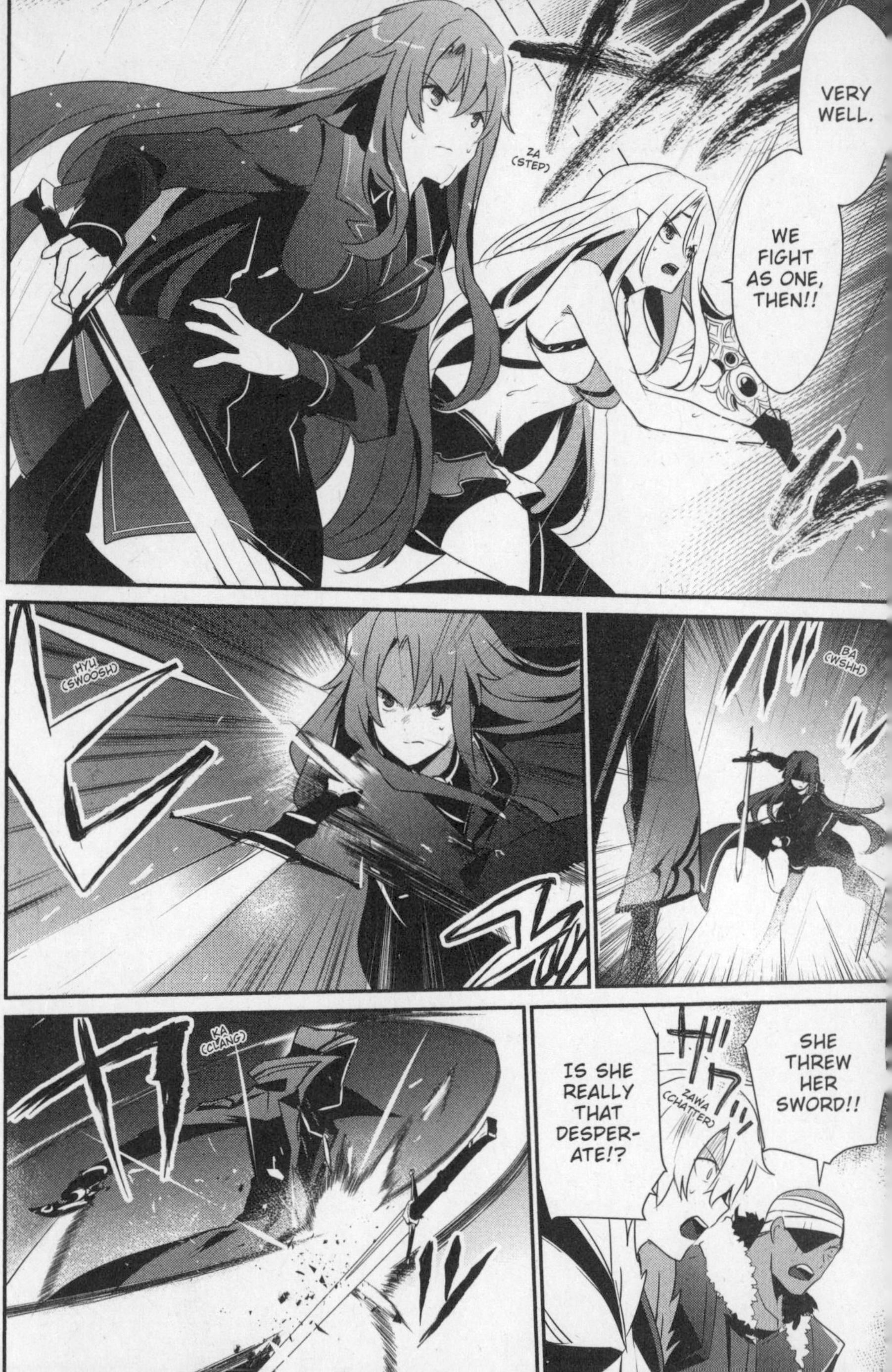
VERY WELL.
ZA (STEP)
WE FIGHT AS ONE, THEN!!
BA (WSHH)
HYU (SWOOSH)
SHE THREW HER SWORD!!
ZAWA (CHATTER)
IS SHE REALLY THAT DESPERATE!?
KA (CLANG)

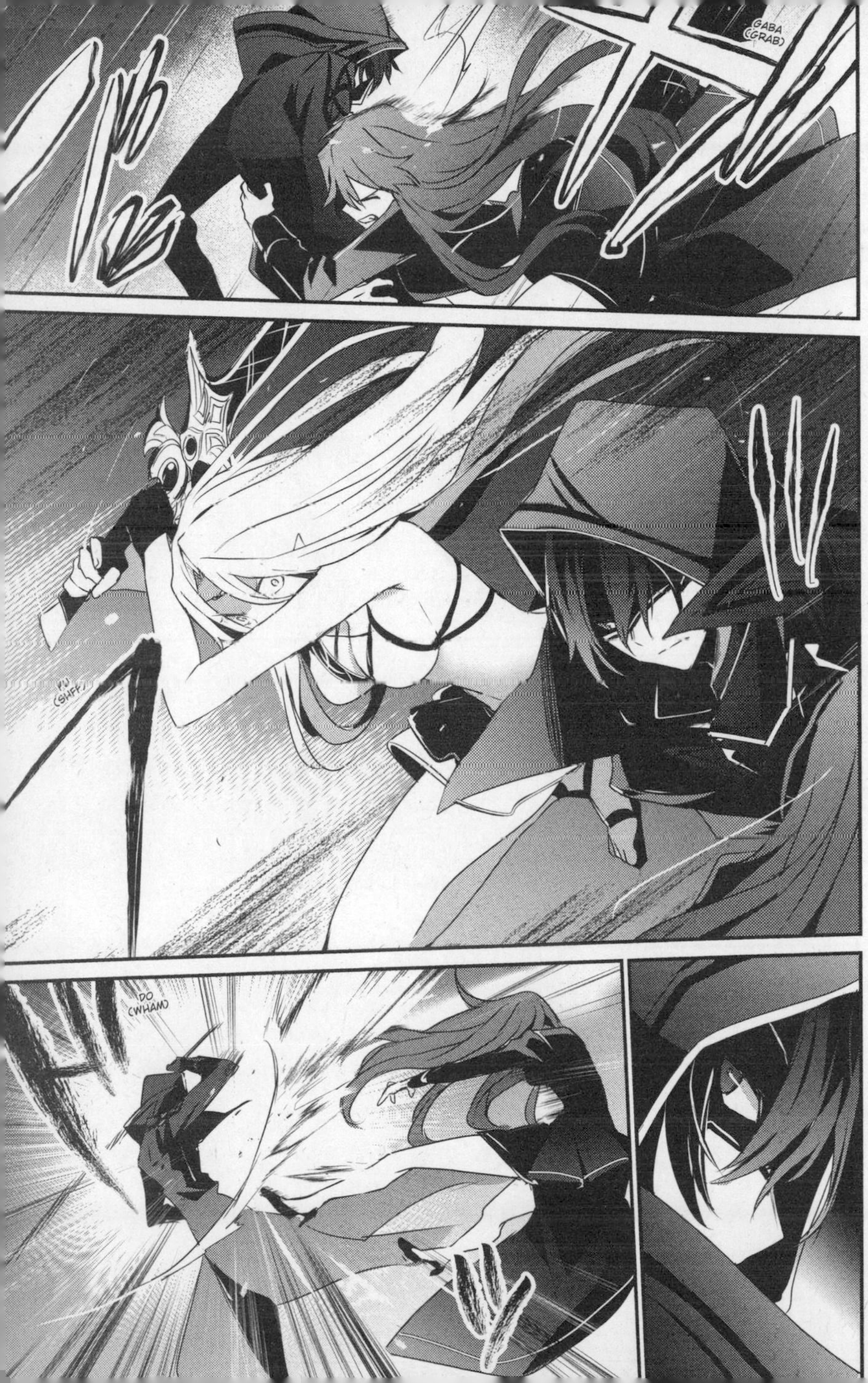
GABA (GRAB)
FU (SHFF)
DO (WHAM)

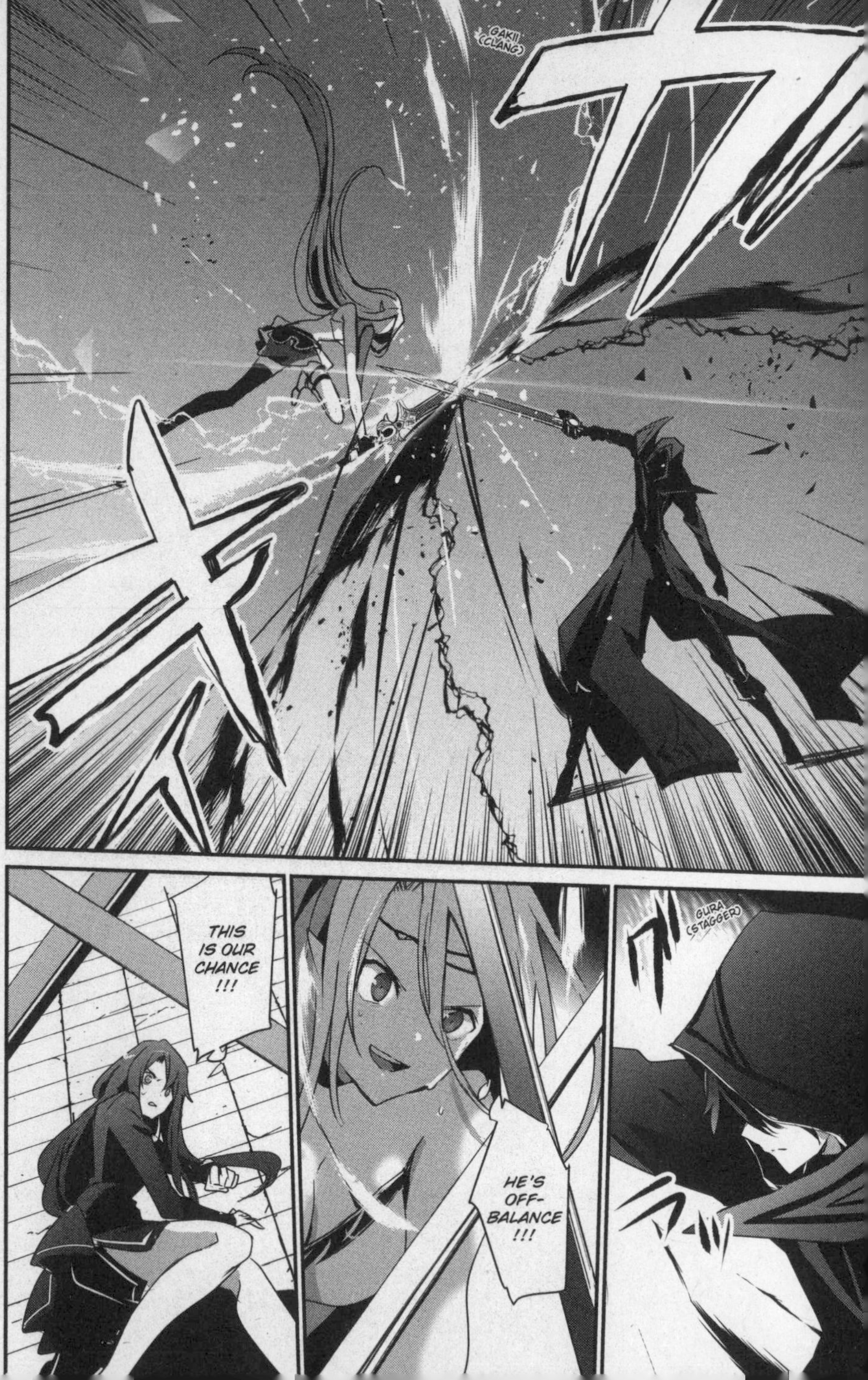
GAKI! (CLANG)
GURA (STAGGER)
HE'S OFF-BALANCE!!!
THIS IS OUR CHANCE!!!

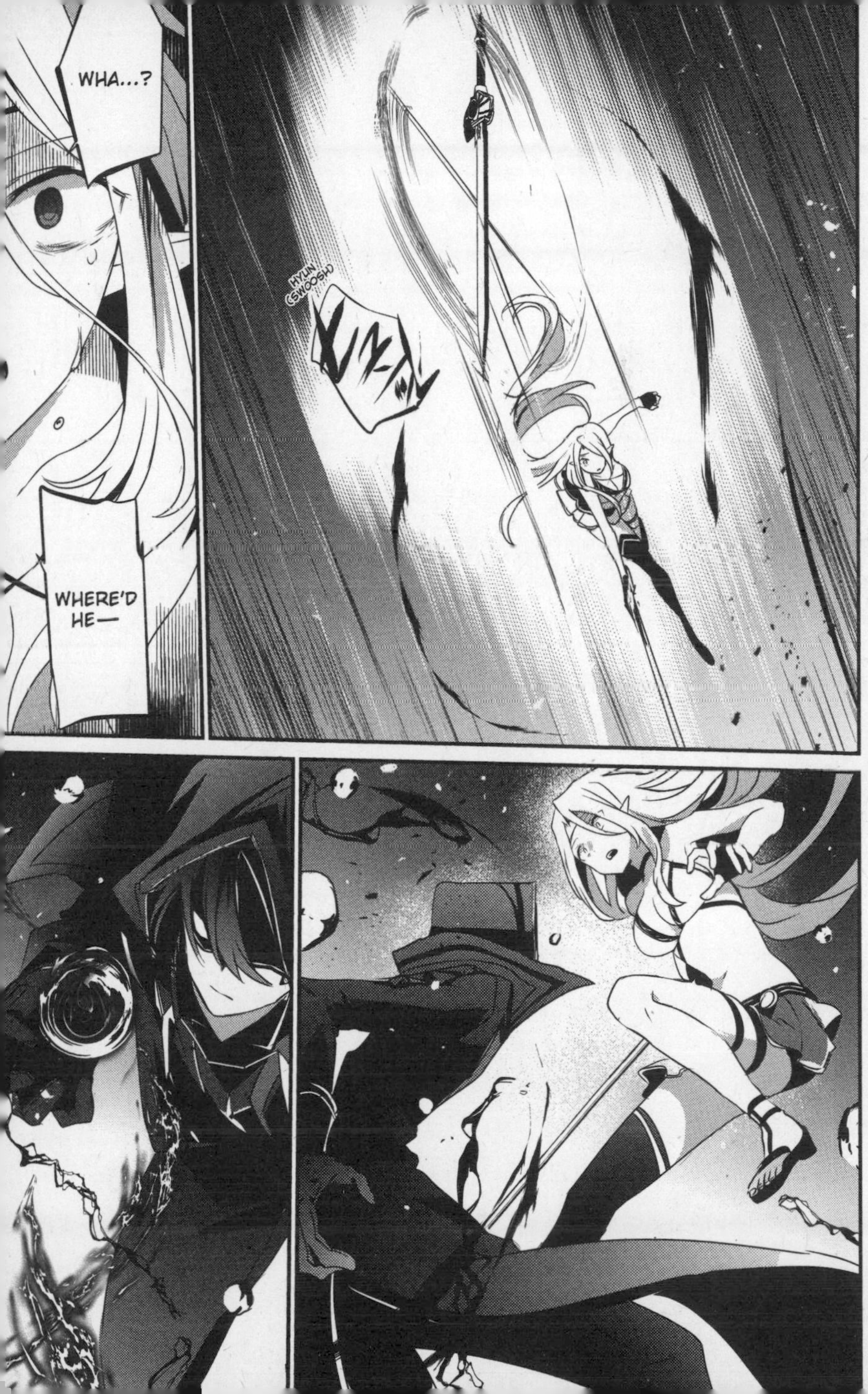
HYUN (SWOOSH)
WHA...?
WHERE'D HE—

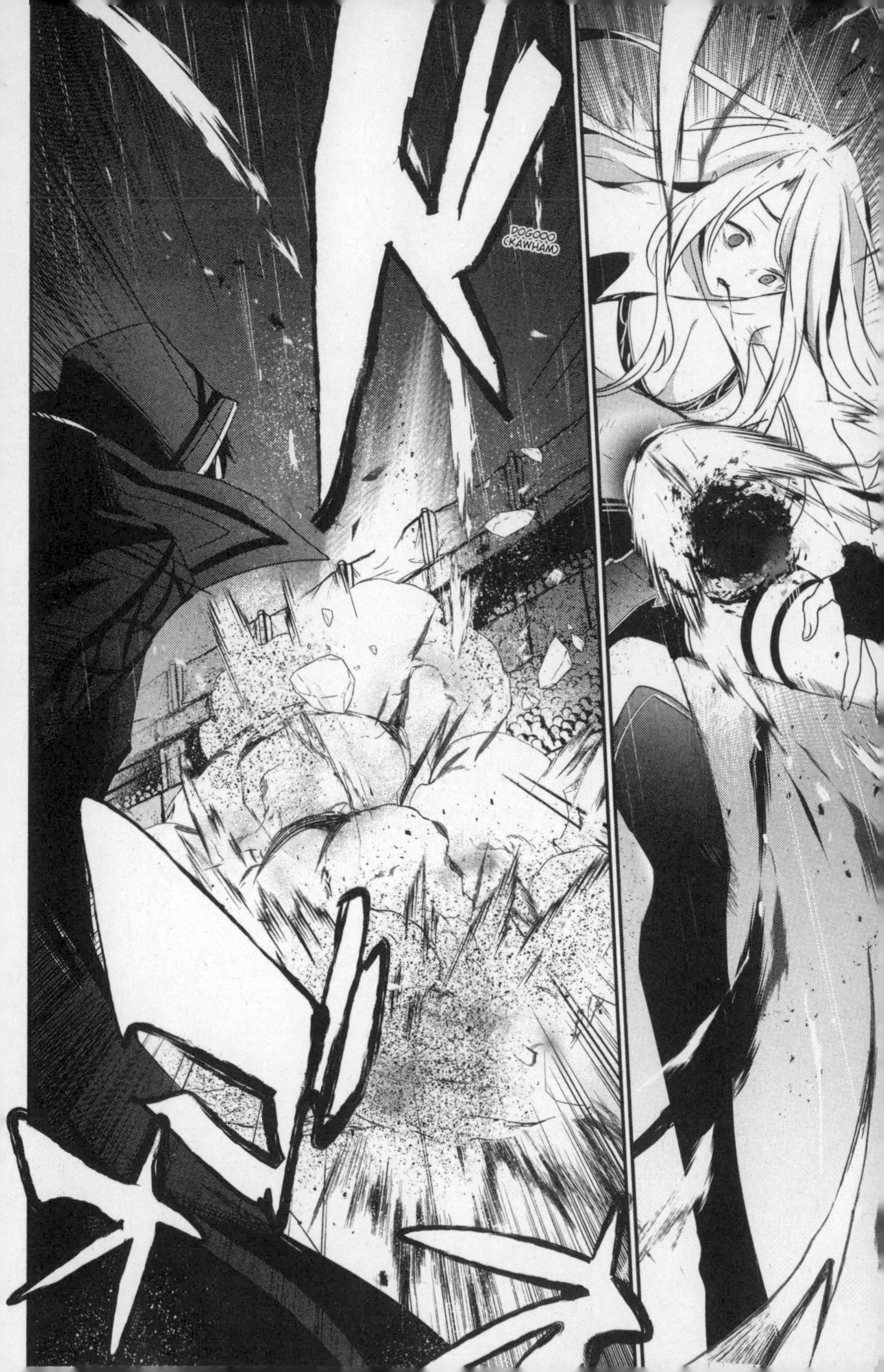
DOGOOO (KAWHAM)

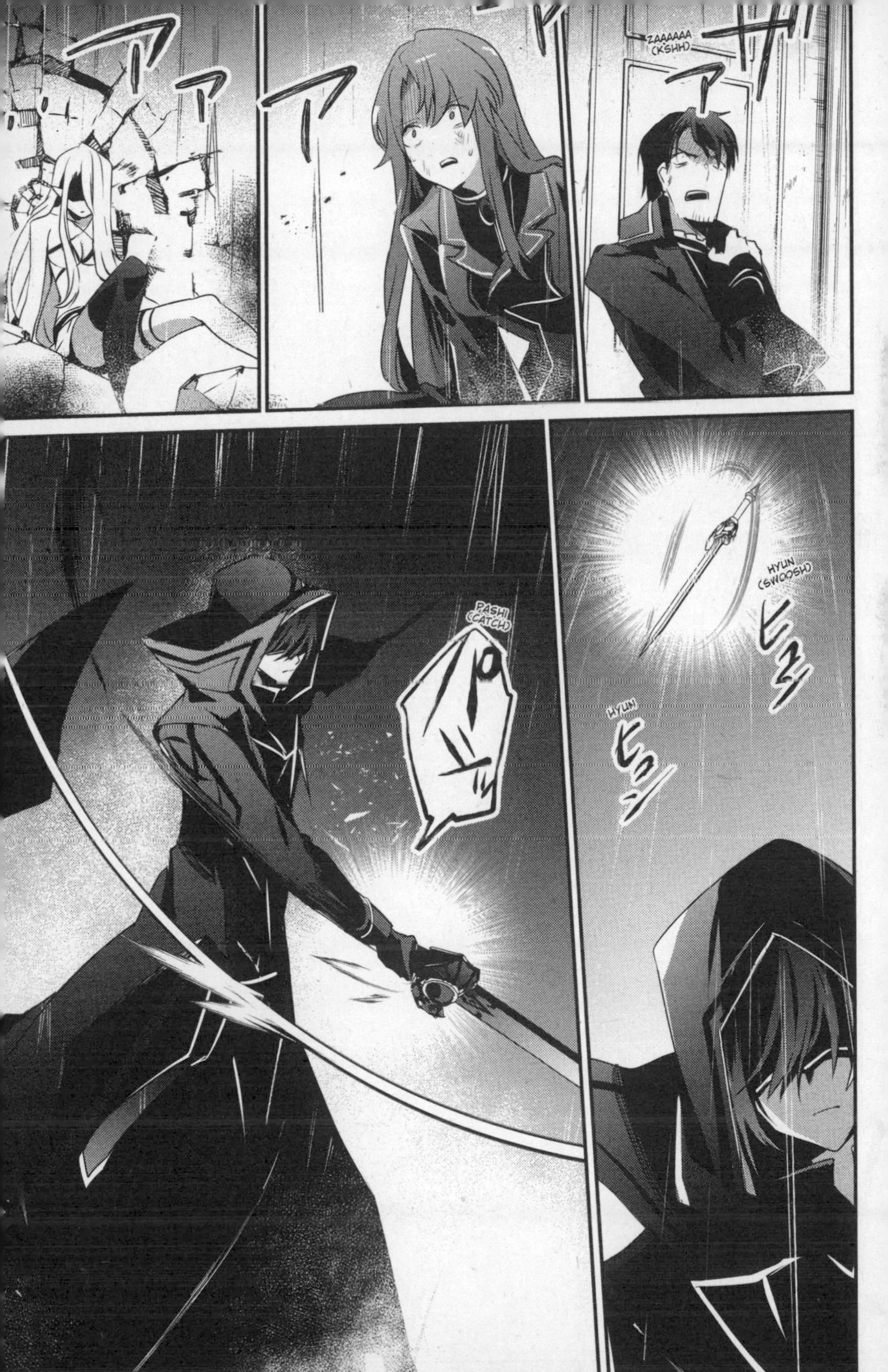
ZAAAAAA (KSHH)
HYUN (SWOOSH)
HYUN
PASHI (CATCH)

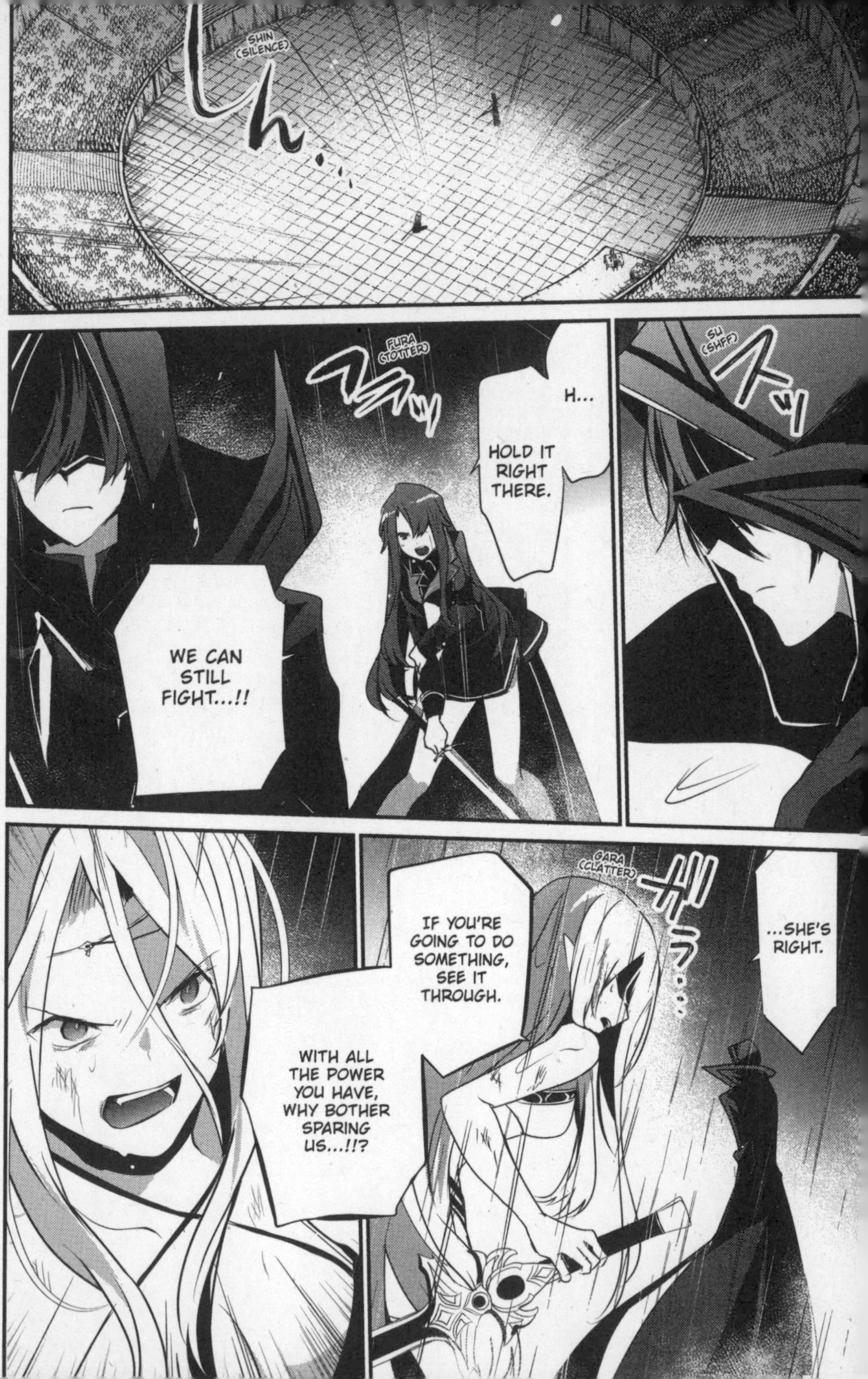
SHIN (SILENCE)
しん…
SU (SHFF)
スッ
FURA (TOTTER)
フラッ
H...
HOLD IT RIGHT THERE.
WE CAN STILL FIGHT...!!
GARA (CLATTER)
ガラ…
...SHE'S RIGHT.
IF YOU'RE GOING TO DO SOMETHING, SEE IT THROUGH.
WITH ALL THE POWER YOU HAVE, WHY BOTHER SPARING US...!!?

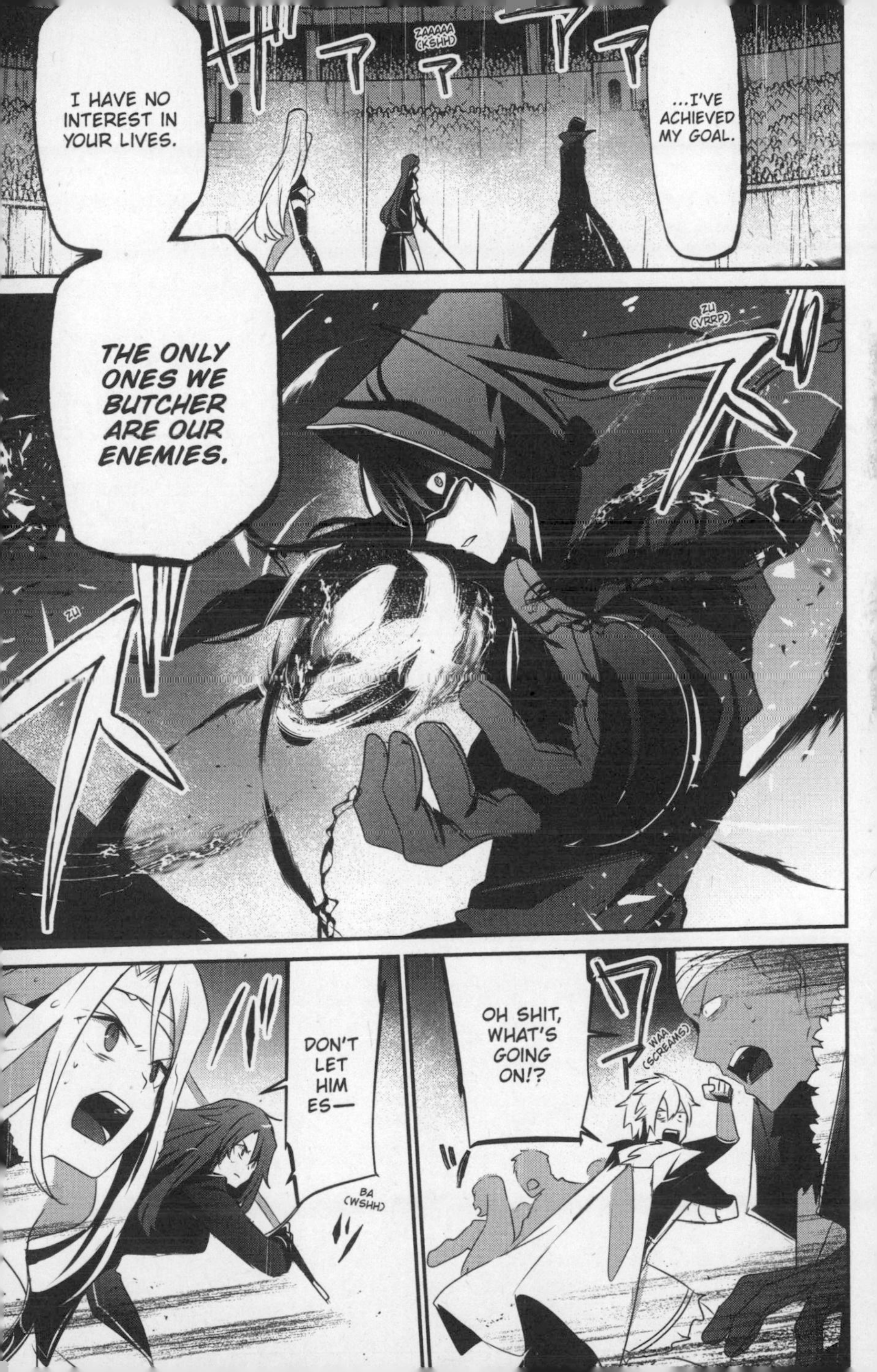
...I'VE ACHIEVED MY GOAL.
ZAAAAA (KSHH)
I HAVE NO INTEREST IN YOUR LIVES.
ZU (VRRP)
THE ONLY ONES WE BUTCHER ARE OUR ENEMIES.
ZU
OH SHIT, WHAT'S GOING ON!?
WAA (SCREAMS)
DON'T LET HIM ES—
BA (WSHH)

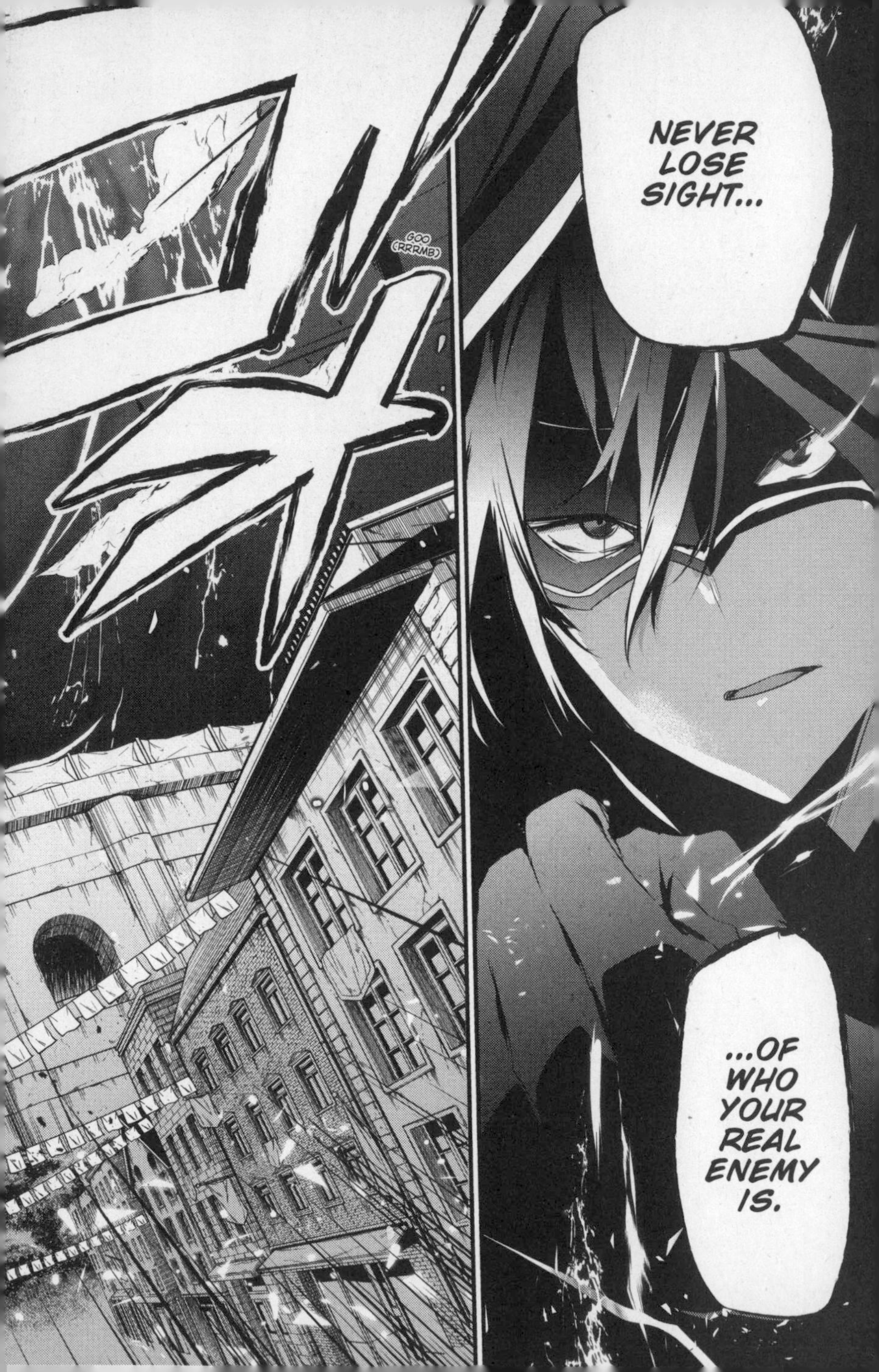
NEVER LOSE SIGHT...
...OF WHO YOUR REAL ENEMY IS.
GOO (RRRMB)

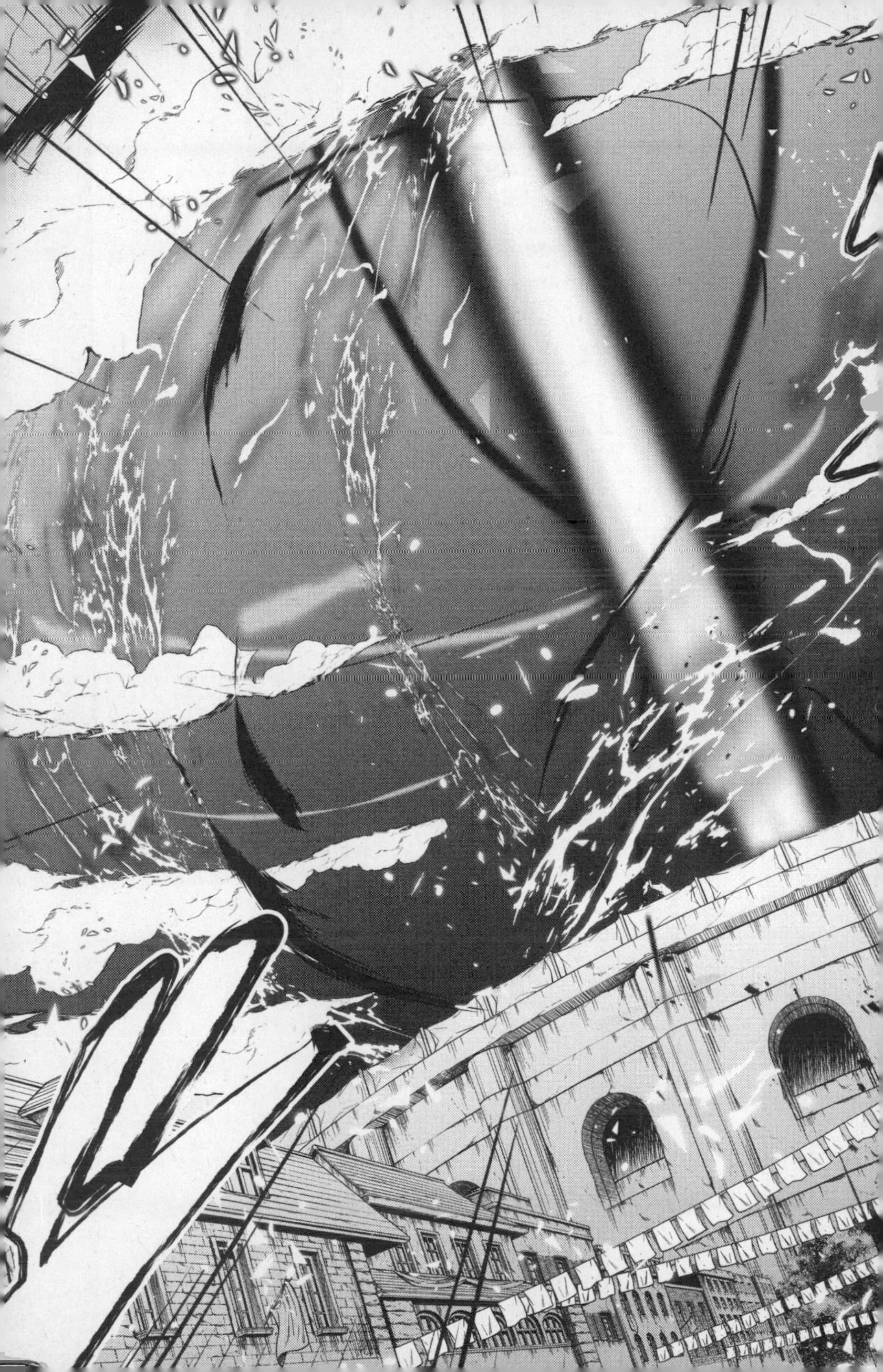

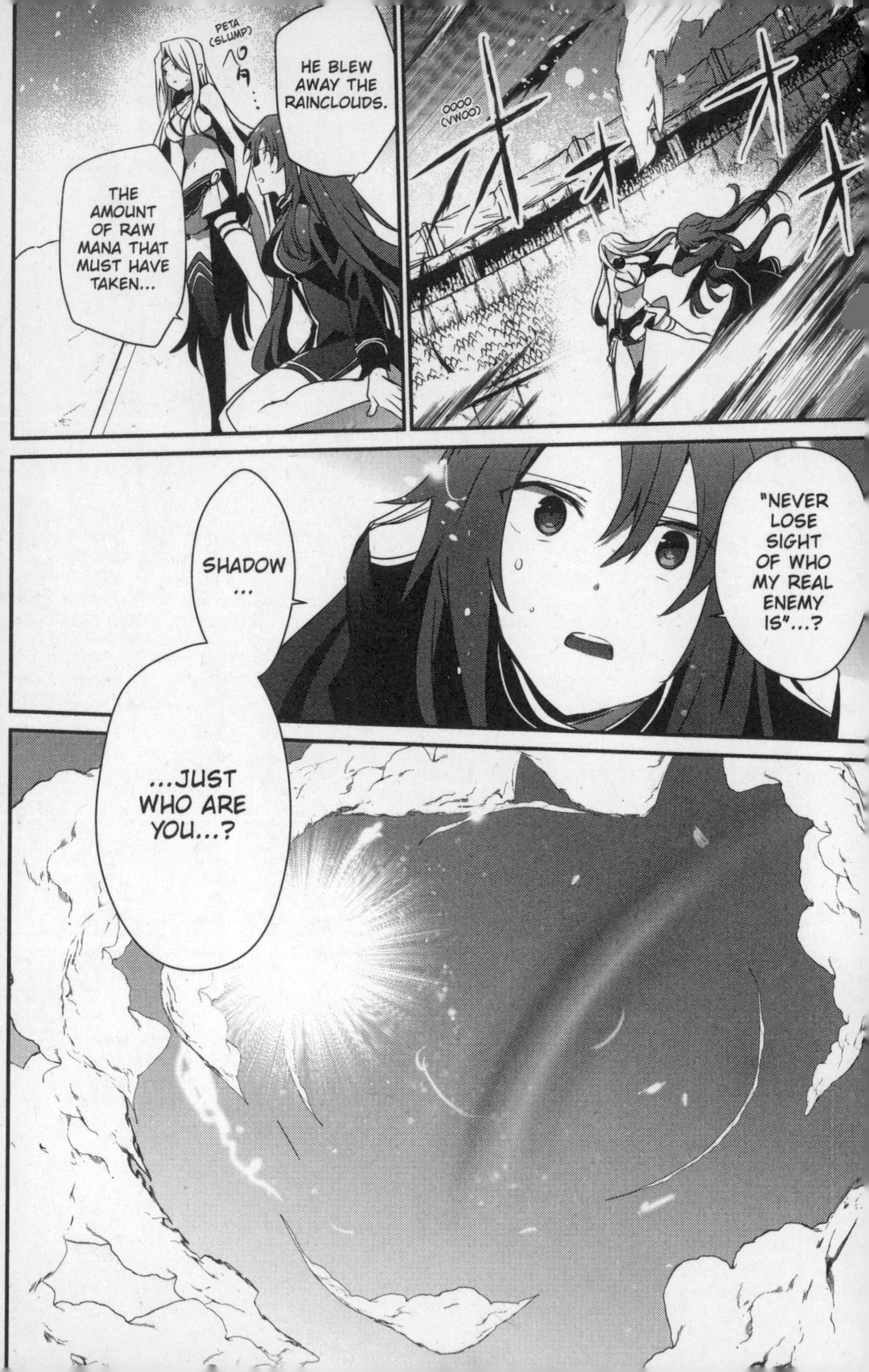
OOOO
(VWOO)
HE BLEW AWAY THE RAINCLOUDS.
PETA
(SLUMP)
THE AMOUNT OF RAW MANA THAT MUST HAVE TAKEN...
"NEVER LOSE SIGHT OF WHO MY REAL ENEMY IS"...?
SHADOW ...
...JUST WHO ARE YOU...?

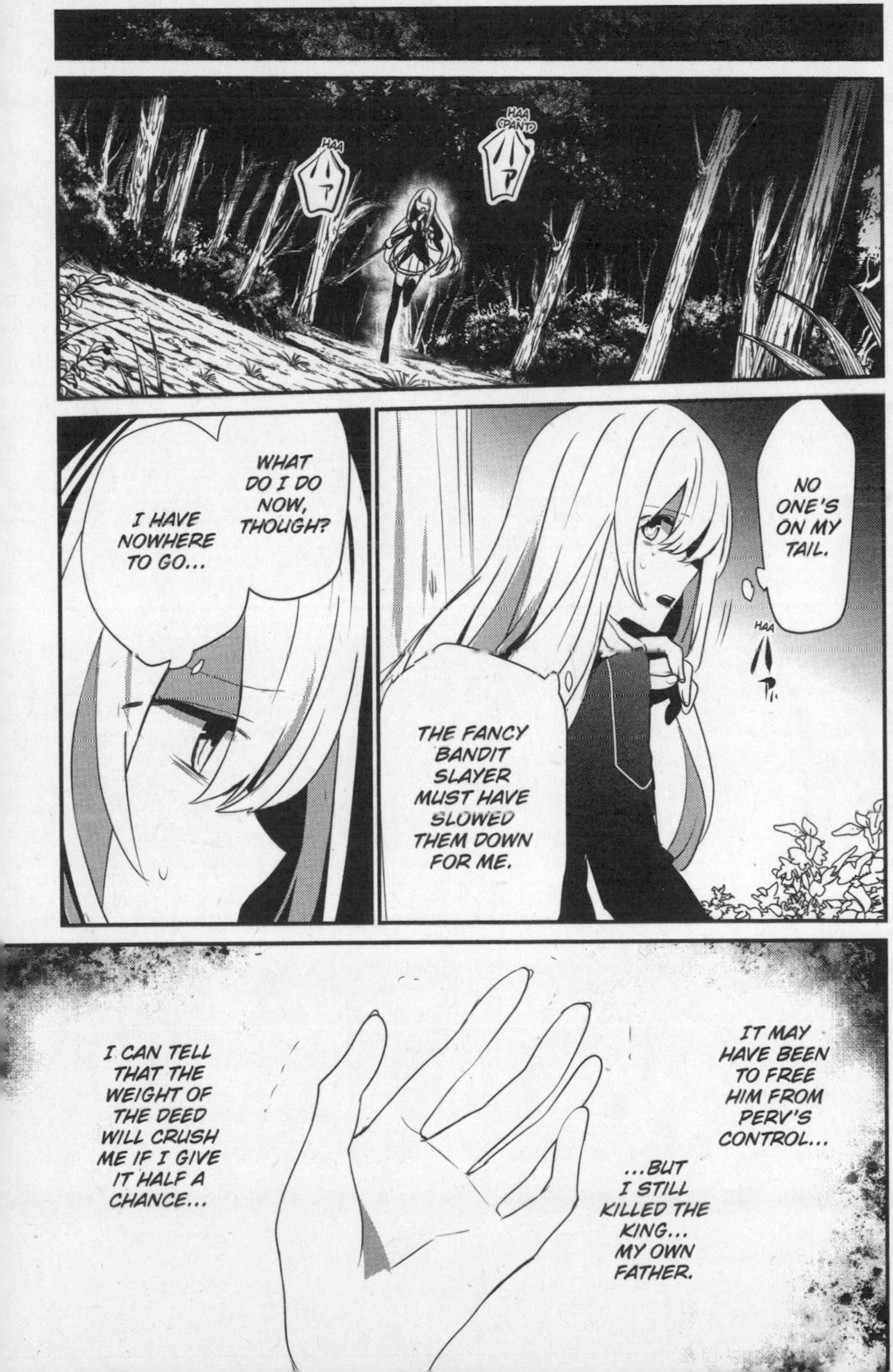
HAA (PANT)
HAA
NO ONE'S ON MY TAIL.
HAA
THE FANCY BANDIT SLAYER MUST HAVE SLOWED THEM DOWN FOR ME.
WHAT DO I DO NOW, THOUGH?
I HAVE NOWHERE TO GO...
IT MAY HAVE BEEN TO FREE HIM FROM PERV'S CONTROL...
...BUT I STILL KILLED THE KING... MY OWN FATHER.
I CAN TELL THAT THE WEIGHT OF THE DEED WILL CRUSH ME IF I GIVE IT HALF A CHANCE...

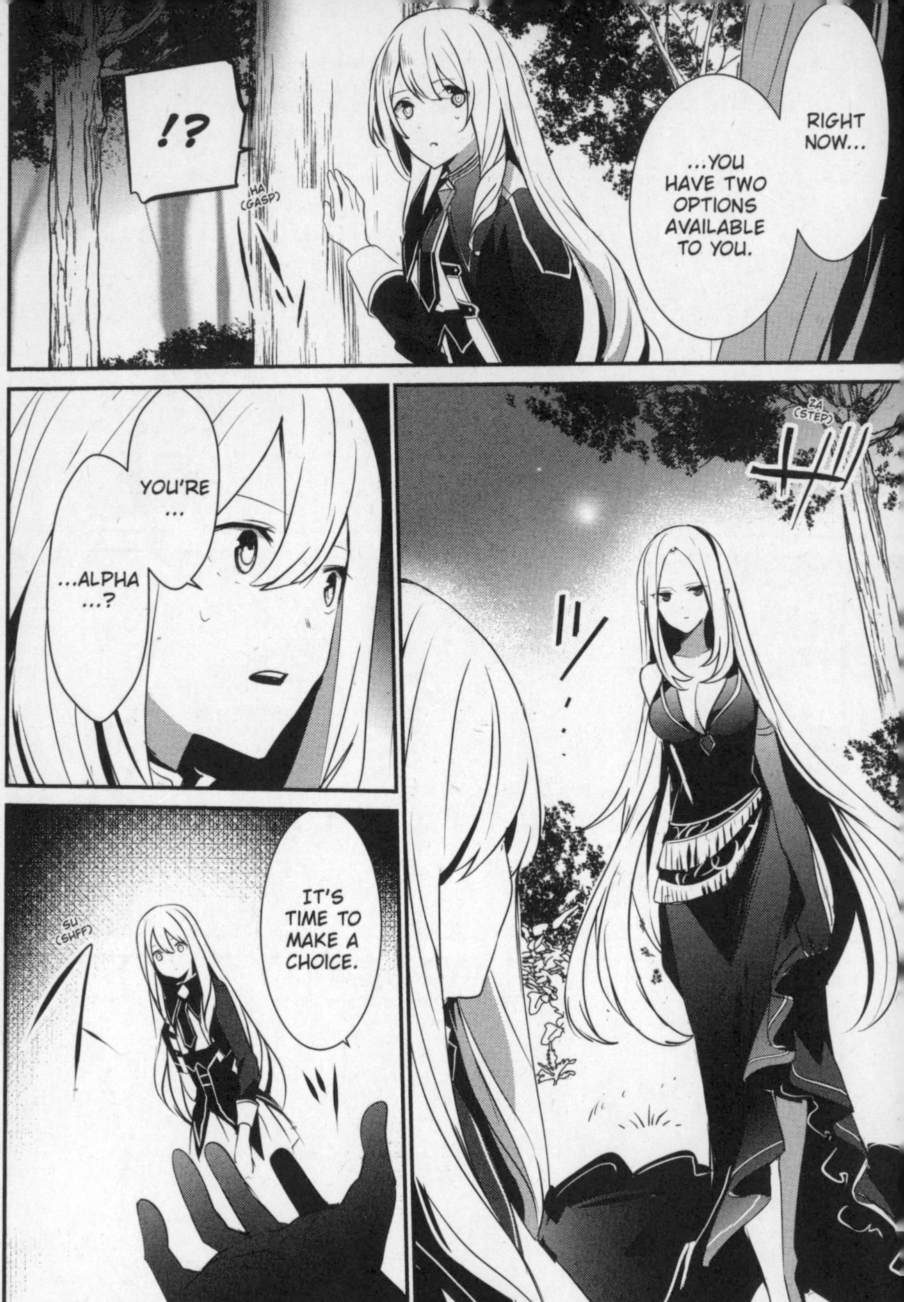
RIGHT NOW...
...YOU HAVE TWO OPTIONS AVAILABLE TO YOU.
!?
HA (GASP)
ZA (STEP)
YOU'RE ...
...ALPHA ...?
IT'S TIME TO MAKE A CHOICE.
SU (SHFF)

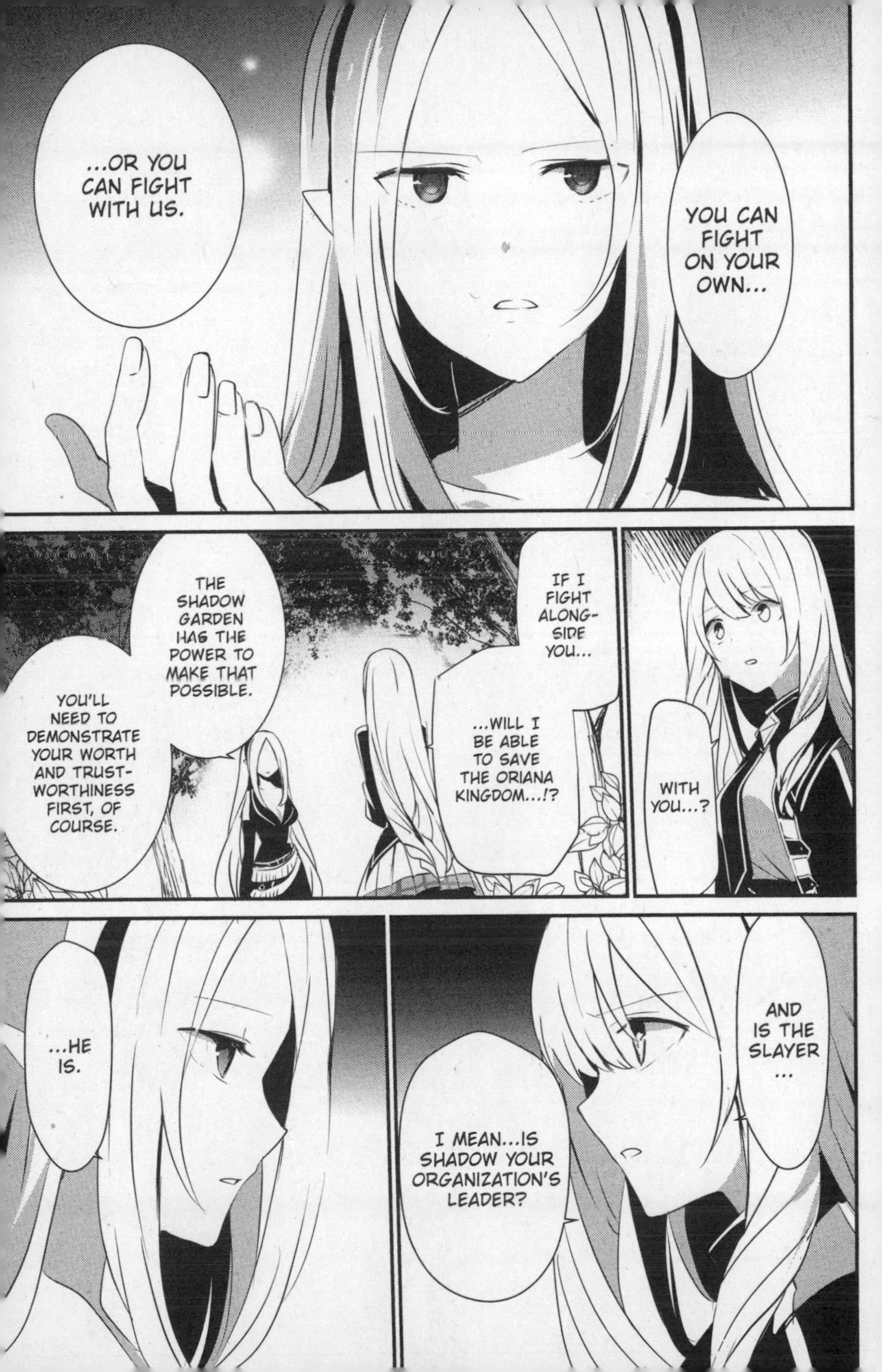
YOU CAN FIGHT ON YOUR OWN...
...OR YOU CAN FIGHT WITH US.
WITH YOU...?
IF I FIGHT ALONG-SIDE YOU...
...WILL I BE ABLE TO SAVE THE ORIANA KINGDOM...!?
THE SHADOW GARDEN HAS THE POWER TO MAKE THAT POSSIBLE.
YOU'LL NEED TO DEMONSTRATE YOUR WORTH AND TRUST-WORTHINESS FIRST, OF COURSE.
AND IS THE SLAYER ...
I MEAN...IS SHADOW YOUR ORGANIZATION'S LEADER?
...HE IS.

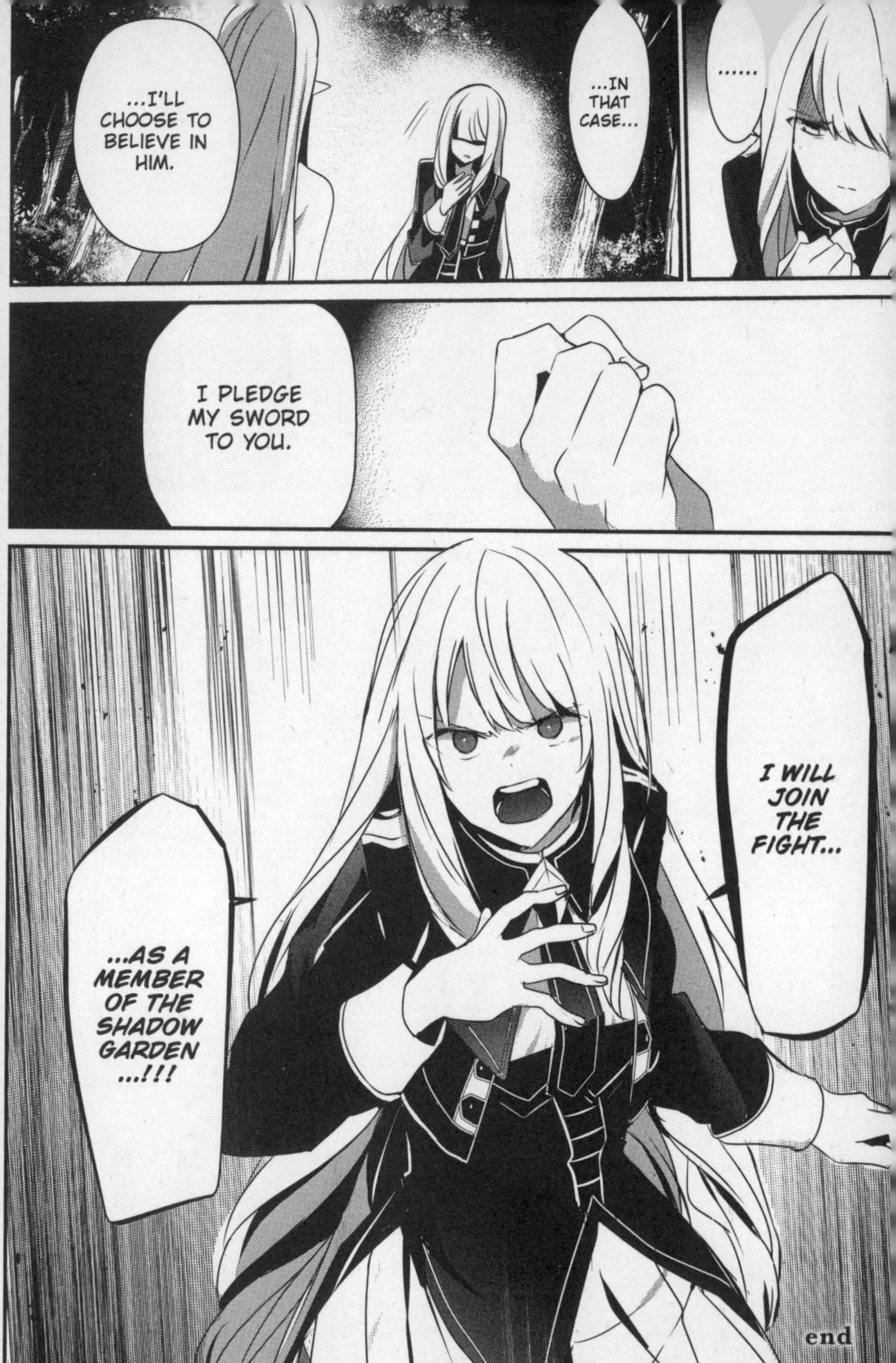
......
...IN THAT CASE...
...I'LL CHOOSE TO BELIEVE IN HIM.
I PLEDGE MY SWORD TO YOU.
I WILL JOIN THE FIGHT...
...AS A MEMBER OF THE SHADOW GARDEN ...!!!
end

Episode.27

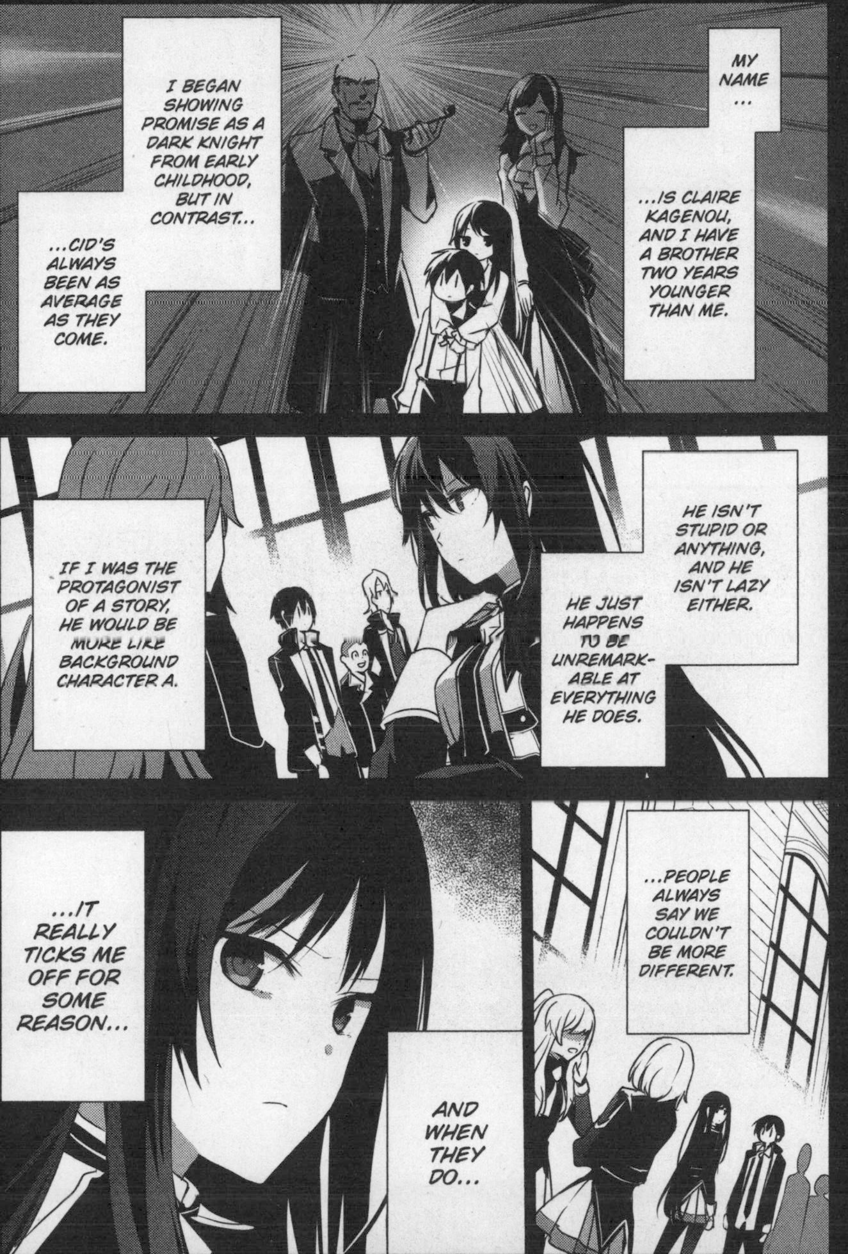
MY NAME ...
...IS CLAIRE KAGENOU, AND I HAVE A BROTHER TWO YEARS YOUNGER THAN ME.
I BEGAN SHOWING PROMISE AS A DARK KNIGHT FROM EARLY CHILDHOOD, BUT IN CONTRAST...
...CID'S ALWAYS BEEN AS AVERAGE AS THEY COME.
HE ISN'T STUPID OR ANYTHING, AND HE ISN'T LAZY EITHER.
HE JUST HAPPENS TO BE UNREMARKABLE AT EVERYTHING HE DOES.
IF I WAS THE PROTAGONIST OF A STORY, HE WOULD BE MORE LIKE BACKGROUND CHARACTER A.
...PEOPLE ALWAYS SAY WE COULDN'T BE MORE DIFFERENT.
AND WHEN THEY DO...
...IT REALLY TICKS ME OFF FOR SOME REASON...

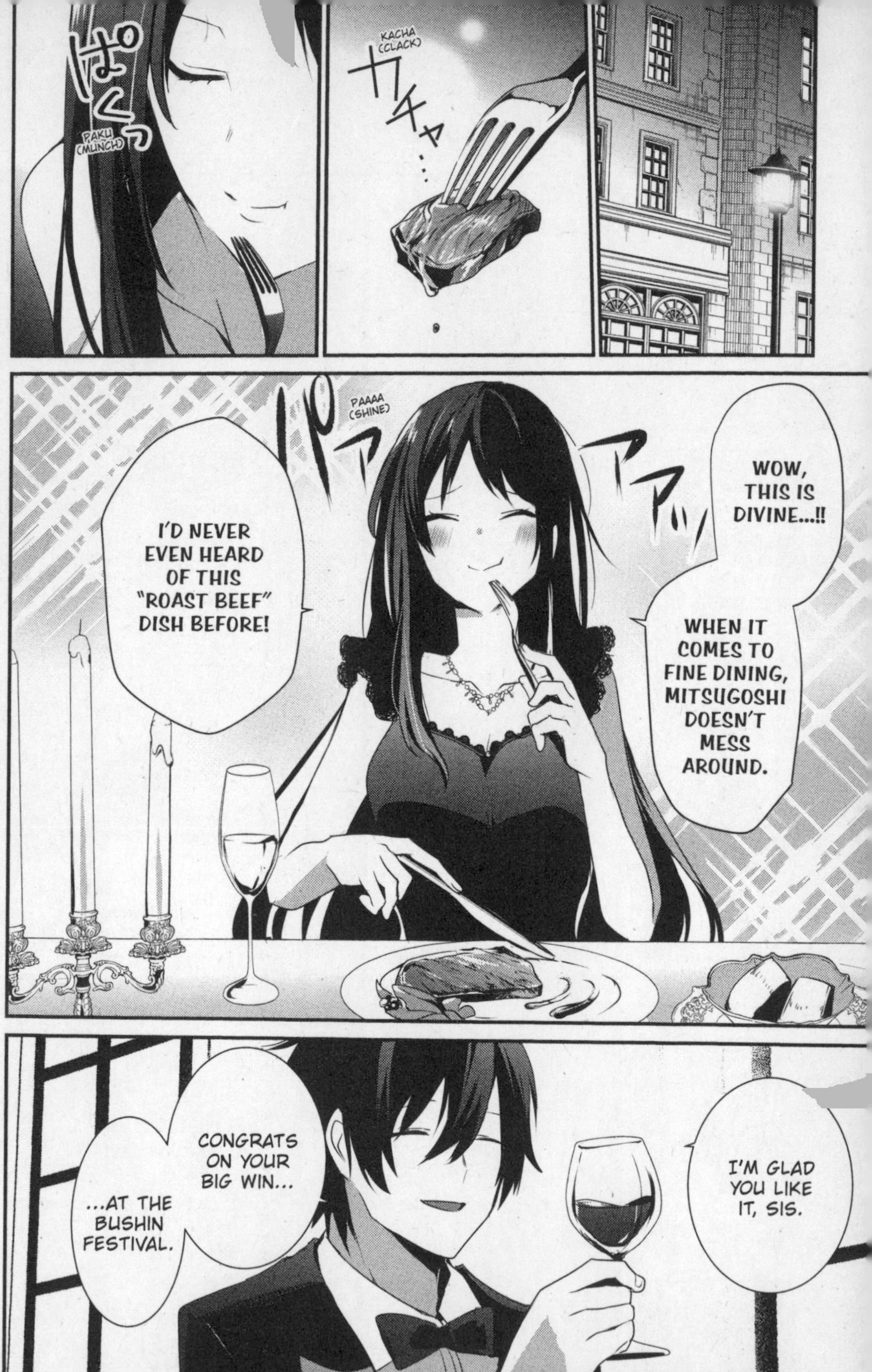
カチャ…
KACHA (CLACK)
ぱくっ
PAKU (MUNCH)
WOW, THIS IS DIVINE...!!
パァァァッ
PAAAA (SHINE)
WHEN IT COMES TO FINE DINING, MITSUGOSHI DOESN'T MESS AROUND.
I'D NEVER EVEN HEARD OF THIS "ROAST BEEF" DISH BEFORE!
I'M GLAD YOU LIKE IT, SIS.
CONGRATS ON YOUR BIG WIN...
...AT THE BUSHIN FESTIVAL.

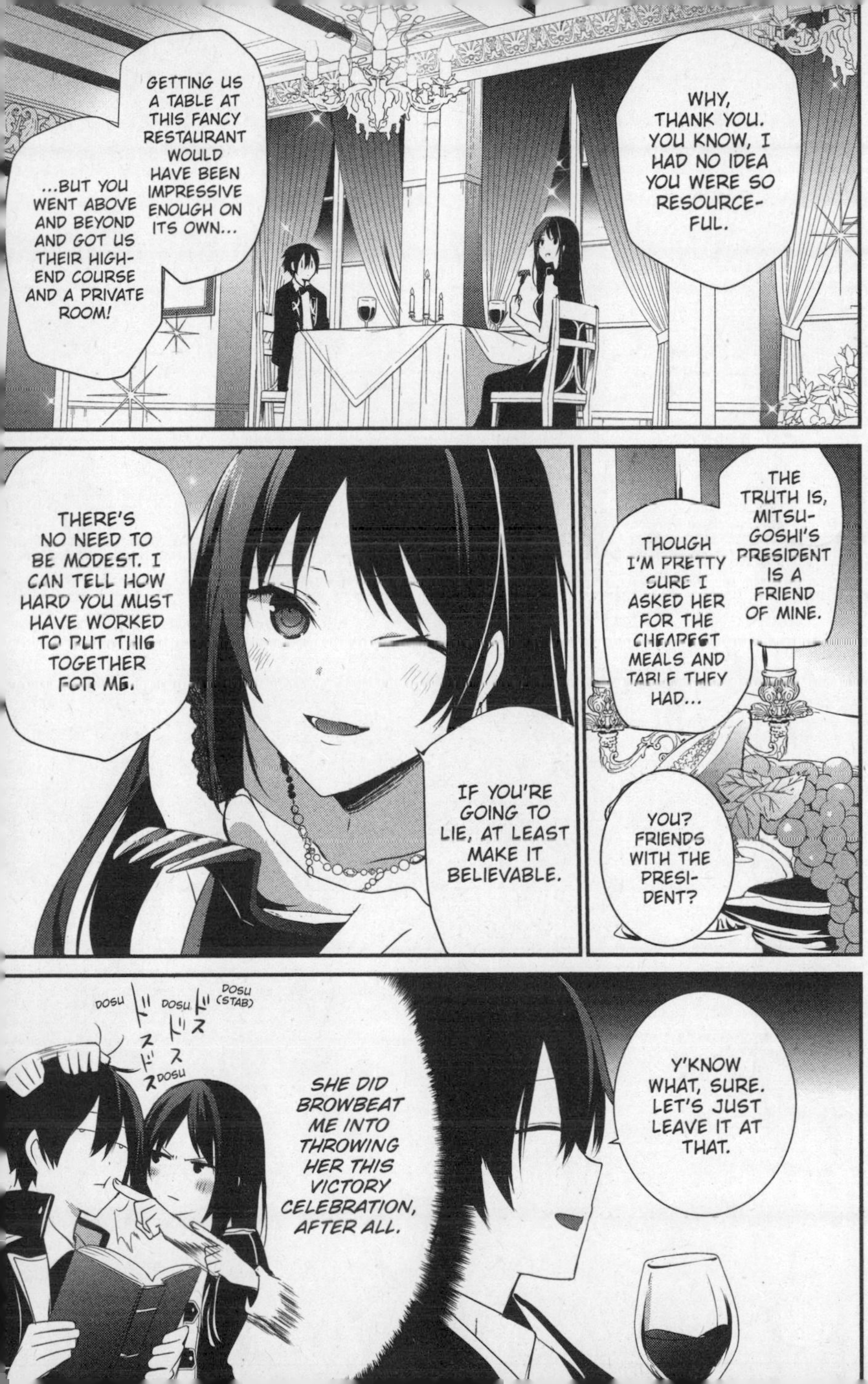
WHY, THANK YOU. YOU KNOW, I HAD NO IDEA YOU WERE SO RESOURCE-FUL.
GETTING US A TABLE AT THIS FANCY RESTAURANT WOULD HAVE BEEN IMPRESSIVE ENOUGH ON ITS OWN...
...BUT YOU WENT ABOVE AND BEYOND AND GOT US THEIR HIGH-END COURSE AND A PRIVATE ROOM!
THE TRUTH IS, MITSU-GOSHI'S PRESIDENT IS A FRIEND OF MINE.
THOUGH I'M PRETTY SURE I ASKED HER FOR THE CHEAPEST MEALS AND TABLE THEY HAD...
YOU? FRIENDS WITH THE PRESI-DENT?
THERE'S NO NEED TO BE MODEST. I CAN TELL HOW HARD YOU MUST HAVE WORKED TO PUT THIS TOGETHER FOR ME.
IF YOU'RE GOING TO LIE, AT LEAST MAKE IT BELIEVABLE.
Y'KNOW WHAT, SURE. LET'S JUST LEAVE IT AT THAT.
SHE DID BROWBEAT ME INTO THROWING HER THIS VICTORY CELEBRATION, AFTER ALL.
DOSU (STAB)
ドスドス
DOSU
ドスドス
DOSU
DOSU

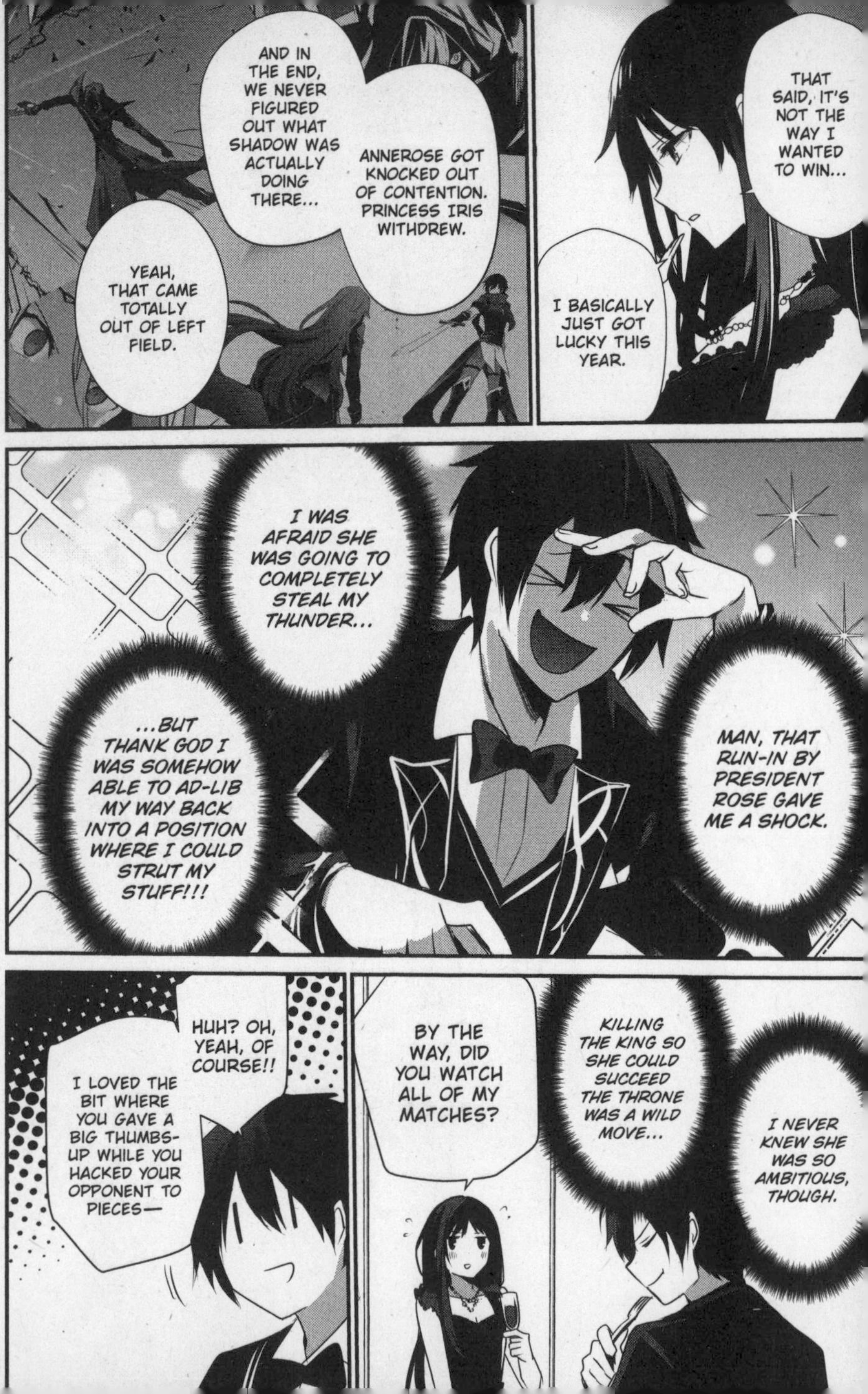
THAT SAID, IT'S NOT THE WAY I WANTED TO WIN...
I BASICALLY JUST GOT LUCKY THIS YEAR.
ANNEROSE GOT KNOCKED OUT OF CONTENTION. PRINCESS IRIS WITHDREW.
AND IN THE END, WE NEVER FIGURED OUT WHAT SHADOW WAS ACTUALLY DOING THERE...
YEAH, THAT CAME TOTALLY OUT OF LEFT FIELD.
MAN, THAT RUN-IN BY PRESIDENT ROSE GAVE ME A SHOCK.
I WAS AFRAID SHE WAS GOING TO COMPLETELY STEAL MY THUNDER...
...BUT THANK GOD I WAS SOMEHOW ABLE TO AD-LIB MY WAY BACK INTO A POSITION WHERE I COULD STRUT MY STUFF!!!
KILLING THE KING SO SHE COULD SUCCEED THE THRONE WAS A WILD MOVE...
I NEVER KNEW SHE WAS SO AMBITIOUS, THOUGH.
BY THE WAY, DID YOU WATCH ALL OF MY MATCHES?
HUH? OH, YEAH, OF COURSE!!
I LOVED THE BIT WHERE YOU GAVE A BIG THUMBS-UP WHILE YOU HACKED YOUR OPPONENT TO PIECES—

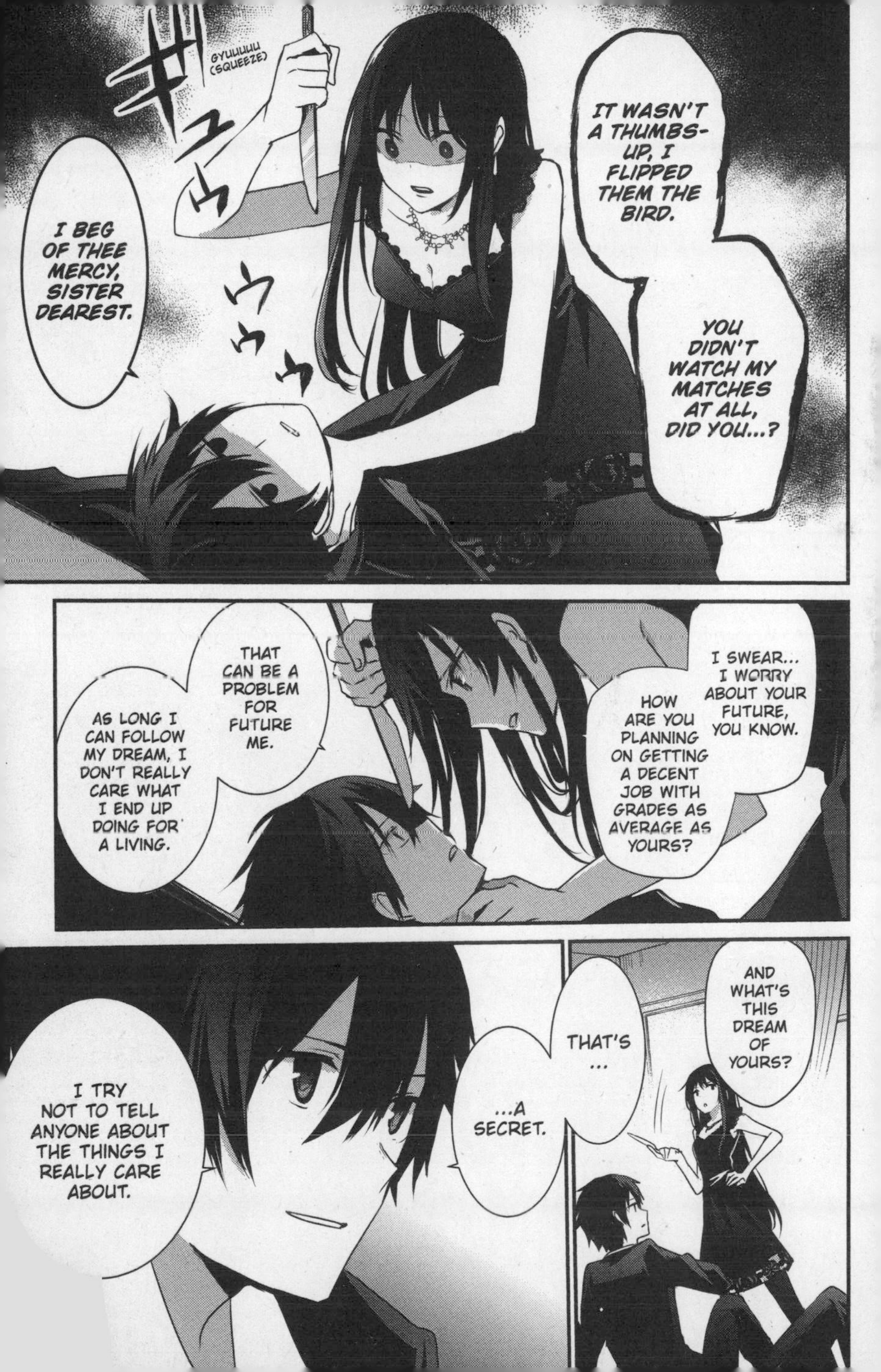
IT WASN'T A THUMBS-UP, I FLIPPED THEM THE BIRD.
YOU DIDN'T WATCH MY MATCHES AT ALL, DID YOU...?
GYUUUUU (SQUEEZE)
I BEG OF THEE MERCY, SISTER DEAREST.
I SWEAR... I WORRY ABOUT YOUR FUTURE, YOU KNOW.
HOW ARE YOU PLANNING ON GETTING A DECENT JOB WITH GRADES AS AVERAGE AS YOURS?
THAT CAN BE A PROBLEM FOR FUTURE ME.
AS LONG I CAN FOLLOW MY DREAM, I DON'T REALLY CARE WHAT I END UP DOING FOR A LIVING.
AND WHAT'S THIS DREAM OF YOURS?
THAT'S ...
...A SECRET.
I TRY NOT TO TELL ANYONE ABOUT THE THINGS I REALLY CARE ABOUT.

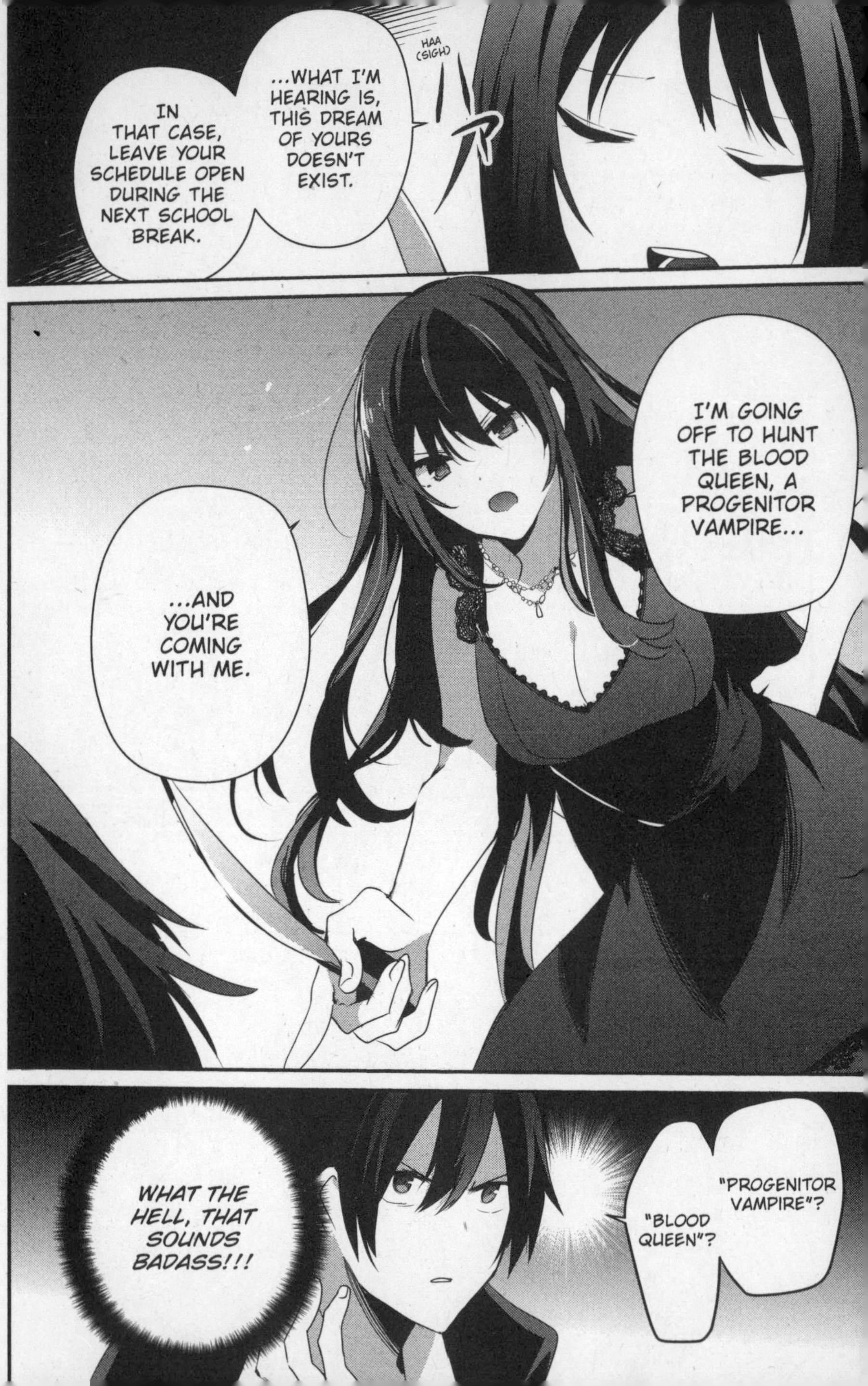
HAA (SIGH)
...WHAT I'M HEARING IS, THIS DREAM OF YOURS DOESN'T EXIST.
IN THAT CASE, LEAVE YOUR SCHEDULE OPEN DURING THE NEXT SCHOOL BREAK.
I'M GOING OFF TO HUNT THE BLOOD QUEEN, A PROGENITOR VAMPIRE...
...AND YOU'RE COMING WITH ME.
"PROGENITOR VAMPIRE"?
"BLOOD QUEEN"?
WHAT THE HELL, THAT SOUNDS BADASS!!!

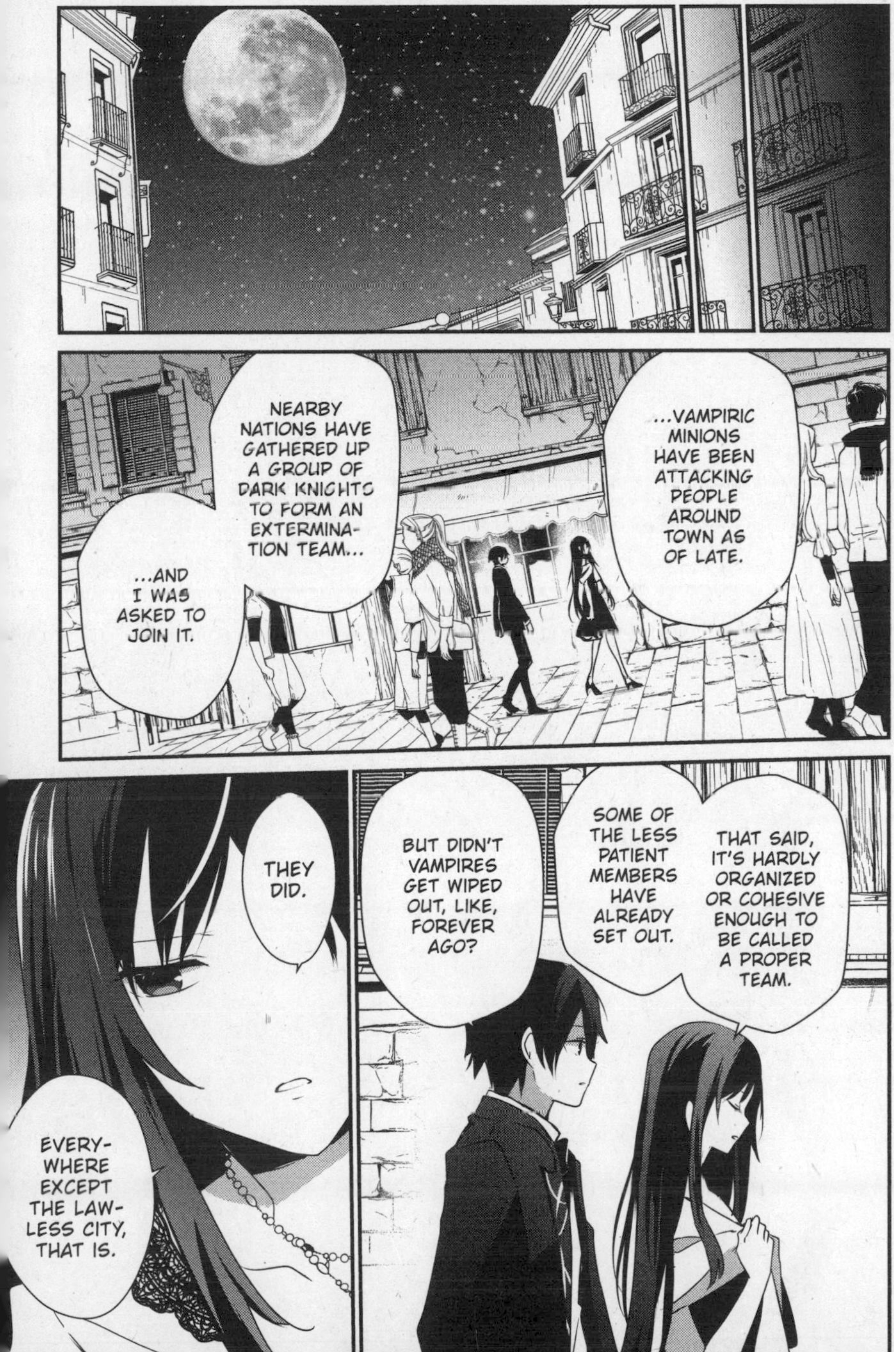
...VAMPIRIC MINIONS HAVE BEEN ATTACKING PEOPLE AROUND TOWN AS OF LATE.
NEARBY NATIONS HAVE GATHERED UP A GROUP OF DARK KNIGHTS TO FORM AN EXTERMINATION TEAM...
...AND I WAS ASKED TO JOIN IT.
THAT SAID, IT'S HARDLY ORGANIZED OR COHESIVE ENOUGH TO BE CALLED A PROPER TEAM.
SOME OF THE LESS PATIENT MEMBERS HAVE ALREADY SET OUT.
BUT DIDN'T VAMPIRES GET WIPED OUT, LIKE, FOREVER AGO?
THEY DID.
EVERYWHERE EXCEPT THE LAWLESS CITY, THAT IS.

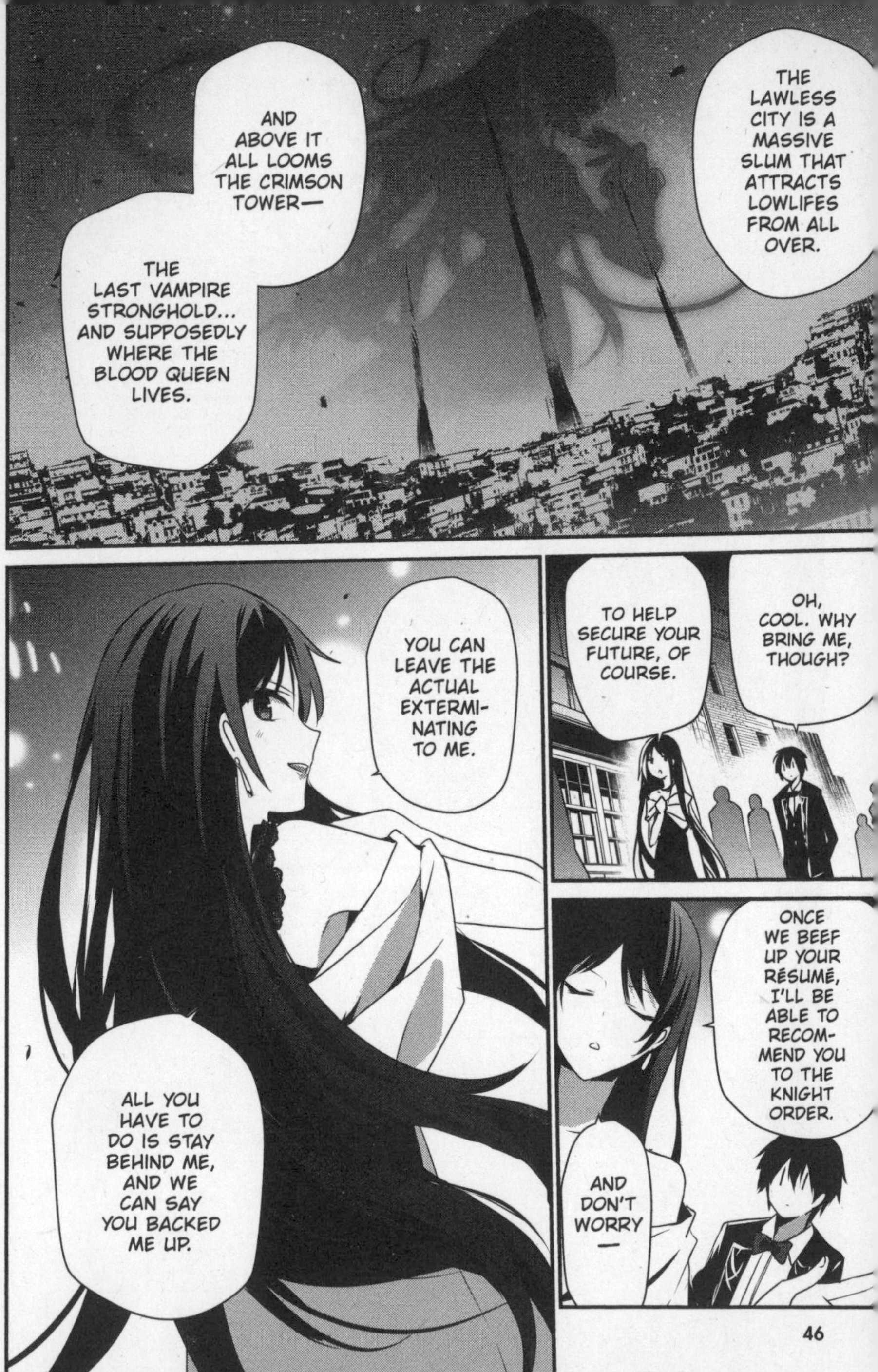
THE LAWLESS CITY IS A MASSIVE SLUM THAT ATTRACTS LOWLIFES FROM ALL OVER.
AND ABOVE IT ALL LOOMS THE CRIMSON TOWER—
THE LAST VAMPIRE STRONGHOLD... AND SUPPOSEDLY WHERE THE BLOOD QUEEN LIVES.
OH, COOL. WHY BRING ME, THOUGH?
TO HELP SECURE YOUR FUTURE, OF COURSE.
ONCE WE BEEF UP YOUR RÉSUMÉ, I'LL BE ABLE TO RECOMMEND YOU TO THE KNIGHT ORDER.
AND DON'T WORRY—
YOU CAN LEAVE THE ACTUAL EXTERMINATING TO ME.
ALL YOU HAVE TO DO IS STAY BEHIND ME, AND WE CAN SAY YOU BACKED ME UP.

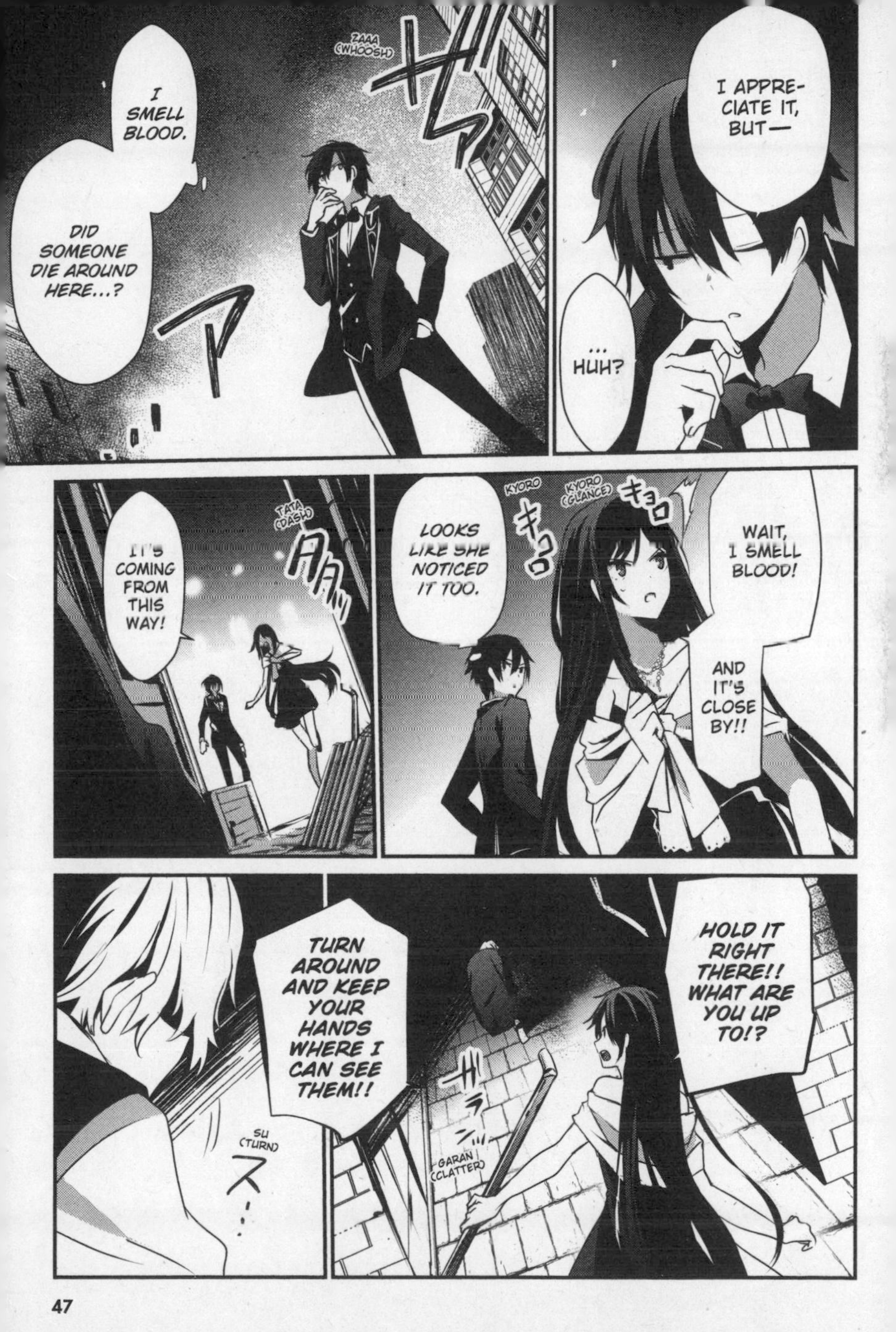
I APPRECIATE IT, BUT—
... HUH?
ZAAA (WHOOSH)
I SMELL BLOOD.
DID SOMEONE DIE AROUND HERE...?
KYORO
KYORO (GLANCE)
WAIT, I SMELL BLOOD!
AND IT'S CLOSE BY!!
LOOKS LIKE SHE NOTICED IT TOO.
TATA (DASH)
IT'S COMING FROM THIS WAY!
HOLD IT RIGHT THERE!! WHAT ARE YOU UP TO!?
GARAN (CLATTER)
TURN AROUND AND KEEP YOUR HANDS WHERE I CAN SEE THEM!!
SU (TURN)

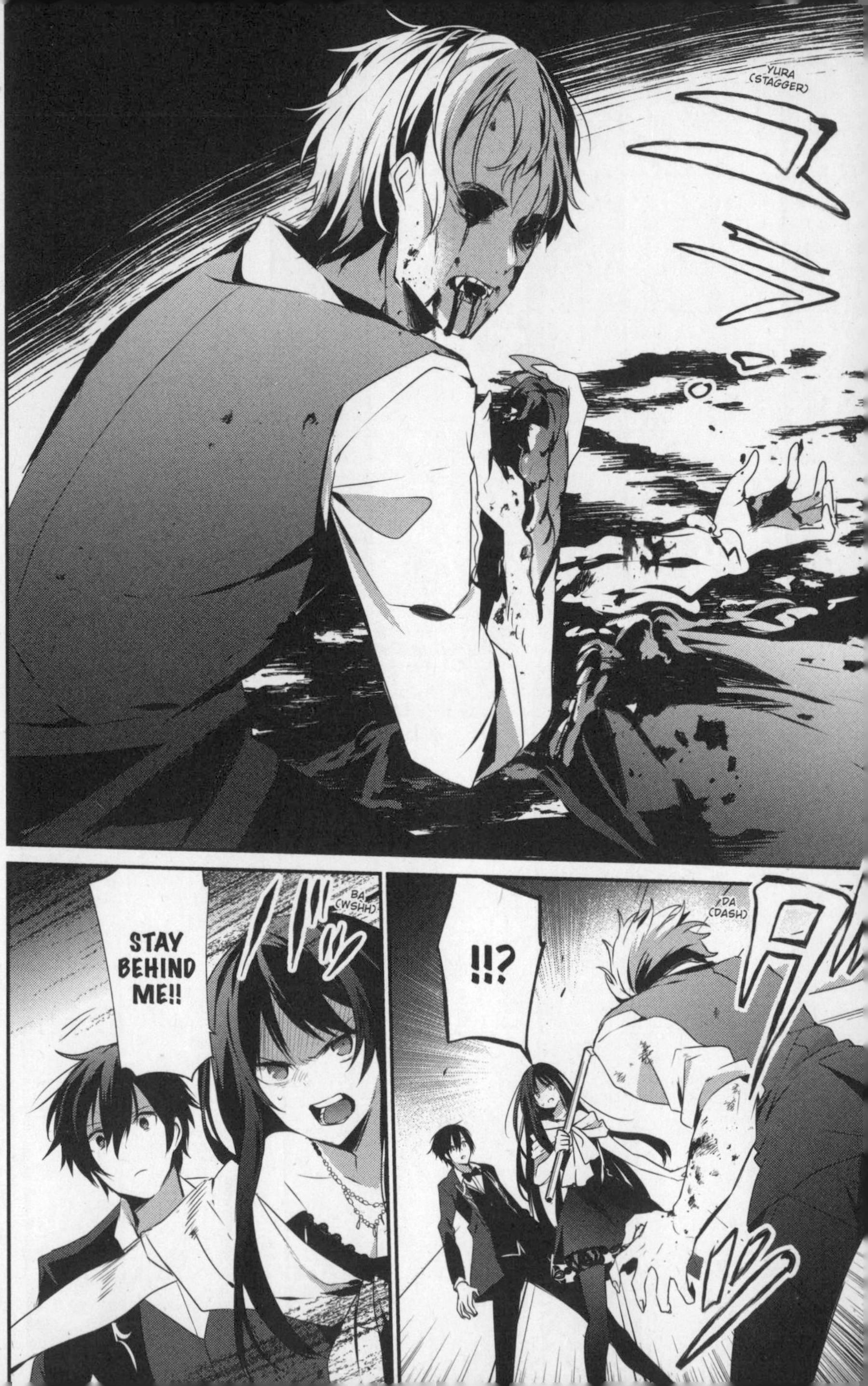
YURA (STAGGER)
DA (DASH)
!!?
BA (WSHH)
STAY BEHIND ME!!

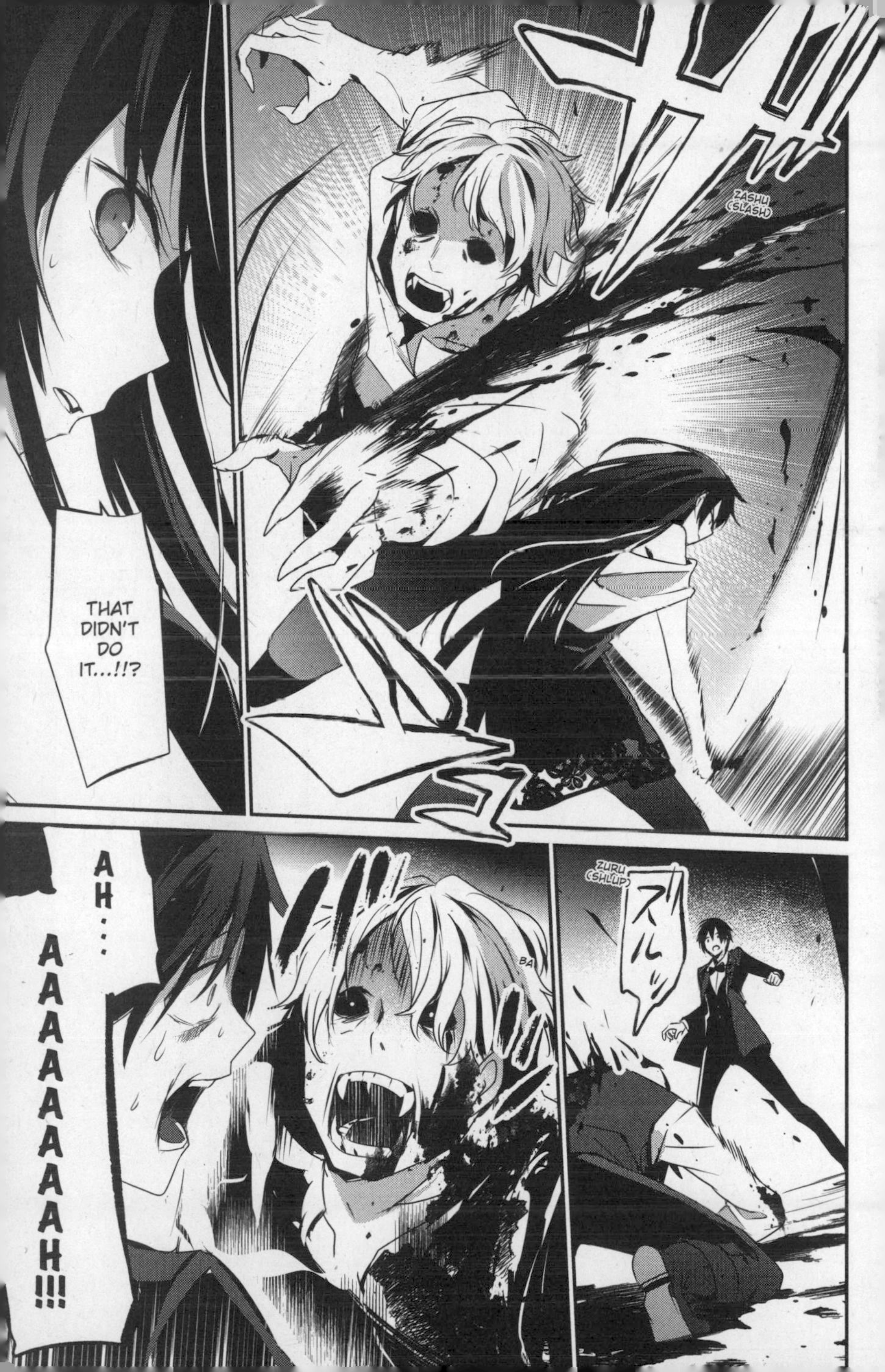
ZASHU (SLASH)
THAT DIDN'T DO IT...!!?
ZURU (SHLUP)
BA
AH...
AAAAAAAAH!!!

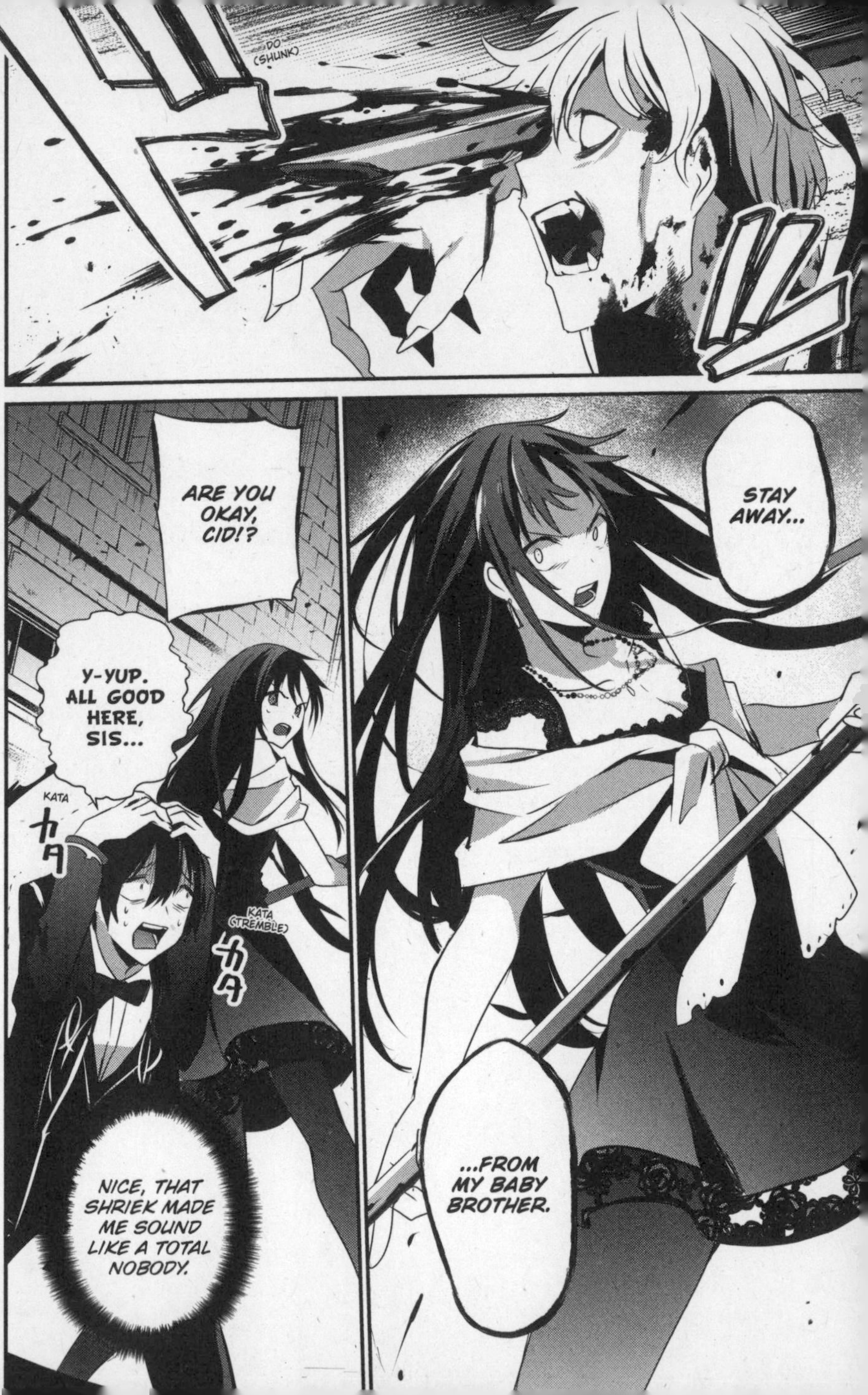
DO
(SHUNK)
STAY AWAY...
...FROM MY BABY BROTHER.
ARE YOU OKAY, CID!?
Y-YUP. ALL GOOD HERE, SIS...
KATA
カタ
KATA
(TREMBLE)
カタ
NICE, THAT SHRIEK MADE ME SOUND LIKE A TOTAL NOBODY.

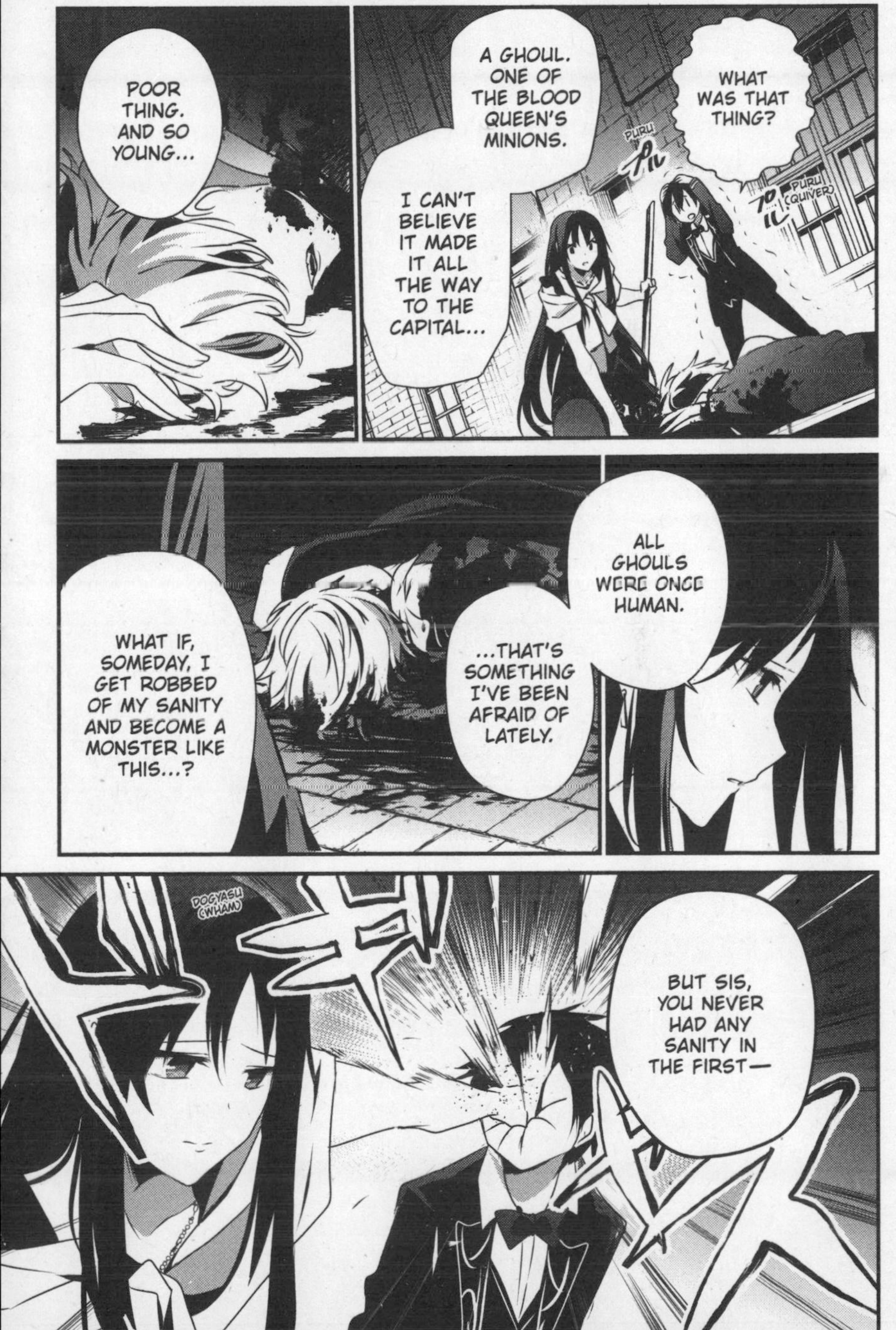
WHAT WAS THAT THING?
PURU
PURU (QUIVER)
A GHOUL. ONE OF THE BLOOD QUEEN'S MINIONS.
I CAN'T BELIEVE IT MADE IT ALL THE WAY TO THE CAPITAL...
POOR THING. AND SO YOUNG...
ALL GHOULS WERE ONCE HUMAN.
...THAT'S SOMETHING I'VE BEEN AFRAID OF LATELY.
WHAT IF, SOMEDAY, I GET ROBBED OF MY SANITY AND BECOME A MONSTER LIKE THIS...?
BUT SIS, YOU NEVER HAD ANY SANITY IN THE FIRST—
DOGYASU (WHAM)

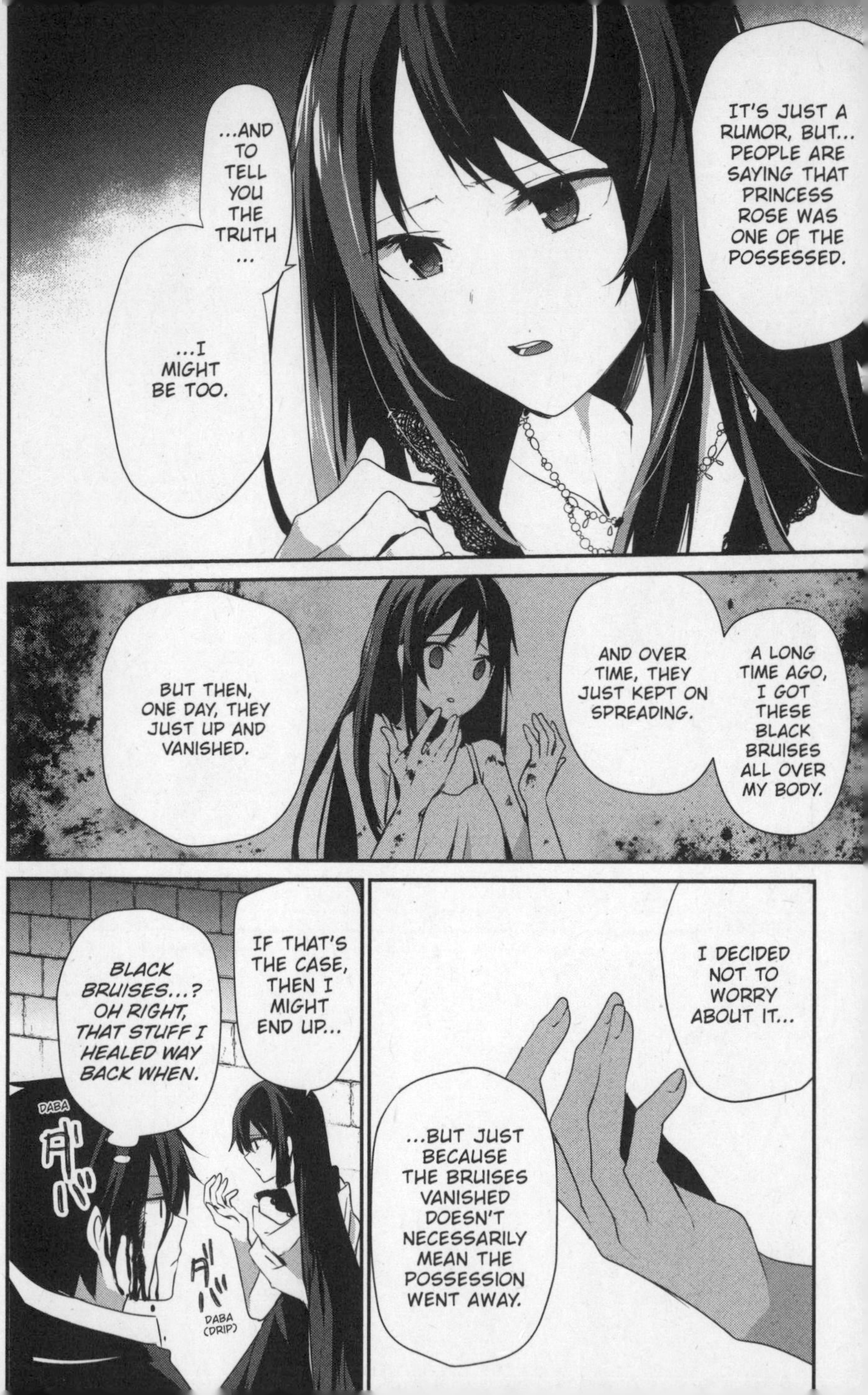
IT'S JUST A RUMOR, BUT... PEOPLE ARE SAYING THAT PRINCESS ROSE WAS ONE OF THE POSSESSED.
...AND TO TELL YOU THE TRUTH...
...I MIGHT BE TOO.
A LONG TIME AGO, I GOT THESE BLACK BRUISES ALL OVER MY BODY.
AND OVER TIME, THEY JUST KEPT ON SPREADING.
BUT THEN, ONE DAY, THEY JUST UP AND VANISHED.
I DECIDED NOT TO WORRY ABOUT IT...
...BUT JUST BECAUSE THE BRUISES VANISHED DOESN'T NECESSARILY MEAN THE POSSESSION WENT AWAY.
IF THAT'S THE CASE, THEN I MIGHT END UP...
BLACK BRUISES...? OH RIGHT, THAT STUFF I HEALED WAY BACK WHEN.
DABA
DABA (DRIP)

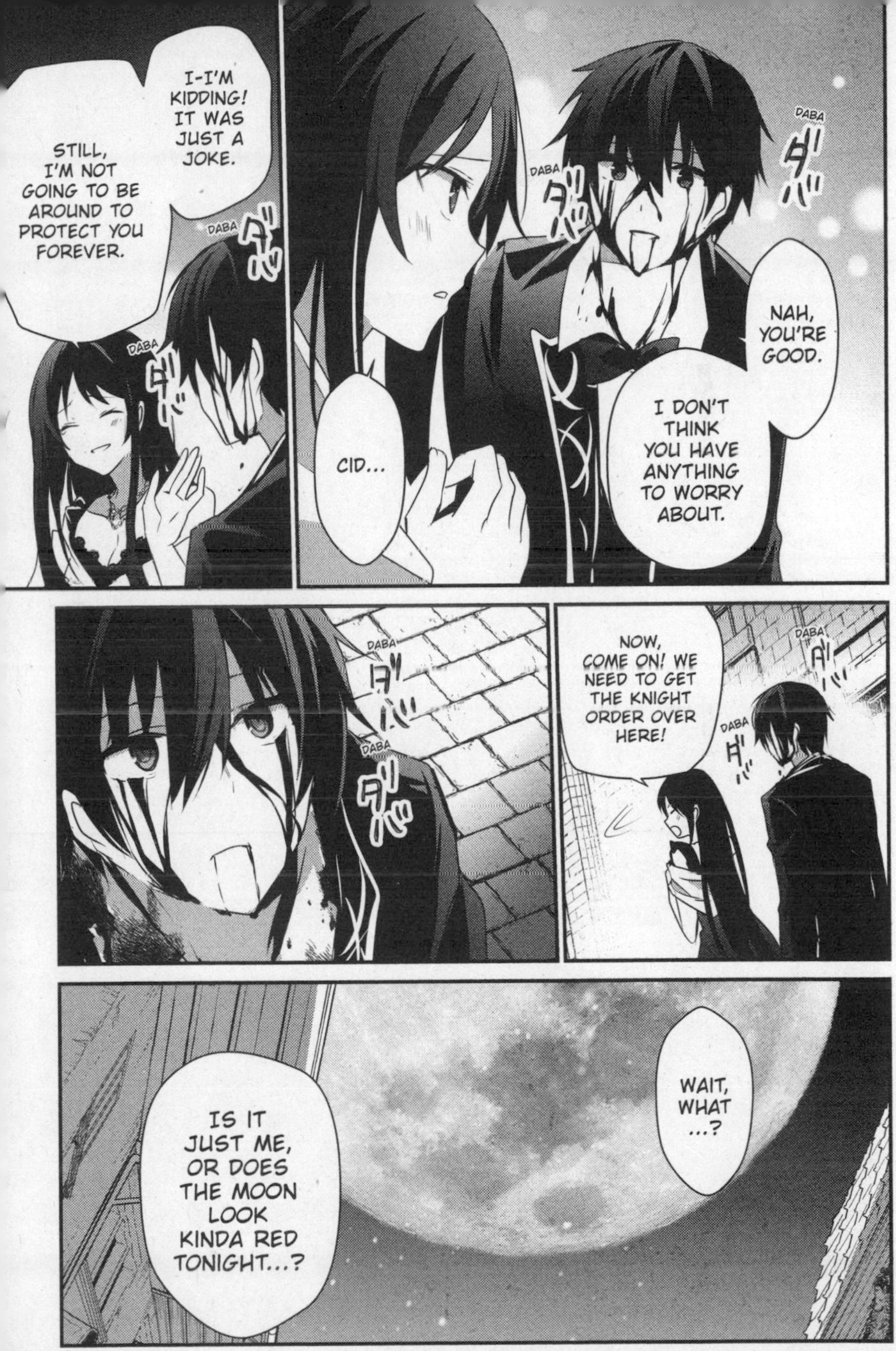
DABA
DABA
NAH, YOU'RE GOOD.
I DON'T THINK YOU HAVE ANYTHING TO WORRY ABOUT.
CID...
I-I'M KIDDING! IT WAS JUST A JOKE.
STILL, I'M NOT GOING TO BE AROUND TO PROTECT YOU FOREVER.
DABA
DABA
DABA
NOW, COME ON! WE NEED TO GET THE KNIGHT ORDER OVER HERE!
DABA
DABA
DABA
WAIT, WHAT ...?
IS IT JUST ME, OR DOES THE MOON LOOK KINDA RED TONIGHT...?

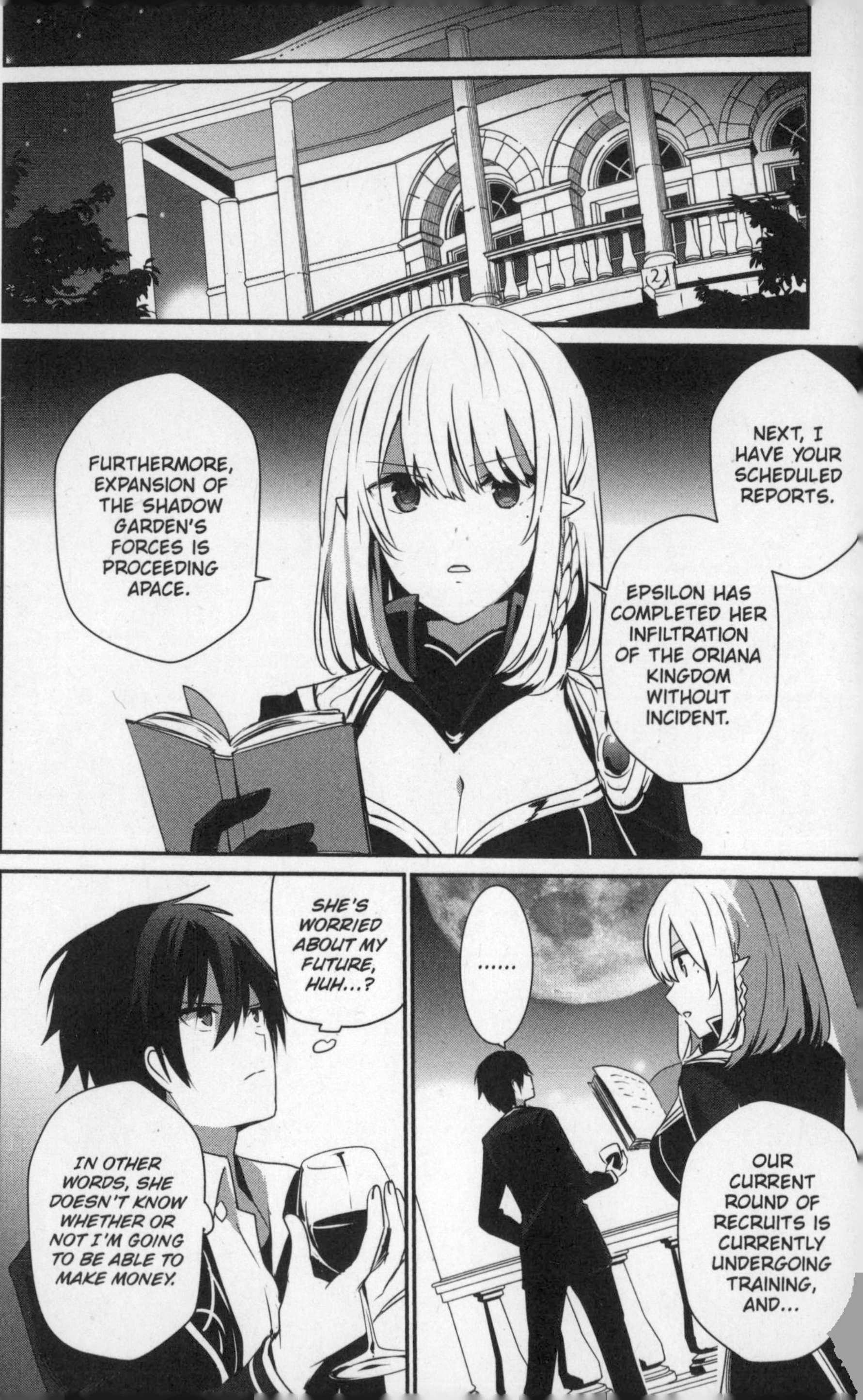
NEXT, I HAVE YOUR SCHEDULED REPORTS.
EPSILON HAS COMPLETED HER INFILTRATION OF THE ORIANA KINGDOM WITHOUT INCIDENT.
FURTHERMORE, EXPANSION OF THE SHADOW GARDEN'S FORCES IS PROCEEDING APACE.
OUR CURRENT ROUND OF RECRUITS IS CURRENTLY UNDERGOING TRAINING, AND...
......
SHE'S WORRIED ABOUT MY FUTURE, HUH...?
IN OTHER WORDS, SHE DOESN'T KNOW WHETHER OR NOT I'M GOING TO BE ABLE TO MAKE MONEY.

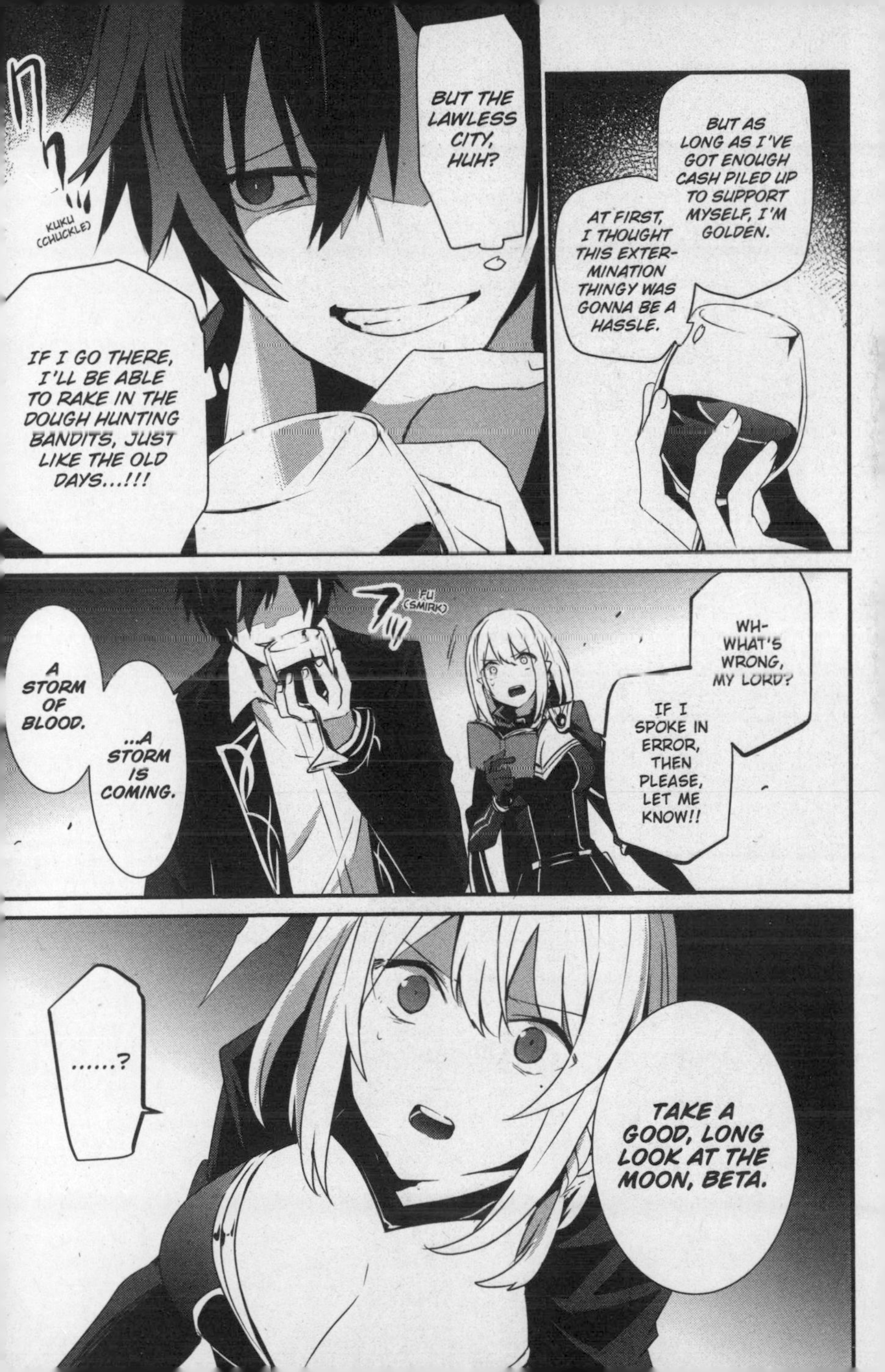
BUT AS LONG AS I'VE GOT ENOUGH CASH PILED UP TO SUPPORT MYSELF, I'M GOLDEN.
AT FIRST, I THOUGHT THIS EXTERMINATION THINGY WAS GONNA BE A HASSLE.
BUT THE LAWLESS CITY, HUH?
KUKU (CHUCKLE)
IF I GO THERE, I'LL BE ABLE TO RAKE IN THE DOUGH HUNTING BANDITS, JUST LIKE THE OLD DAYS...!!!
WH-WHAT'S WRONG, MY LORD?
IF I SPOKE IN ERROR, THEN PLEASE, LET ME KNOW!!
FU (SMIRK)
A STORM OF BLOOD.
...A STORM IS COMING.
TAKE A GOOD, LONG LOOK AT THE MOON, BETA.
......?

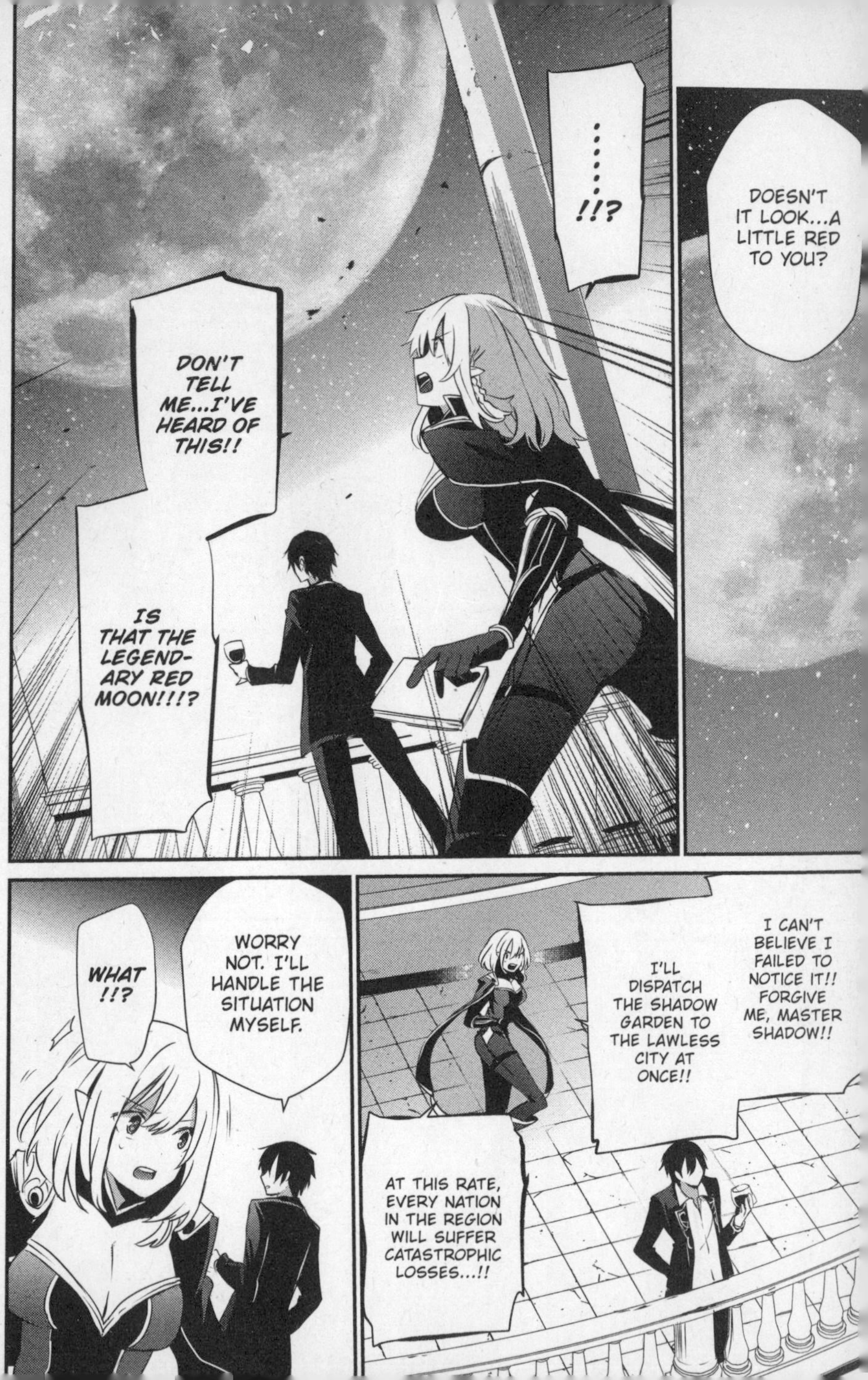
DOESN'T IT LOOK...A LITTLE RED TO YOU?
......!!?
DON'T TELL ME...I'VE HEARD OF THIS!!
IS THAT THE LEGENDARY RED MOON!!!?
I CAN'T BELIEVE I FAILED TO NOTICE IT!! FORGIVE ME, MASTER SHADOW!!
I'LL DISPATCH THE SHADOW GARDEN TO THE LAWLESS CITY AT ONCE!!
AT THIS RATE, EVERY NATION IN THE REGION WILL SUFFER CATASTROPHIC LOSSES...!!
WORRY NOT. I'LL HANDLE THE SITUATION MYSELF.
WHAT!!?

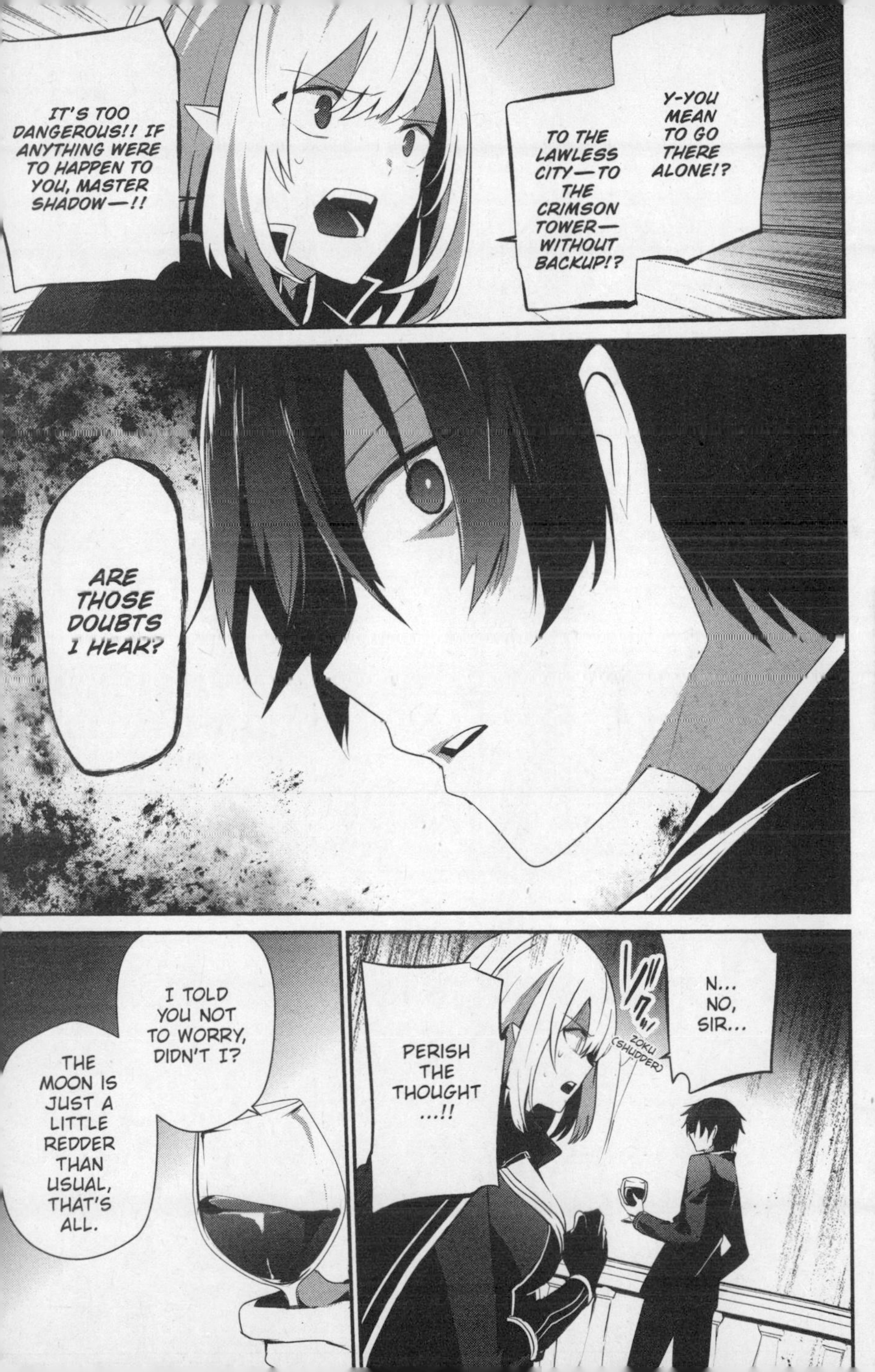
Y-YOU MEAN TO GO THERE ALONE!?
TO THE LAWLESS CITY—TO THE CRIMSON TOWER—WITHOUT BACKUP!?
IT'S TOO DANGEROUS!! IF ANYTHING WERE TO HAPPEN TO YOU, MASTER SHADOW—!!
ARE THOSE DOUBTS I HEAR?
N... NO, SIR...
ZOKU (SHUDDER)
PERISH THE THOUGHT ...!!
I TOLD YOU NOT TO WORRY, DIDN'T I?
THE MOON IS JUST A LITTLE REDDER THAN USUAL, THAT'S ALL.

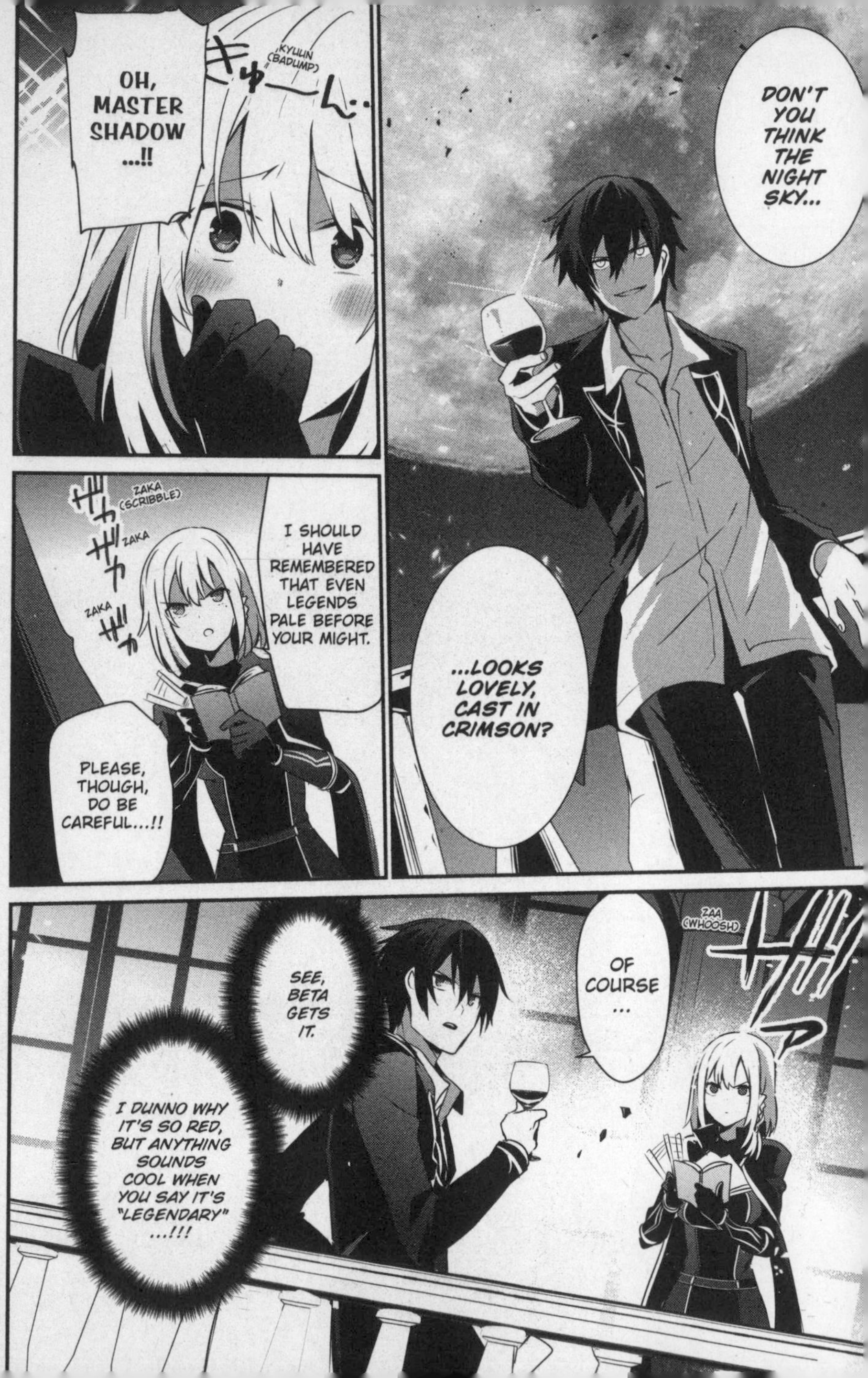
DON'T YOU THINK THE NIGHT SKY...
...LOOKS LOVELY, CAST IN CRIMSON?
KYUUN (BADUMP)
OH, MASTER SHADOW ...!!
ZAKA (SCRIBBLE)
ZAKA
ZAKA
I SHOULD HAVE REMEMBERED THAT EVEN LEGENDS PALE BEFORE YOUR MIGHT.
PLEASE, THOUGH, DO BE CAREFUL...!!
ZAA (WHOOSH)
OF COURSE ...
SEE, BETA GETS IT.
I DUNNO WHY IT'S SO RED, BUT ANYTHING SOUNDS COOL WHEN YOU SAY IT'S "LEGENDARY" ...!!!

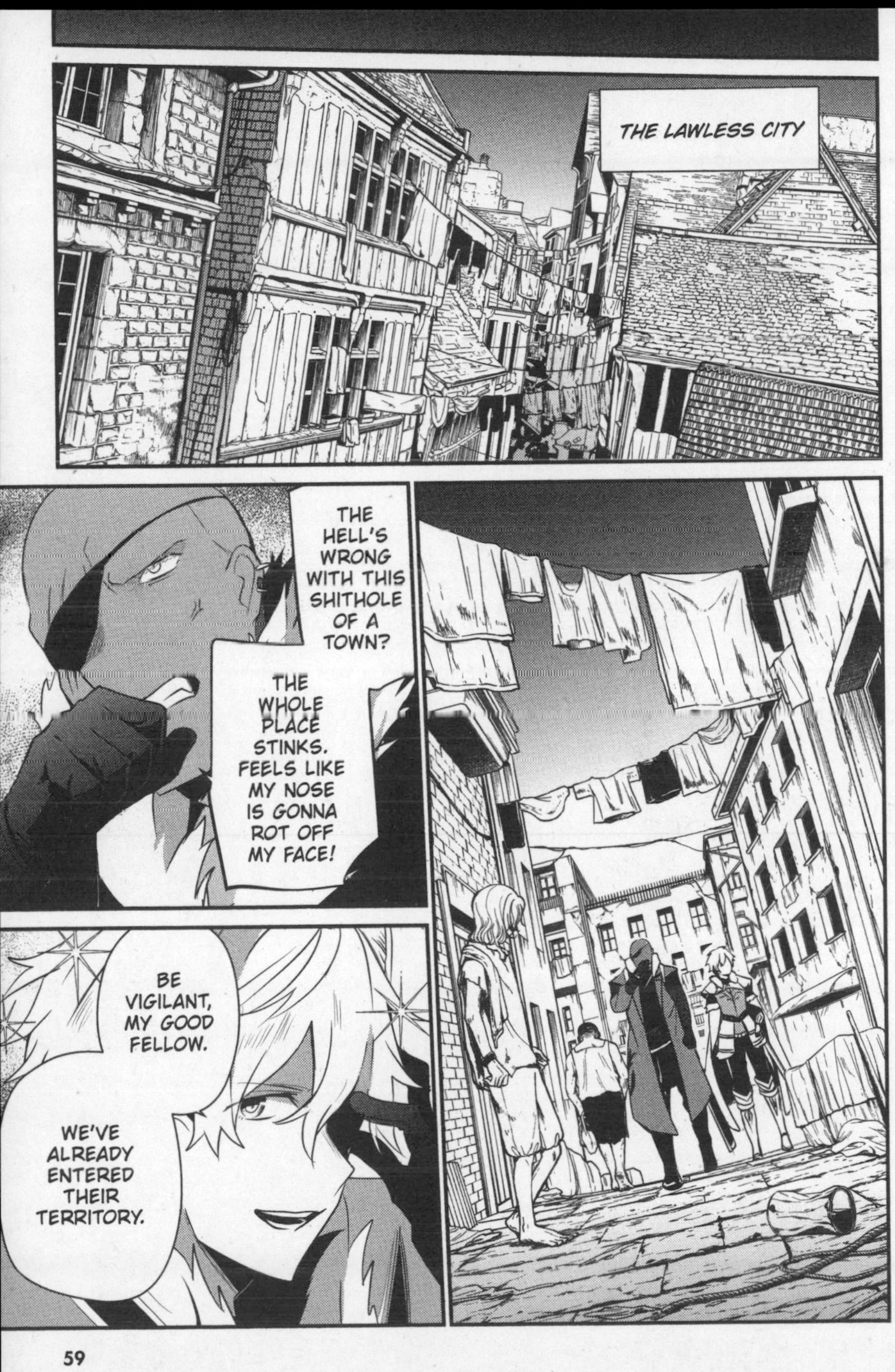
THE LAWLESS CITY
THE HELL'S WRONG WITH THIS SHITHOLE OF A TOWN?
THE WHOLE PLACE STINKS. FEELS LIKE MY NOSE IS GONNA ROT OFF MY FACE!
BE VIGILANT, MY GOOD FELLOW.
WE'VE ALREADY ENTERED THEIR TERRITORY.

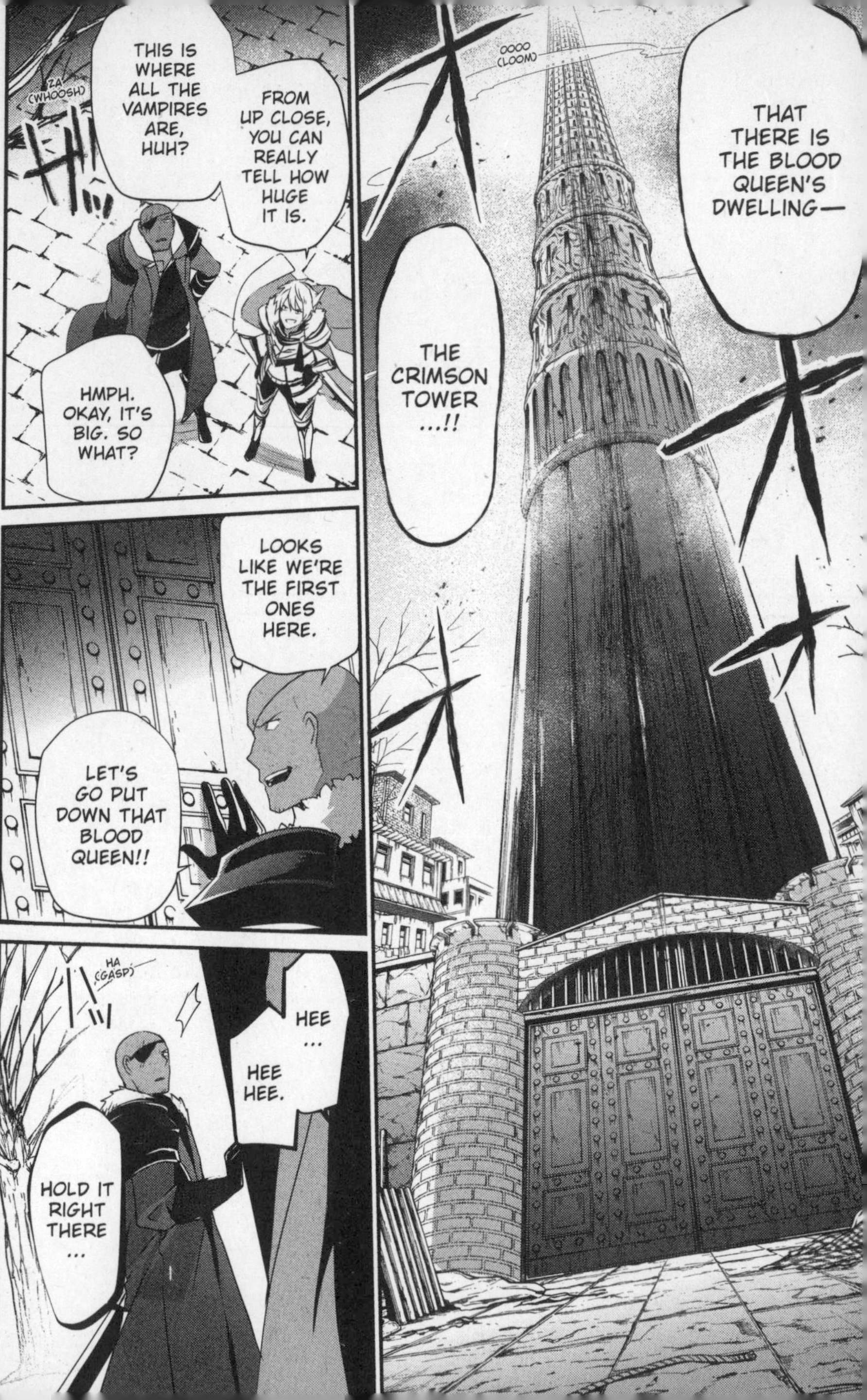
OOOO (LOOM)
THAT THERE IS THE BLOOD QUEEN'S DWELLING—
THE CRIMSON TOWER ...!!
ZA (WHOOSH)
THIS IS WHERE ALL THE VAMPIRES ARE, HUH?
FROM UP CLOSE, YOU CAN REALLY TELL HOW HUGE IT IS.
HMPH. OKAY, IT'S BIG. SO WHAT?
LOOKS LIKE WE'RE THE FIRST ONES HERE.
LET'S GO PUT DOWN THAT BLOOD QUEEN!!
HA (GASP)
HEE ...
HEE HEE.
HOLD IT RIGHT THERE ...

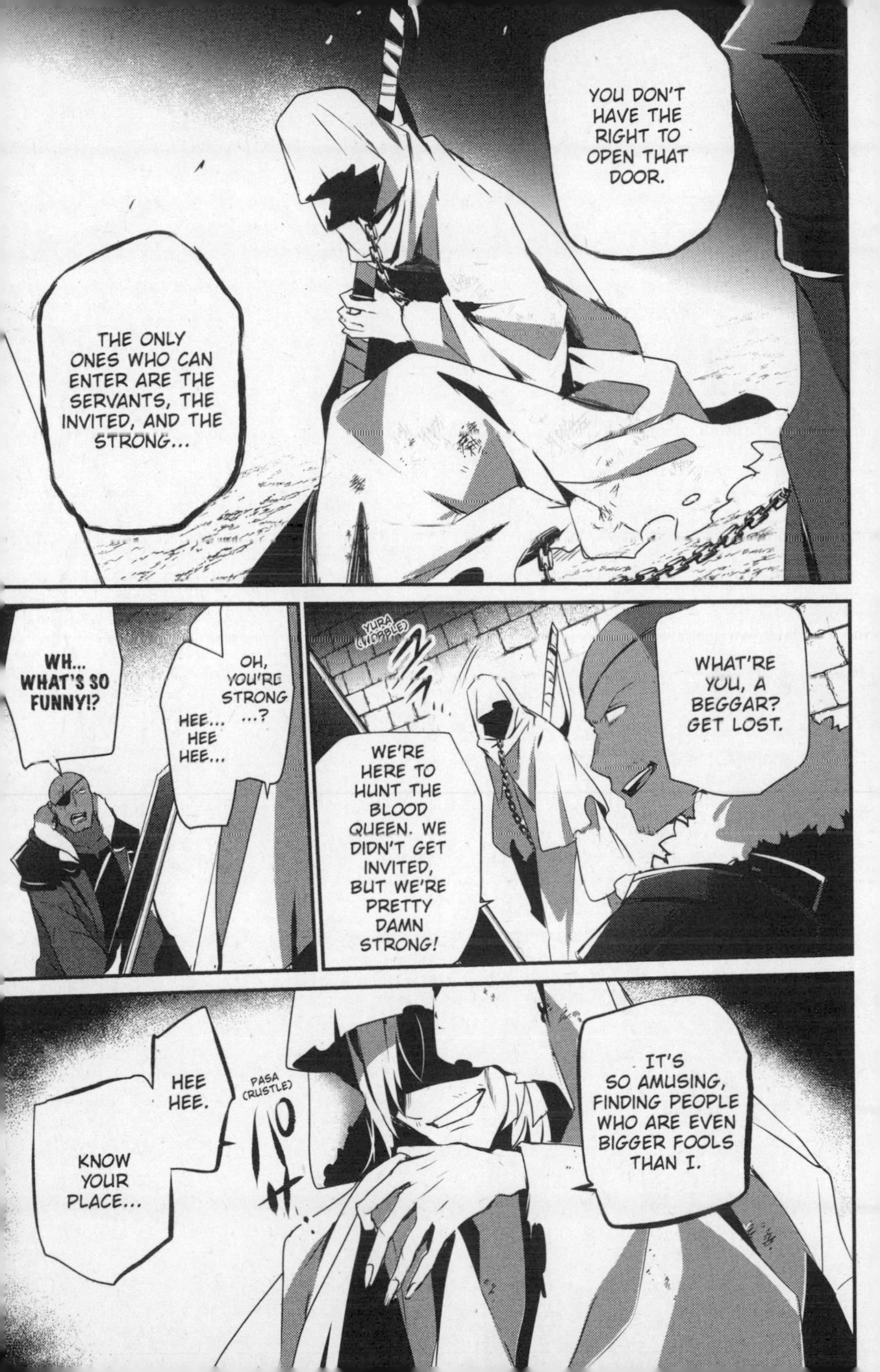
YOU DON'T HAVE THE RIGHT TO OPEN THAT DOOR.
THE ONLY ONES WHO CAN ENTER ARE THE SERVANTS, THE INVITED, AND THE STRONG...
WHAT'RE YOU, A BEGGAR? GET LOST.
YURA (WOBBLE)
WE'RE HERE TO HUNT THE BLOOD QUEEN. WE DIDN'T GET INVITED, BUT WE'RE PRETTY DAMN STRONG!
OH, YOU'RE STRONG ...?
HEE... HEE HEE...
WH... WHAT'S SO FUNNY!?
IT'S SO AMUSING, FINDING PEOPLE WHO ARE EVEN BIGGER FOOLS THAN I.
PASA (RUSTLE)
HEE HEE.
KNOW YOUR PLACE...

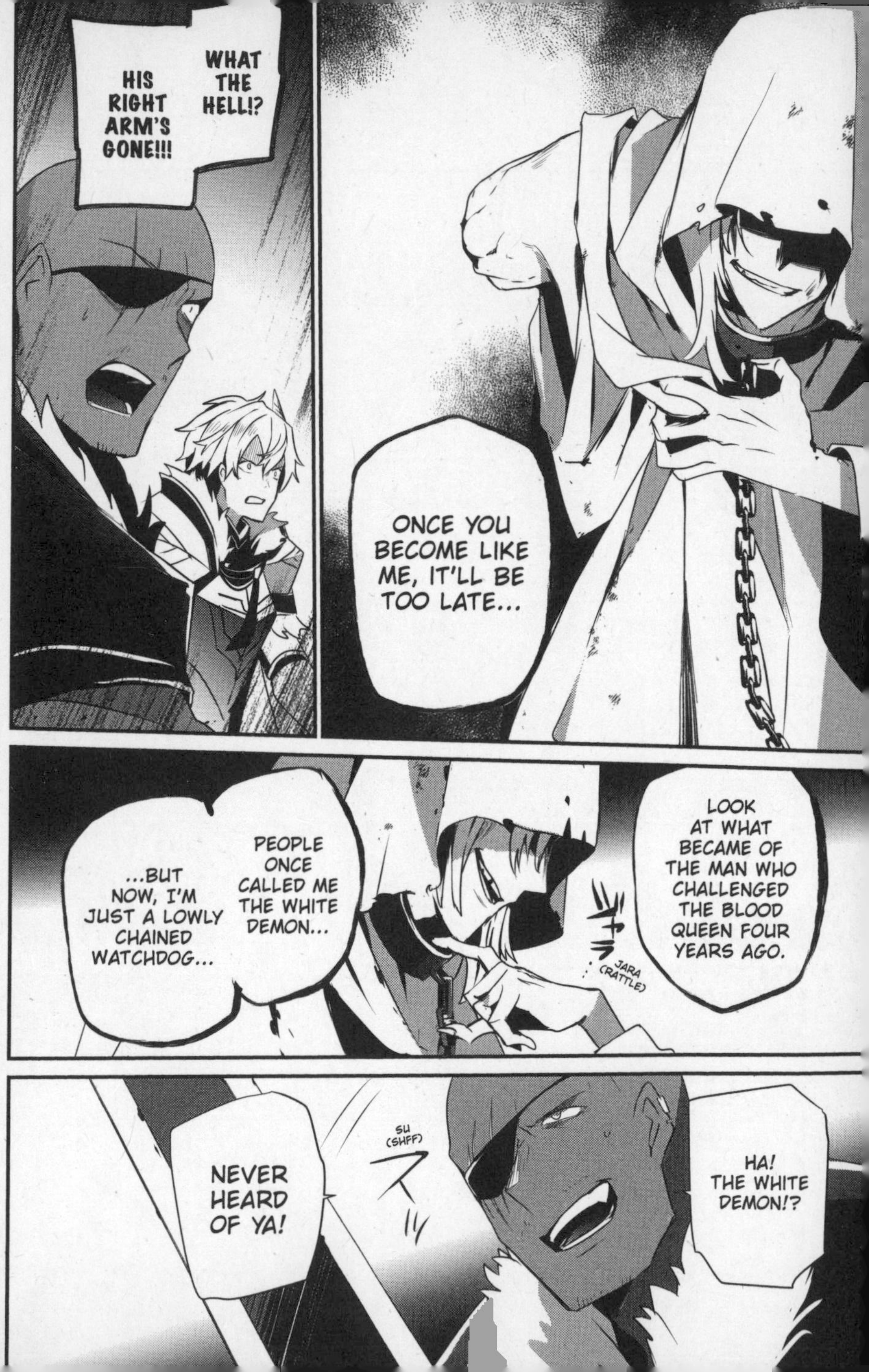
ONCE YOU BECOME LIKE ME, IT'LL BE TOO LATE...
WHAT THE HELL!?
HIS RIGHT ARM'S GONE!!!
LOOK AT WHAT BECAME OF THE MAN WHO CHALLENGED THE BLOOD QUEEN FOUR YEARS AGO.
JARA (RATTLE)
PEOPLE ONCE CALLED ME THE WHITE DEMON...
...BUT NOW, I'M JUST A LOWLY CHAINED WATCHDOG...
HA! THE WHITE DEMON!?
SU (SHFF)
NEVER HEARD OF YA!

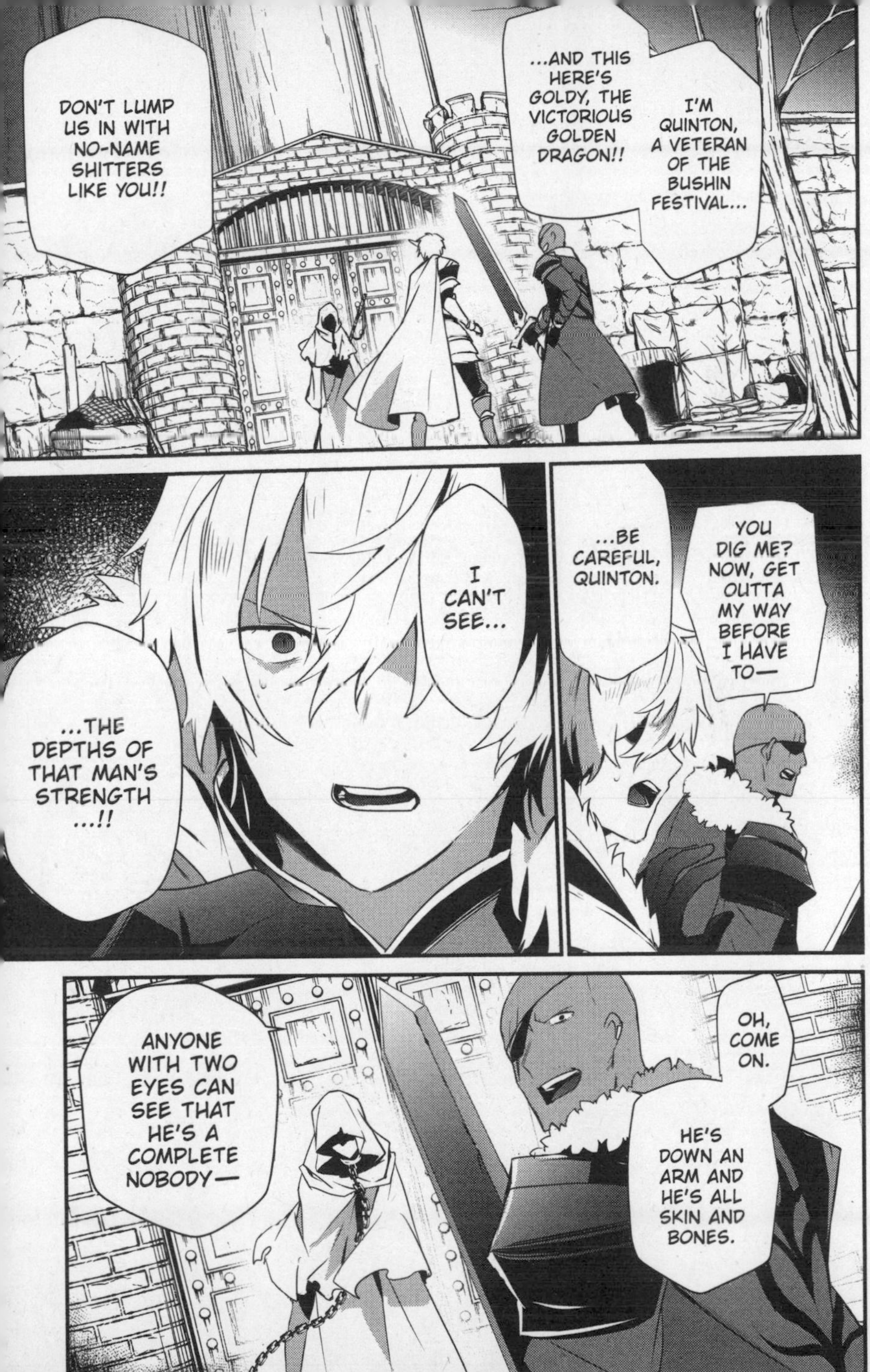
I'M QUINTON, A VETERAN OF THE BUSHIN FESTIVAL...
...AND THIS HERE'S GOLDY, THE VICTORIOUS GOLDEN DRAGON!!
DON'T LUMP US IN WITH NO-NAME SHITTERS LIKE YOU!!
YOU DIG ME? NOW, GET OUTTA MY WAY BEFORE I HAVE TO—
...BE CAREFUL, QUINTON.
I CAN'T SEE...
...THE DEPTHS OF THAT MAN'S STRENGTH...!!
OH, COME ON.
HE'S DOWN AN ARM AND HE'S ALL SKIN AND BONES.
ANYONE WITH TWO EYES CAN SEE THAT HE'S A COMPLETE NOBODY—

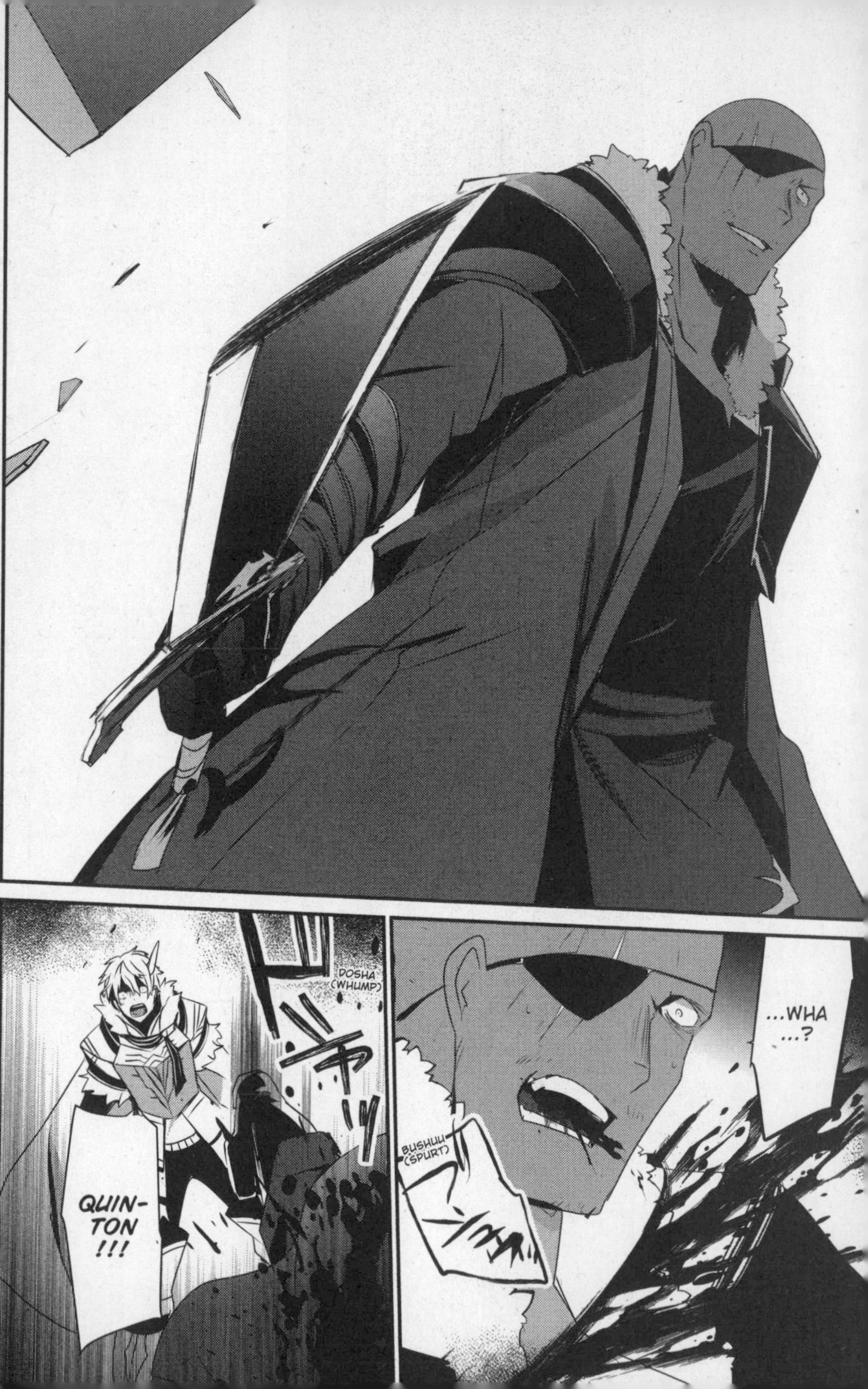
...WHA ...?
BUSHUU (SPURT)
DOSHA (WHUMP)
QUIN-TON !!!

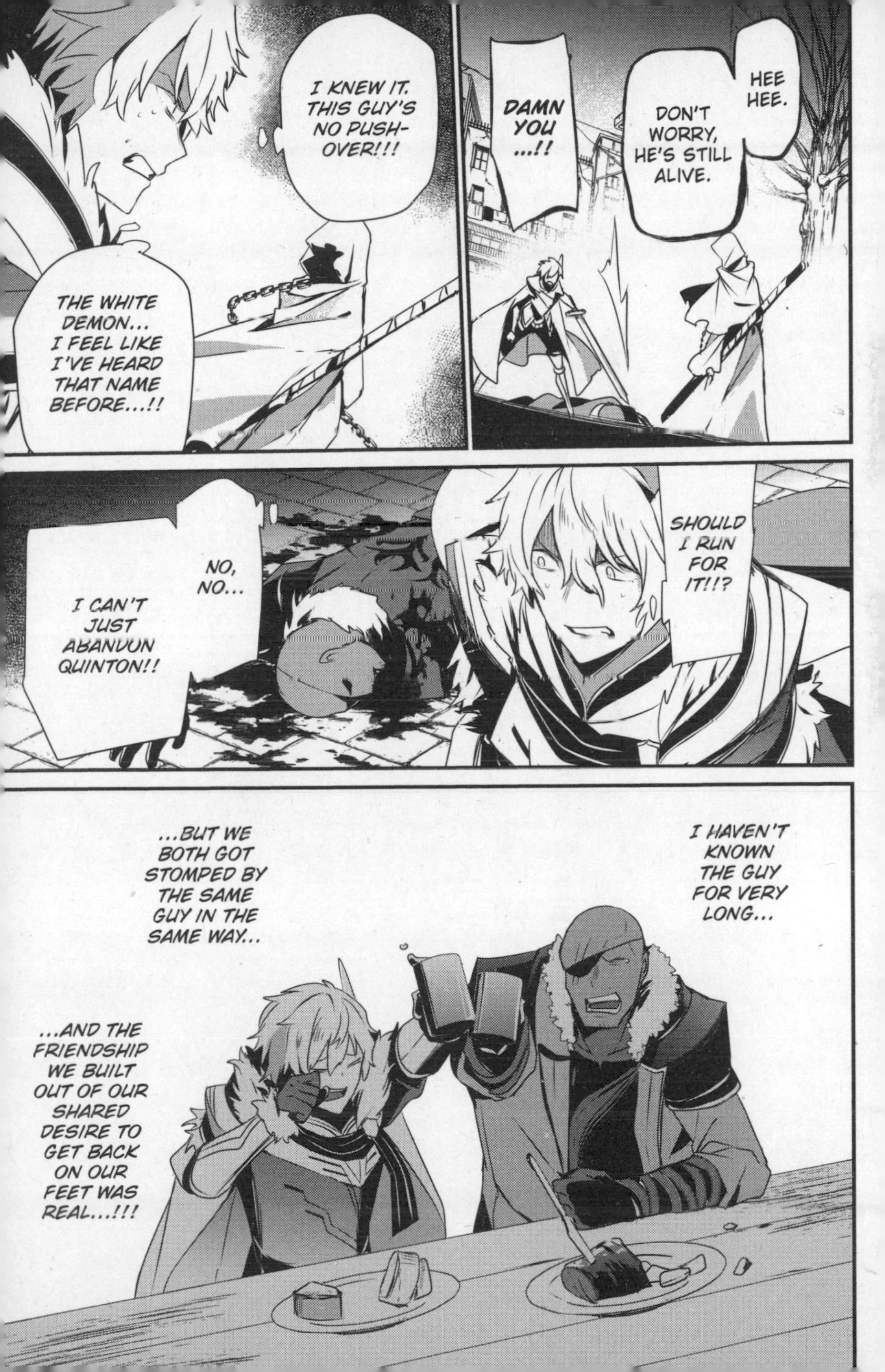
HEE HEE.
DON'T WORRY, HE'S STILL ALIVE.
DAMN YOU ...!!
I KNEW IT. THIS GUY'S NO PUSH-OVER!!!
THE WHITE DEMON... I FEEL LIKE I'VE HEARD THAT NAME BEFORE...!!
SHOULD I RUN FOR IT!!?
NO, NO...
I CAN'T JUST ABANDON QUINTON!!
I HAVEN'T KNOWN THE GUY FOR VERY LONG...
...BUT WE BOTH GOT STOMPED BY THE SAME GUY IN THE SAME WAY...
...AND THE FRIENDSHIP WE BUILT OUT OF OUR SHARED DESIRE TO GET BACK ON OUR FEET WAS REAL...!!!

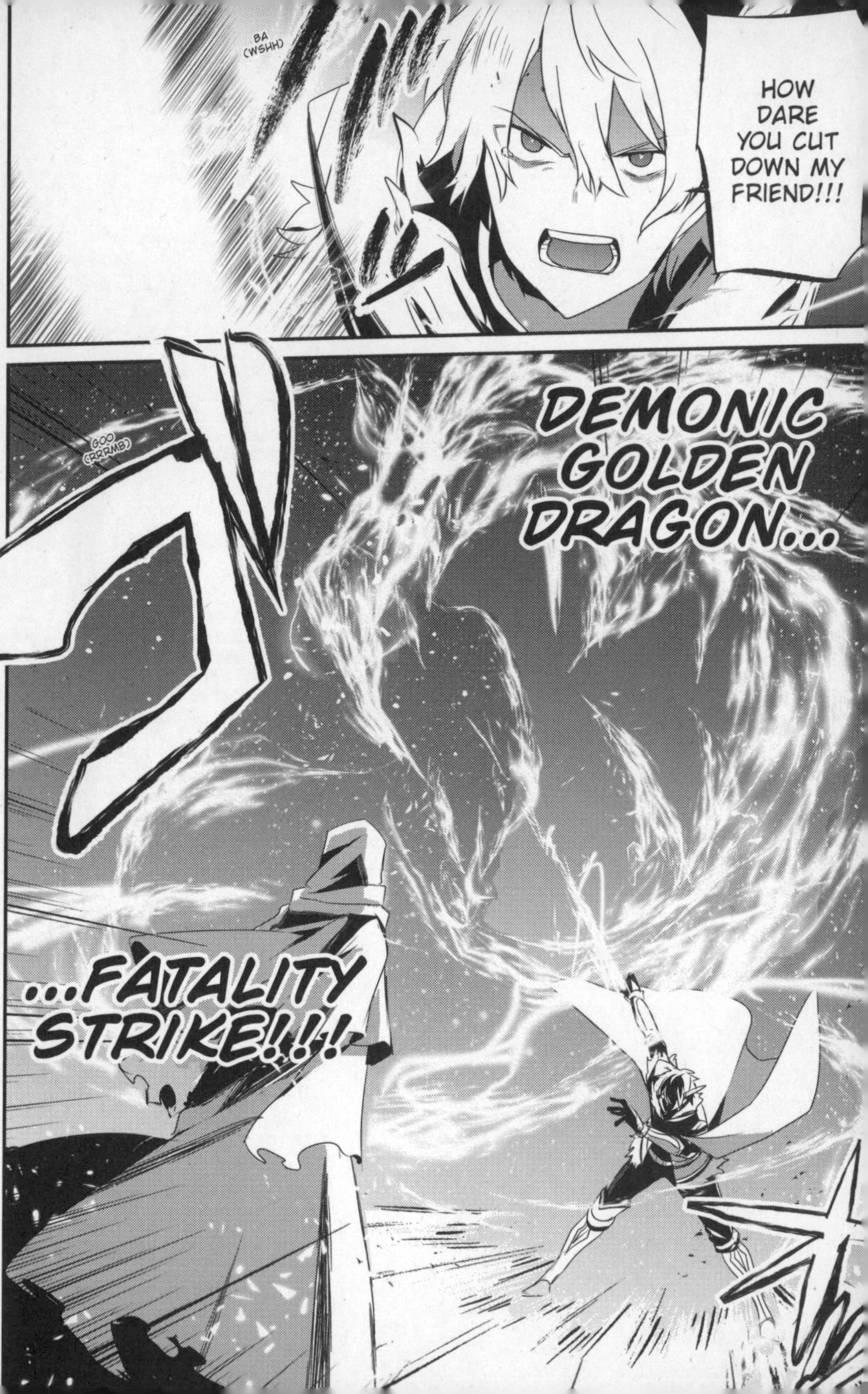
HOW DARE YOU CUT DOWN MY FRIEND!!!
BA (WSHH)
DEMONIC GOLDEN DRAGON...
GOO (RRRMB)
...FATALITY STRIKE!!!

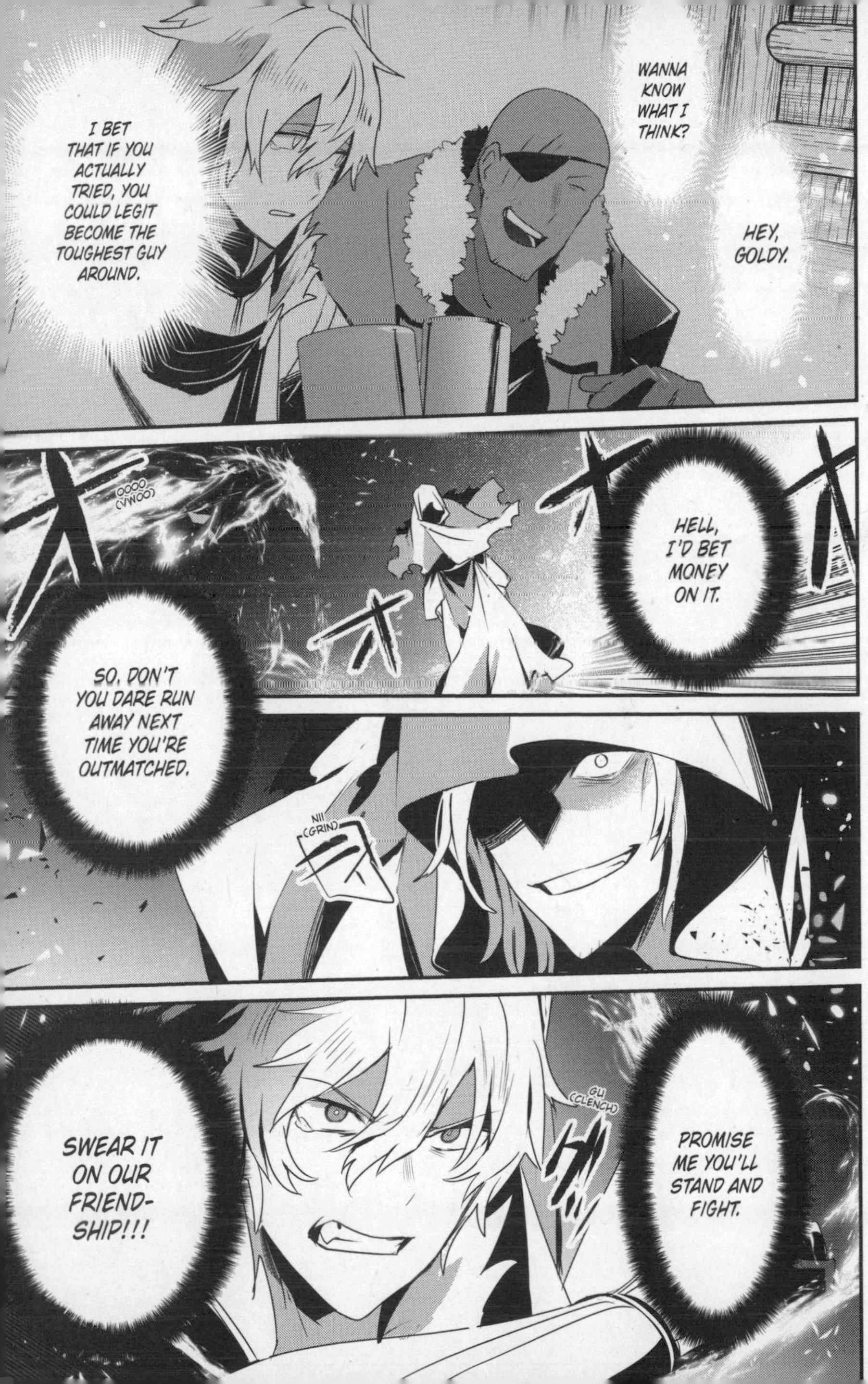
HEY, GOLDY.
WANNA KNOW WHAT I THINK?
I BET THAT IF YOU ACTUALLY TRIED, YOU COULD LEGIT BECOME THE TOUGHEST GUY AROUND.
HELL, I'D BET MONEY ON IT.
OOOO (VWOO)
SO, DON'T YOU DARE RUN AWAY NEXT TIME YOU'RE OUTMATCHED.
NII (GRIN)
PROMISE ME YOU'LL STAND AND FIGHT.
GU (CLENCH)
SWEAR IT ON OUR FRIEND-SHIP!!!

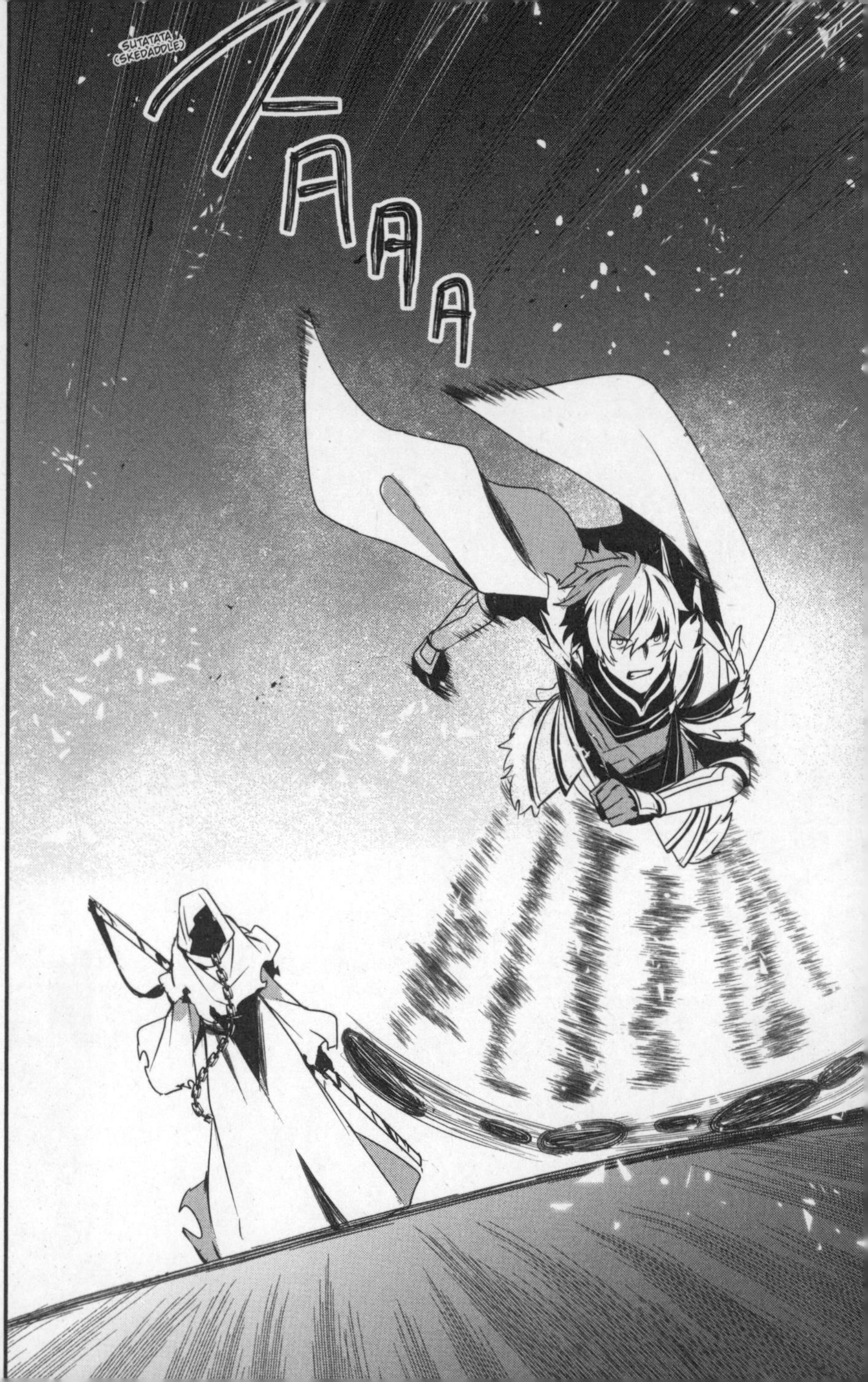
SUTATATA (SKEDADDLE)

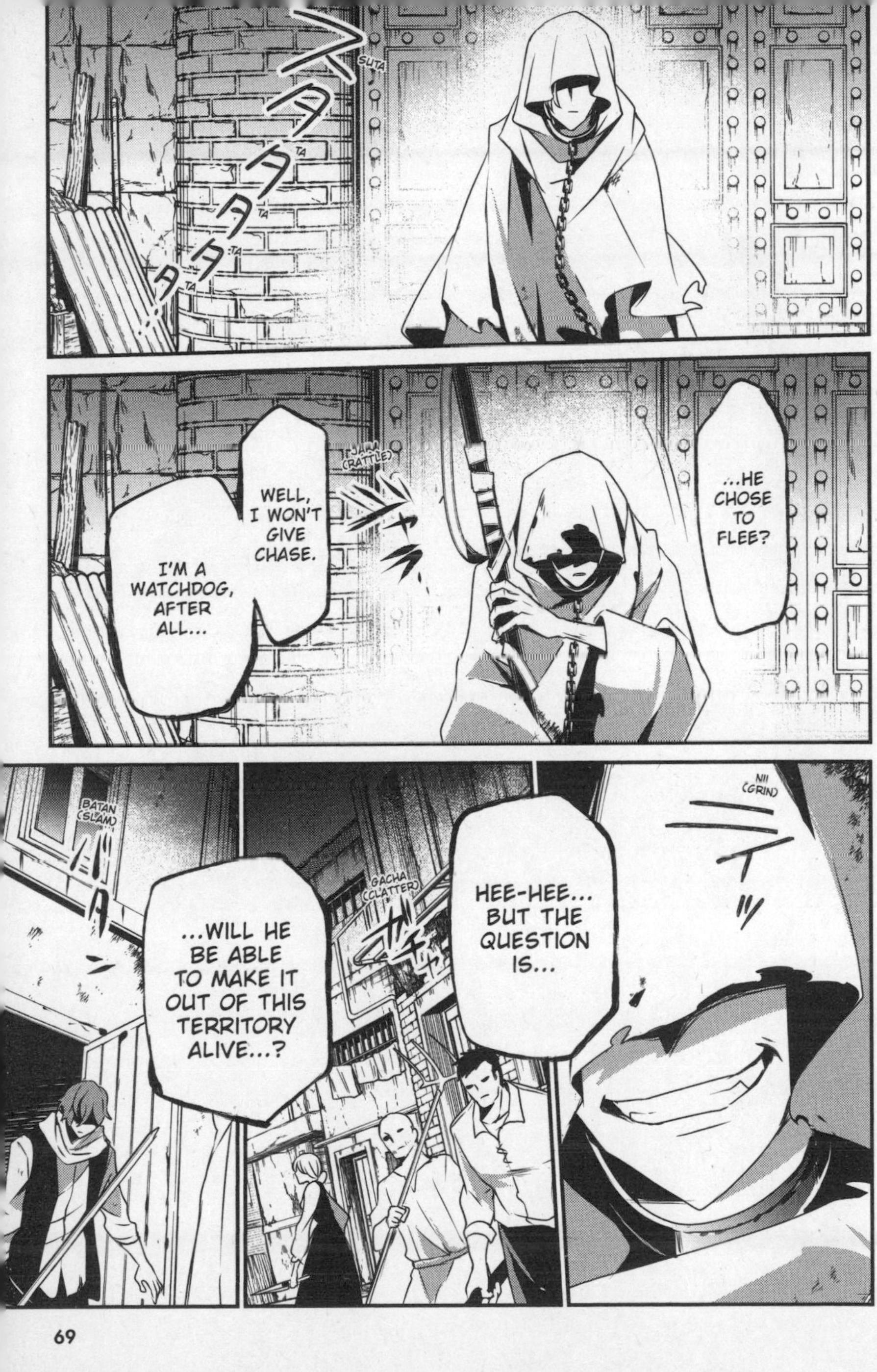
SUTA
TA
TA
TA
TA
...HE CHOSE TO FLEE?
JARA (RATTLE)
WELL, I WON'T GIVE CHASE.
I'M A WATCHDOG, AFTER ALL...
NII (GRIN)
HEE-HEE... BUT THE QUESTION IS...
GACHA (CLATTER)
...WILL HE BE ABLE TO MAKE IT OUT OF THIS TERRITORY ALIVE...?
BATAN (SLAM)

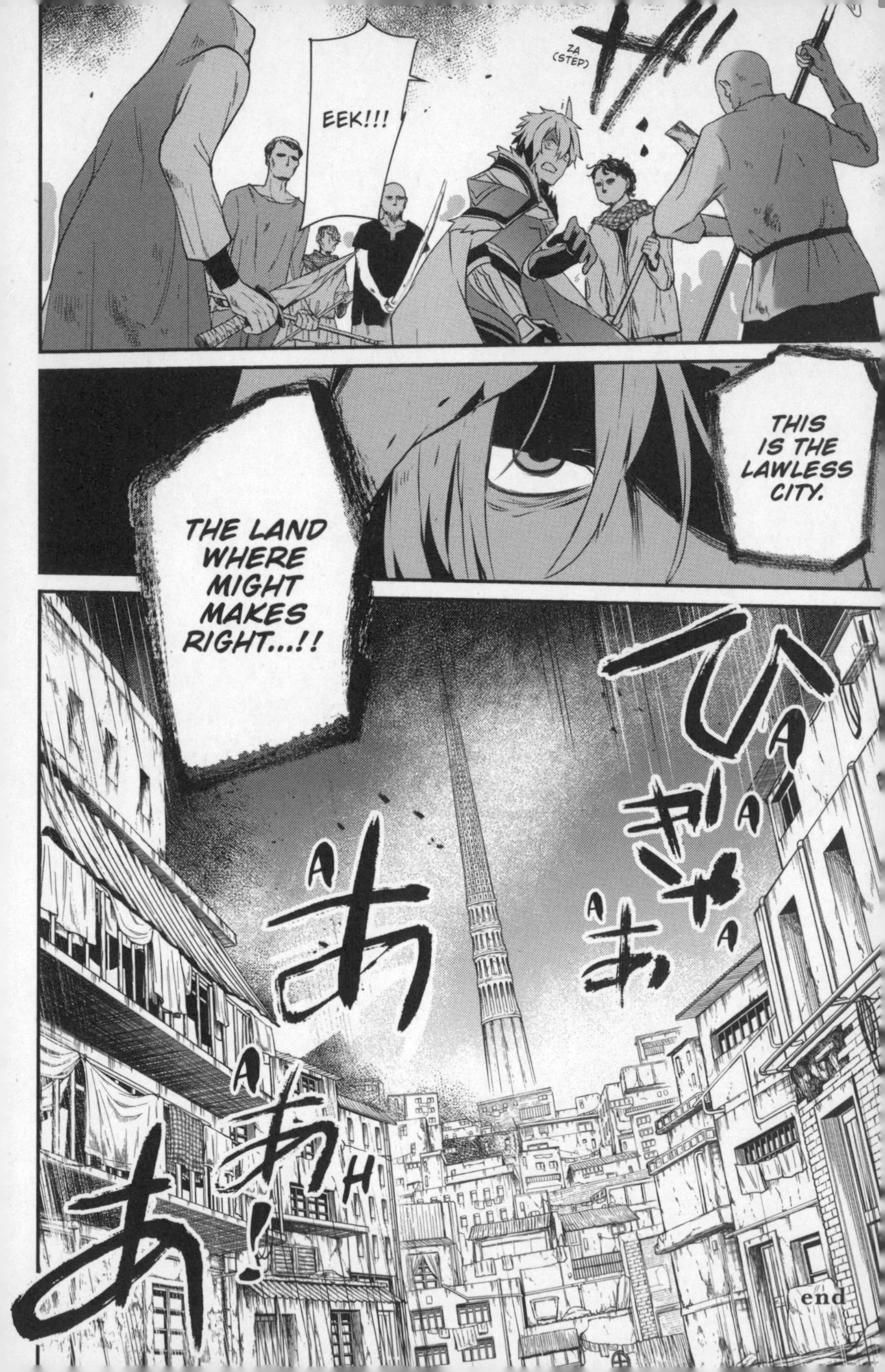

ZA (STEP)
EEK!!!
THIS IS THE LAWLESS CITY.
THE LAND WHERE MIGHT MAKES RIGHT...!!
ひゃあ
A A A A
あああ!
A A H !
end

Episode.28

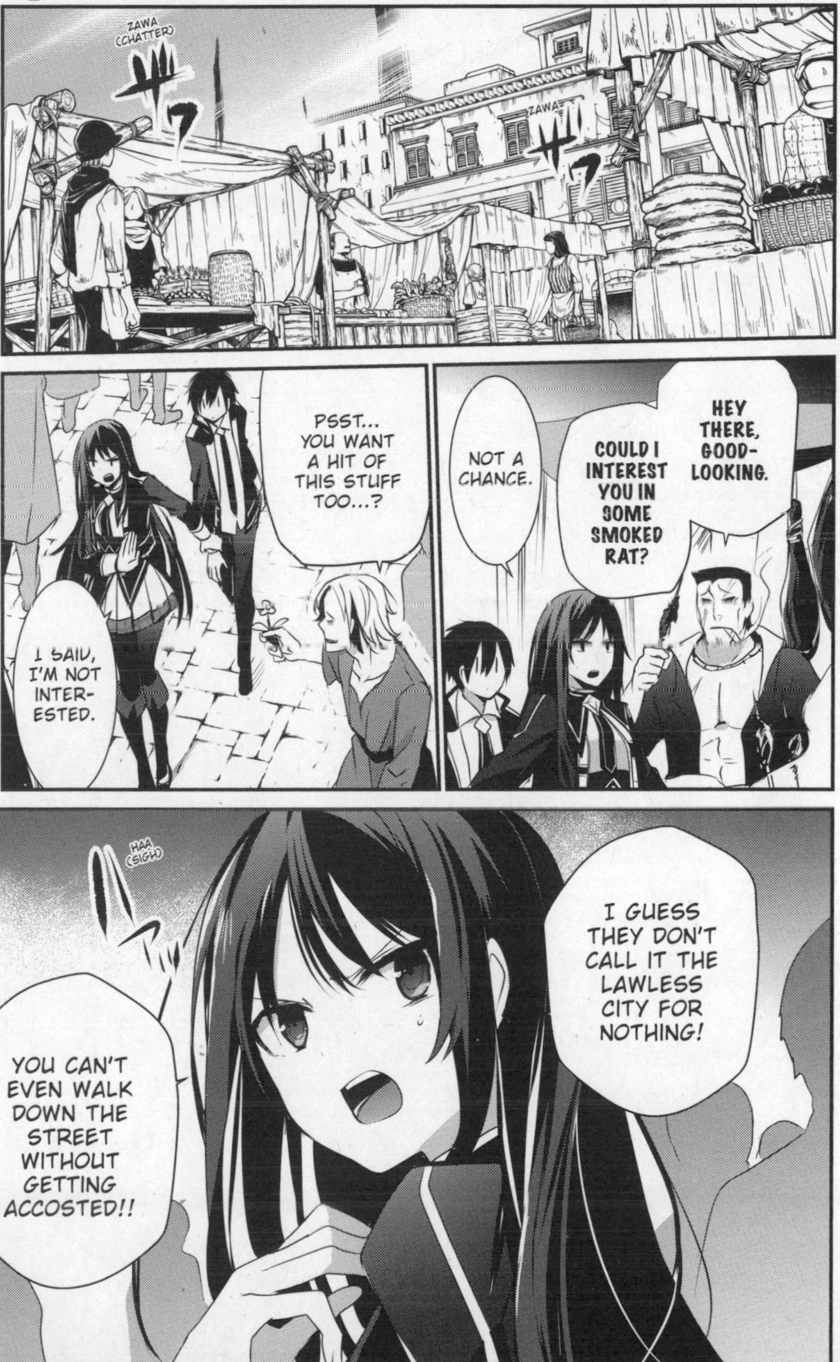
ZAWA (CHATTER)
ZAWA
HEY THERE, GOOD-LOOKING.
COULD I INTEREST YOU IN SOME SMOKED RAT?
NOT A CHANCE.
PSST... YOU WANT A HIT OF THIS STUFF TOO...?
I SAID, I'M NOT INTERESTED.
I GUESS THEY DON'T CALL IT THE LAWLESS CITY FOR NOTHING!
HAA (SIGH)
YOU CAN'T EVEN WALK DOWN THE STREET WITHOUT GETTING ACCOSTED!!

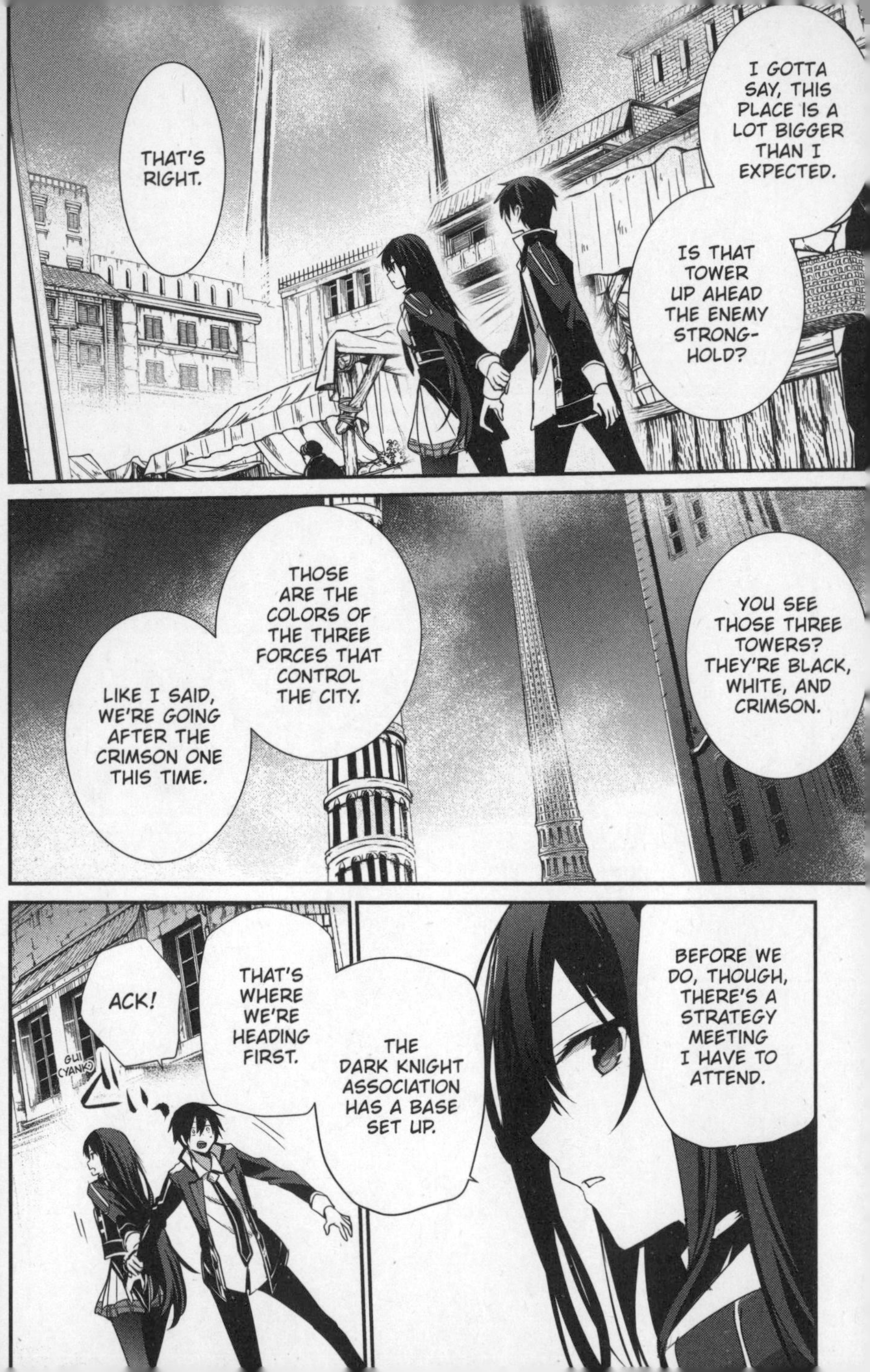
I GOTTA SAY, THIS PLACE IS A LOT BIGGER THAN I EXPECTED.
IS THAT TOWER UP AHEAD THE ENEMY STRONG-HOLD?
THAT'S RIGHT.
YOU SEE THOSE THREE TOWERS? THEY'RE BLACK, WHITE, AND CRIMSON.
THOSE ARE THE COLORS OF THE THREE FORCES THAT CONTROL THE CITY.
LIKE I SAID, WE'RE GOING AFTER THE CRIMSON ONE THIS TIME.
BEFORE WE DO, THOUGH, THERE'S A STRATEGY MEETING I HAVE TO ATTEND.
THE DARK KNIGHT ASSOCIATION HAS A BASE SET UP.
THAT'S WHERE WE'RE HEADING FIRST.
ACK!
GUI CYANK

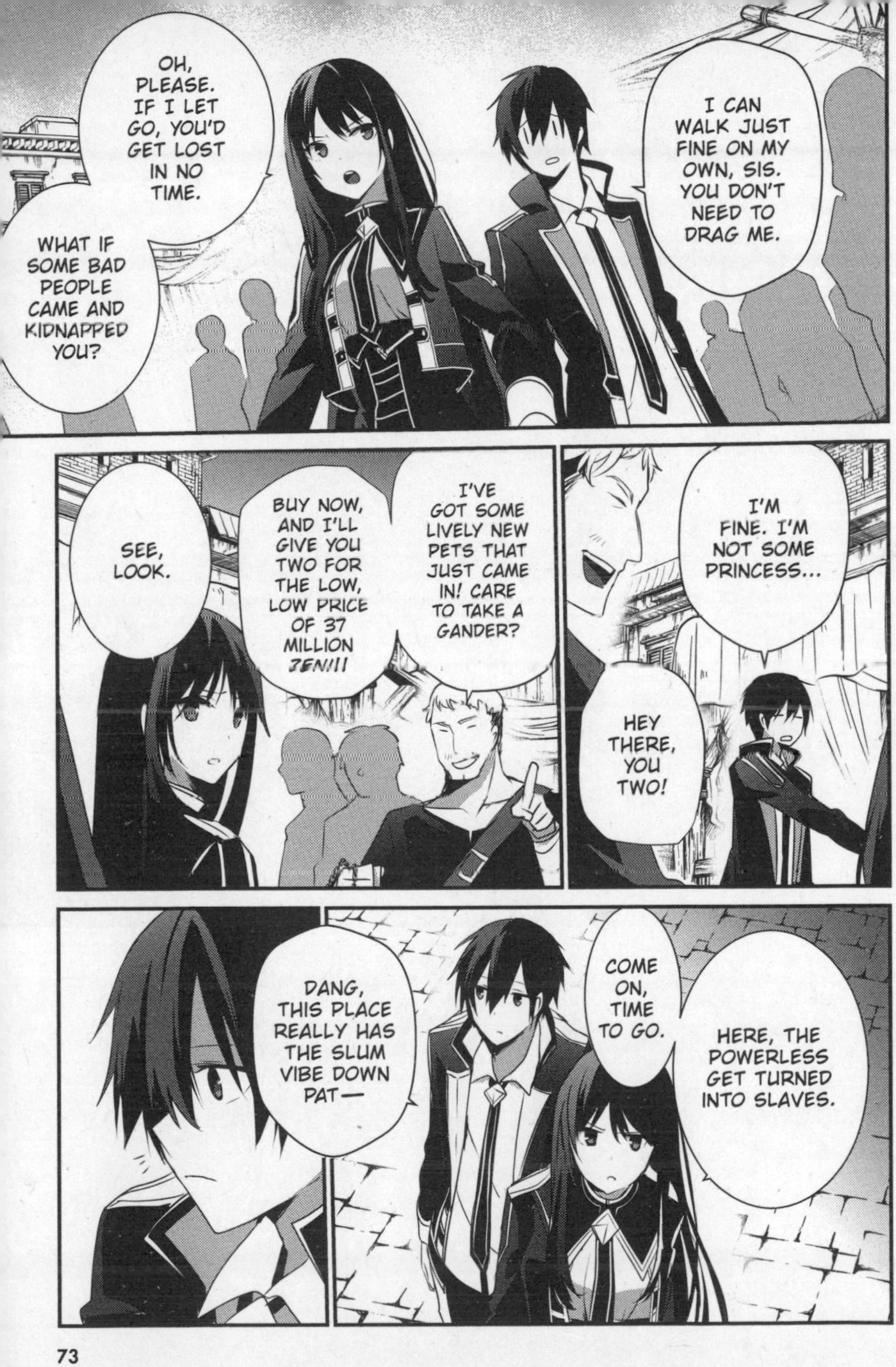
I CAN WALK JUST FINE ON MY OWN, SIS. YOU DON'T NEED TO DRAG ME.
OH, PLEASE. IF I LET GO, YOU'D GET LOST IN NO TIME.
WHAT IF SOME BAD PEOPLE CAME AND KIDNAPPED YOU?
I'M FINE. I'M NOT SOME PRINCESS...
HEY THERE, YOU TWO!
I'VE GOT SOME LIVELY NEW PETS THAT JUST CAME IN! CARE TO TAKE A GANDER?
BUY NOW, AND I'LL GIVE YOU TWO FOR THE LOW, LOW PRICE OF 37 MILLION ZENI!!
SEE, LOOK.
HERE, THE POWERLESS GET TURNED INTO SLAVES.
COME ON, TIME TO GO.
DANG, THIS PLACE REALLY HAS THE SLUM VIBE DOWN PAT—

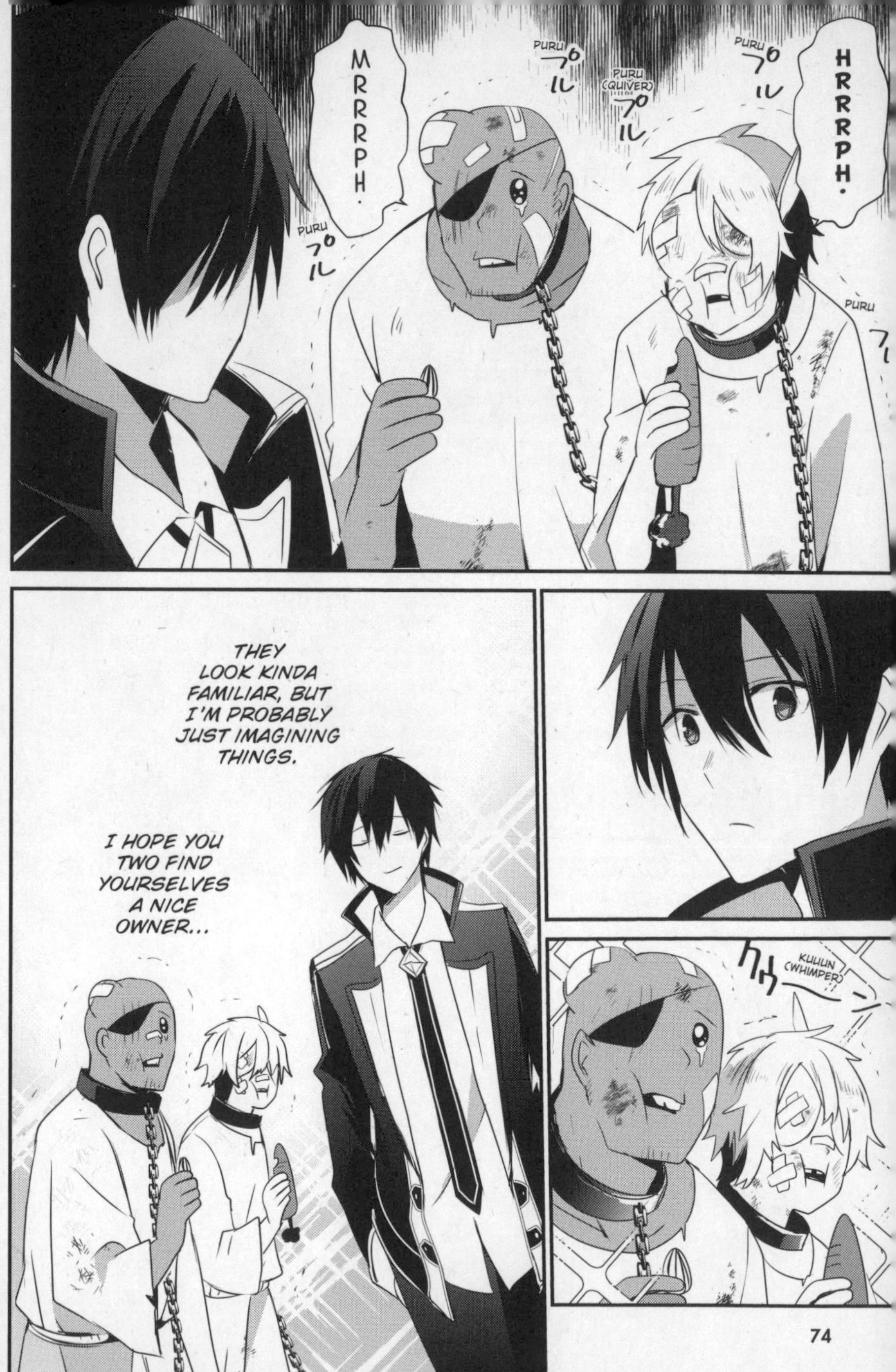
HRRRPH.
Puru プル
Puru (quiver) プル
Puru プル
MRRRPH.
Puru プル
Puru プル
Kuuun (whimper) クゥ
THEY LOOK KINDA FAMILIAR, BUT I'M PROBABLY JUST IMAGINING THINGS.
I HOPE YOU TWO FIND YOURSELVES A NICE OWNER...

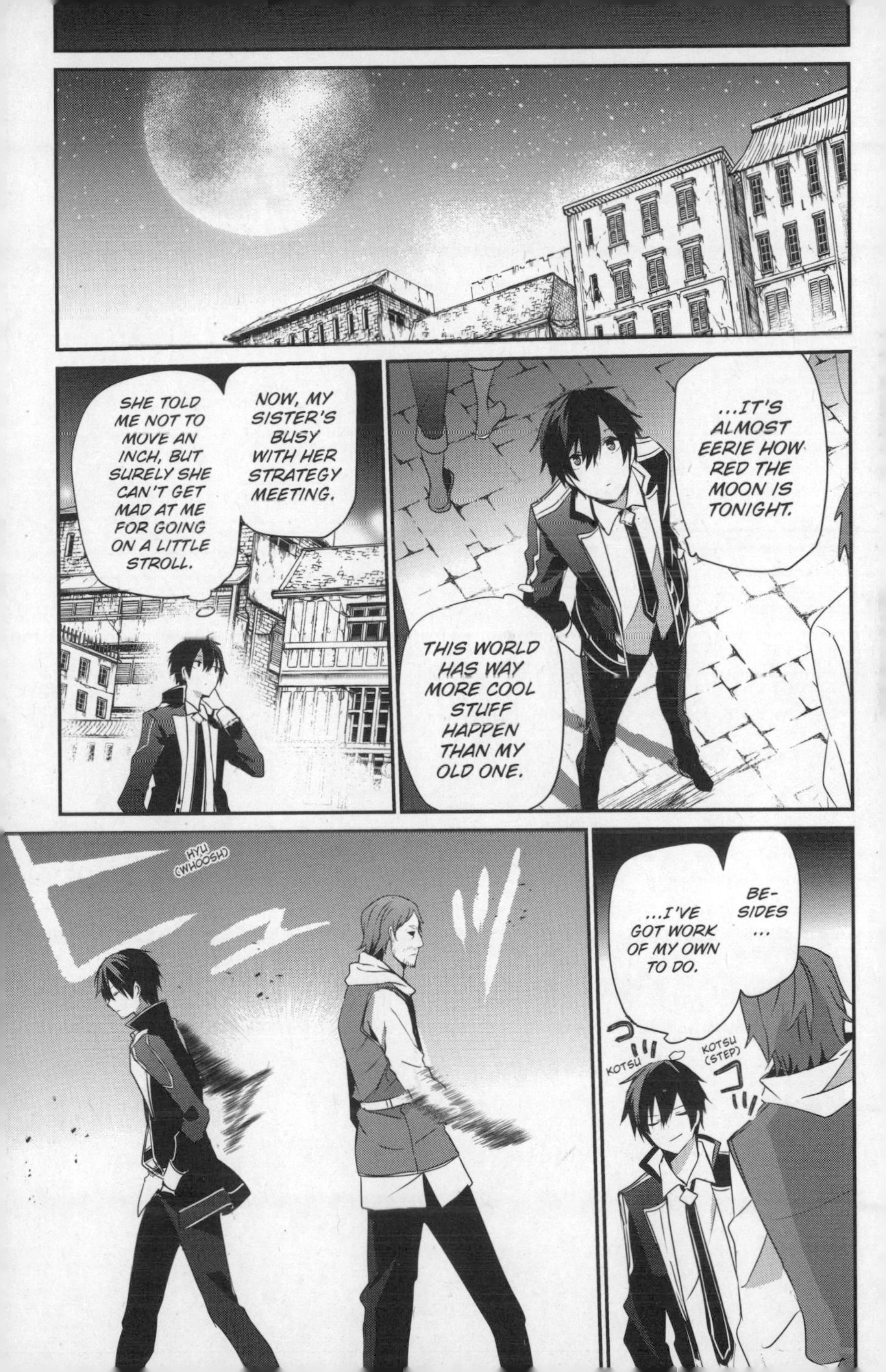
...IT'S ALMOST EERIE HOW RED THE MOON IS TONIGHT.
THIS WORLD HAS WAY MORE COOL STUFF HAPPEN THAN MY OLD ONE.
NOW, MY SISTER'S BUSY WITH HER STRATEGY MEETING.
SHE TOLD ME NOT TO MOVE AN INCH, BUT SURELY SHE CAN'T GET MAD AT ME FOR GOING ON A LITTLE STROLL.
BE-SIDES...
...I'VE GOT WORK OF MY OWN TO DO.
KOTSU (STEP)
KOTSU
HYU (WHOOSH)

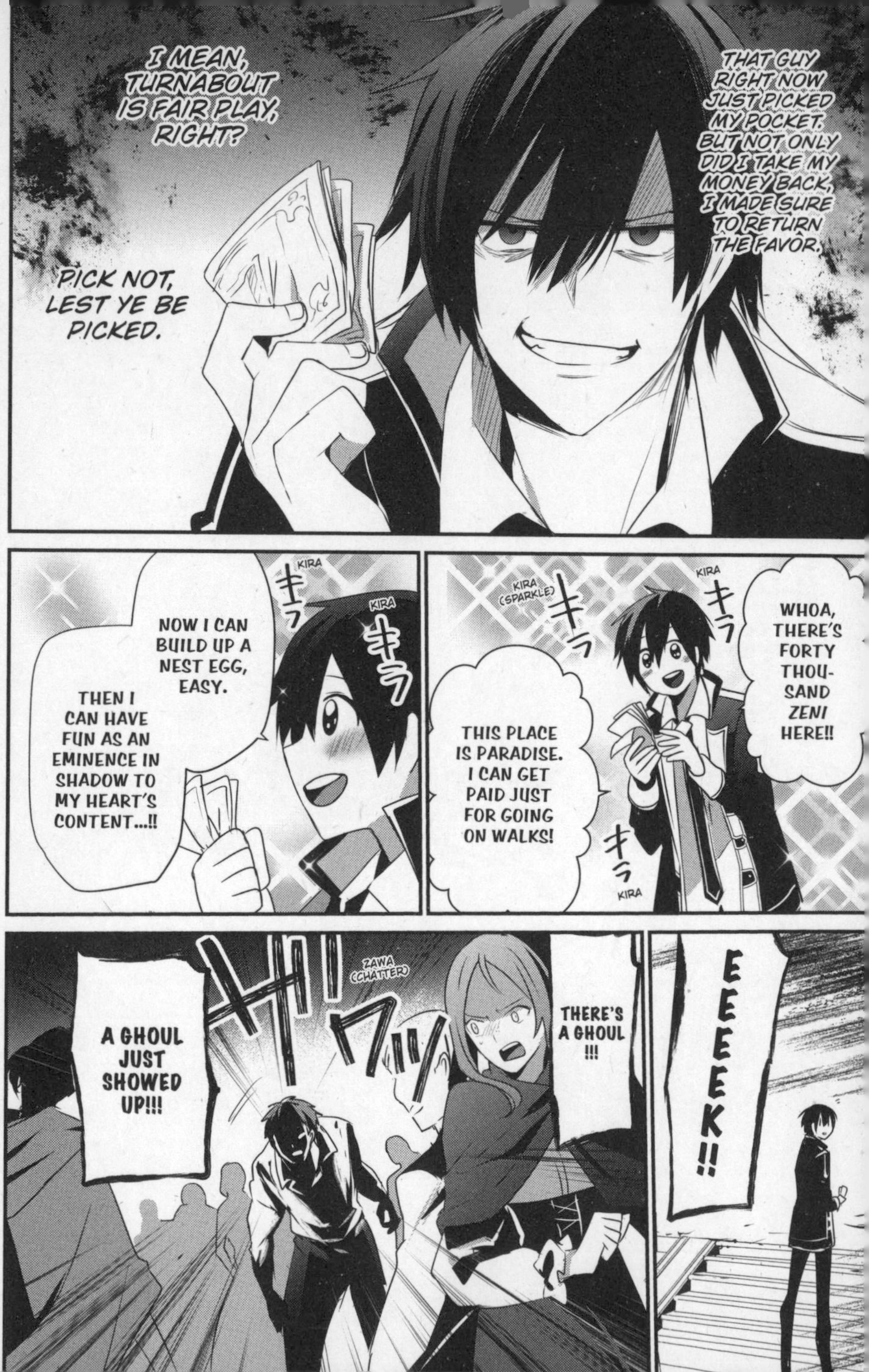
THAT GUY RIGHT NOW JUST PICKED MY POCKET. BUT NOT ONLY DID I TAKE MY MONEY BACK, I MADE SURE TO RETURN THE FAVOR.
I MEAN, TURNABOUT IS FAIR PLAY, RIGHT?
PICK NOT, LEST YE BE PICKED.
KIRA
KIRA (SPARKLE)
WHOA, THERE'S FORTY THOU-SAND ZENI HERE!!
THIS PLACE IS PARADISE. I CAN GET PAID JUST FOR GOING ON WALKS!
KIRA
KIRA
KIRA
NOW I CAN BUILD UP A NEST EGG, EASY.
THEN I CAN HAVE FUN AS AN EMINENCE IN SHADOW TO MY HEART'S CONTENT...!!
EEEEEK!!
THERE'S A GHOUL!!!
ZAWA (CHATTER)
A GHOUL JUST SHOWED UP!!!

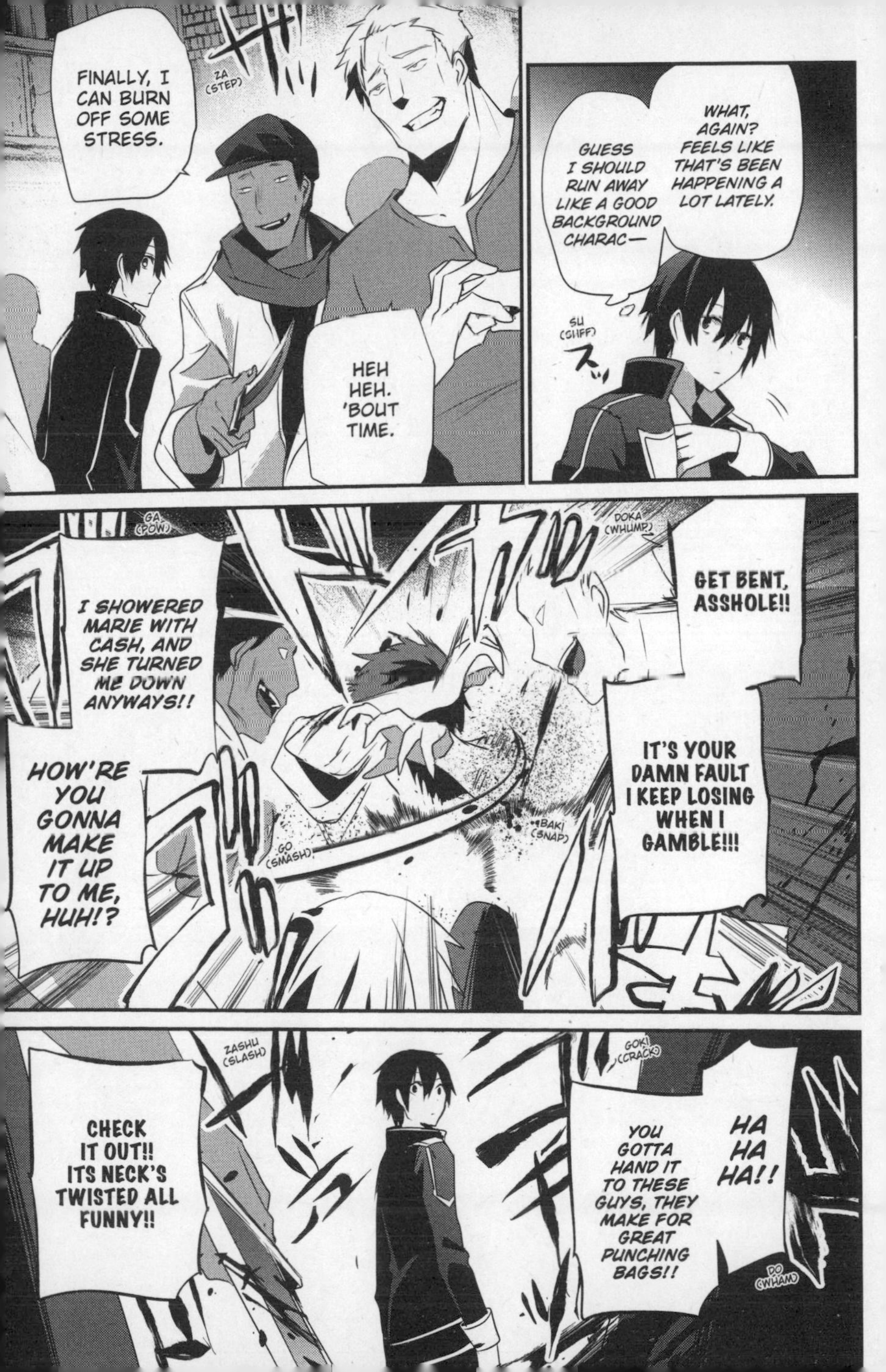
FINALLY, I CAN BURN OFF SOME STRESS.
ZA (STEP)
HEH HEH. 'BOUT TIME.
WHAT, AGAIN? FEELS LIKE THAT'S BEEN HAPPENING A LOT LATELY.
GUESS I SHOULD RUN AWAY LIKE A GOOD BACKGROUND CHARAC—
SU (SHFF)
GA (POW)
I SHOWERED MARIE WITH CASH, AND SHE TURNED ME DOWN ANYWAYS!!
HOW'RE YOU GONNA MAKE IT UP TO ME, HUH!?
GO (SMASH)
BAKI (SNAP)
DOKA (WHUMP)
GET BENT, ASSHOLE!!
IT'S YOUR DAMN FAULT I KEEP LOSING WHEN I GAMBLE!!!
ZASHU (SLASH)
CHECK IT OUT!! ITS NECK'S TWISTED ALL FUNNY!!
GOKI (CRACK)
YOU GOTTA HAND IT TO THESE GUYS, THEY MAKE FOR GREAT PUNCHING BAGS!!
HA HA HA!!
DO (WHAM)

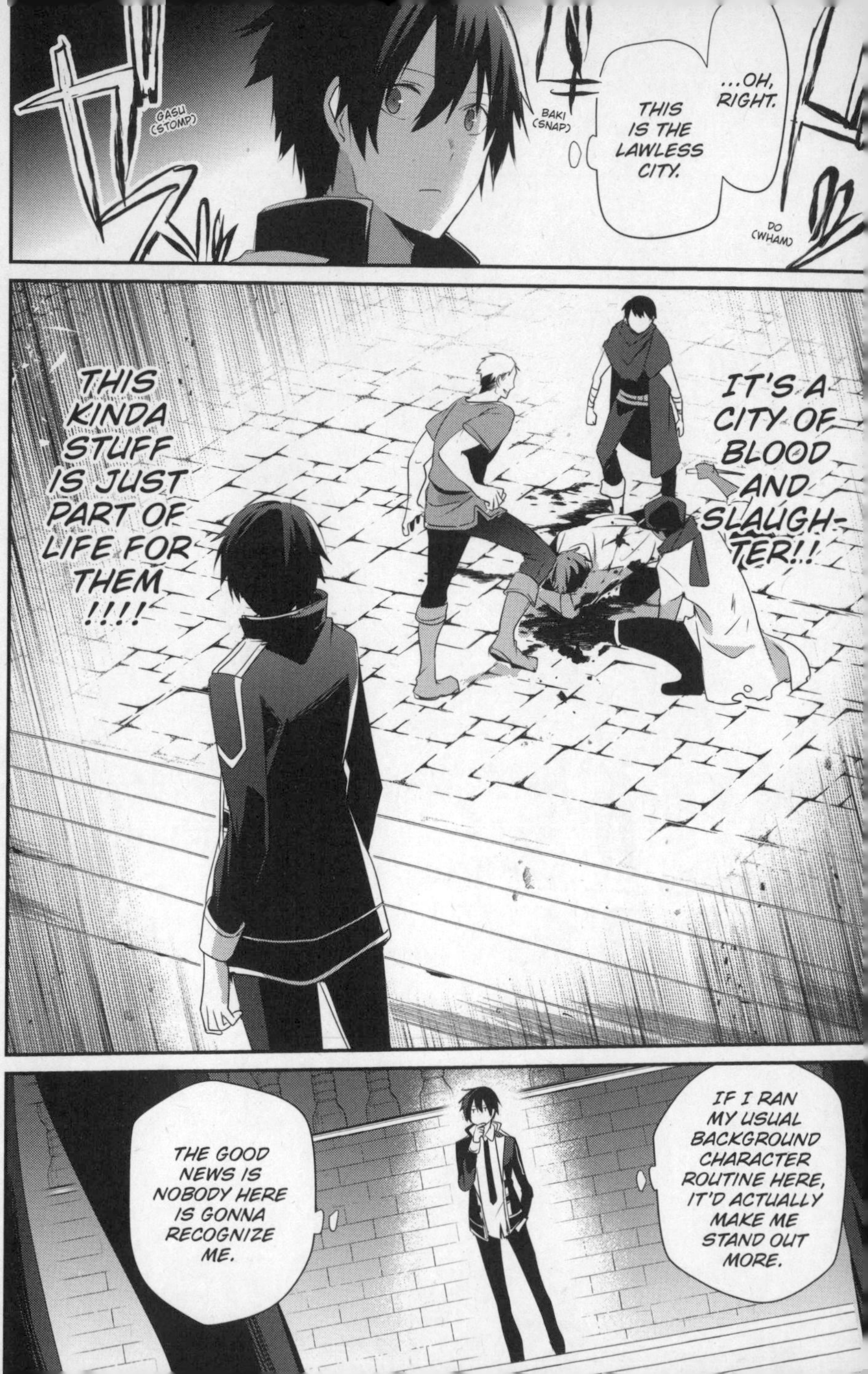
DO (WHAM)
...OH, RIGHT.
THIS IS THE LAWLESS CITY.
BAKI (SNAP)
GASU (STOMP)
IT'S A CITY OF BLOOD AND SLAUGH-TER!!
THIS KINDA STUFF IS JUST PART OF LIFE FOR THEM!!!!
IF I RAN MY USUAL BACKGROUND CHARACTER ROUTINE HERE, IT'D ACTUALLY MAKE ME STAND OUT MORE.
THE GOOD NEWS IS NOBODY HERE IS GONNA RECOGNIZE ME.

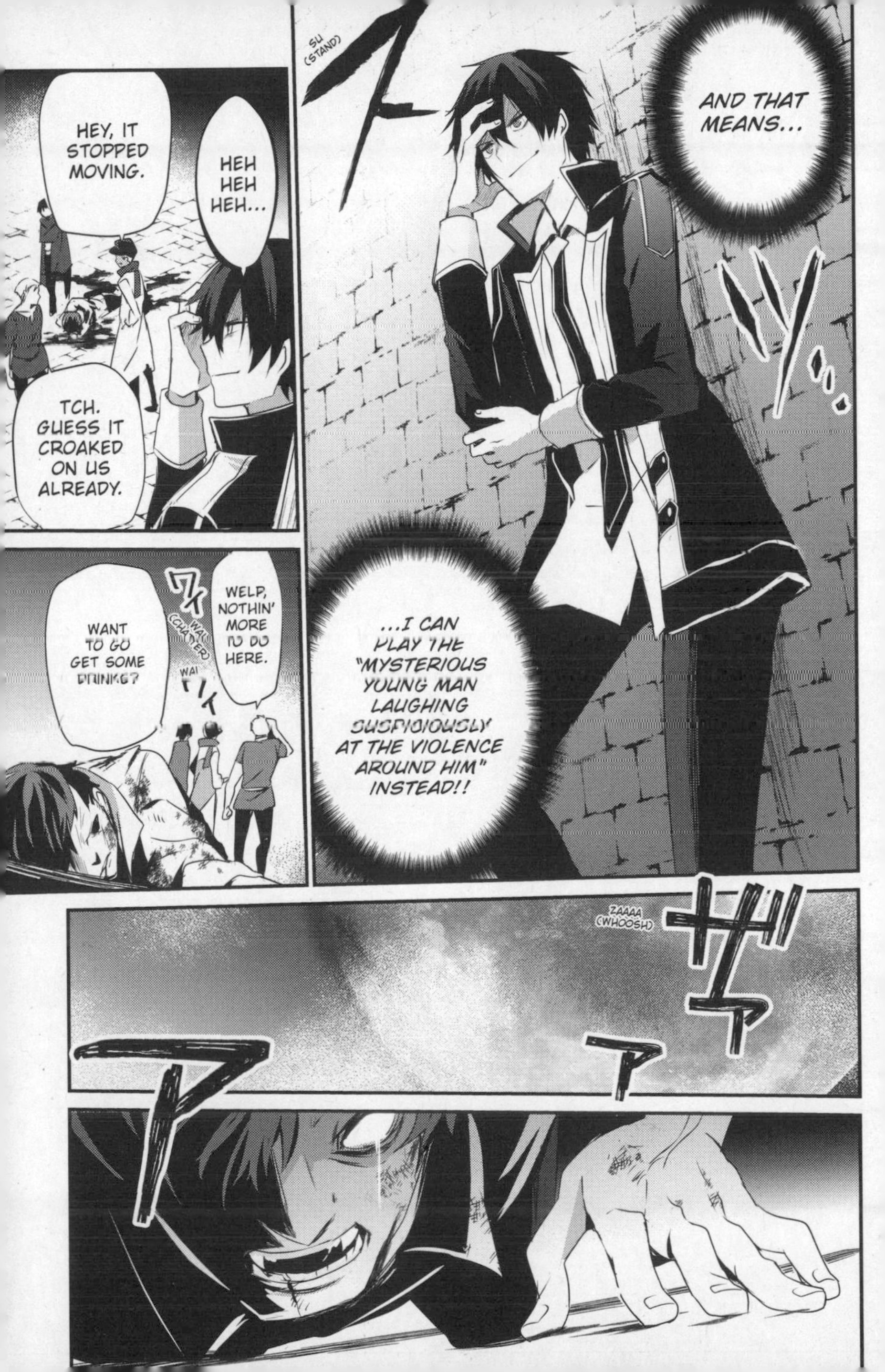

SU (STAND)
AND THAT MEANS...
...I CAN PLAY THE "MYSTERIOUS YOUNG MAN LAUGHING SUSPICIOUSLY AT THE VIOLENCE AROUND HIM" INSTEAD!!
HEH HEH HEH...
HEY, IT STOPPED MOVING.
TCH. GUESS IT CROAKED ON US ALREADY.
WELP, NOTHIN' MORE TO DO HERE.
WAI WAI (CHATTER)
WANT TO GO GET SOME DRINKS?
ZAAAA (WHOOSH)

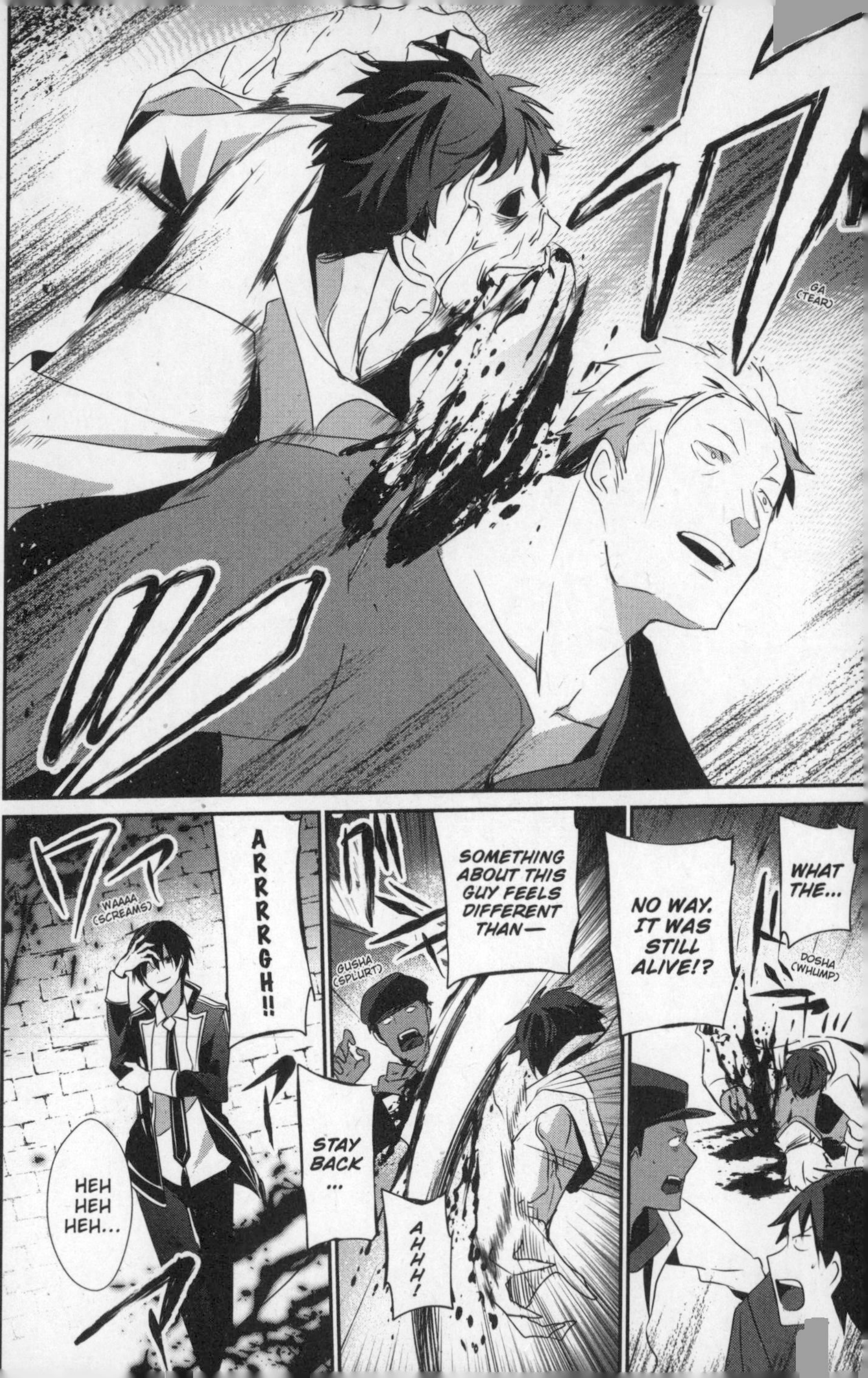
GA (TEAR)
WHAT THE...
DOSHA (WHUMP)
NO WAY. IT WAS STILL ALIVE!?
SOMETHING ABOUT THIS GUY FEELS DIFFERENT THAN—
GUSHA (SPLURT)
STAY BACK ...
AHHH!
ARRRRGH!!
WAAAA (SCREAMS)
HEH HEH HEH...

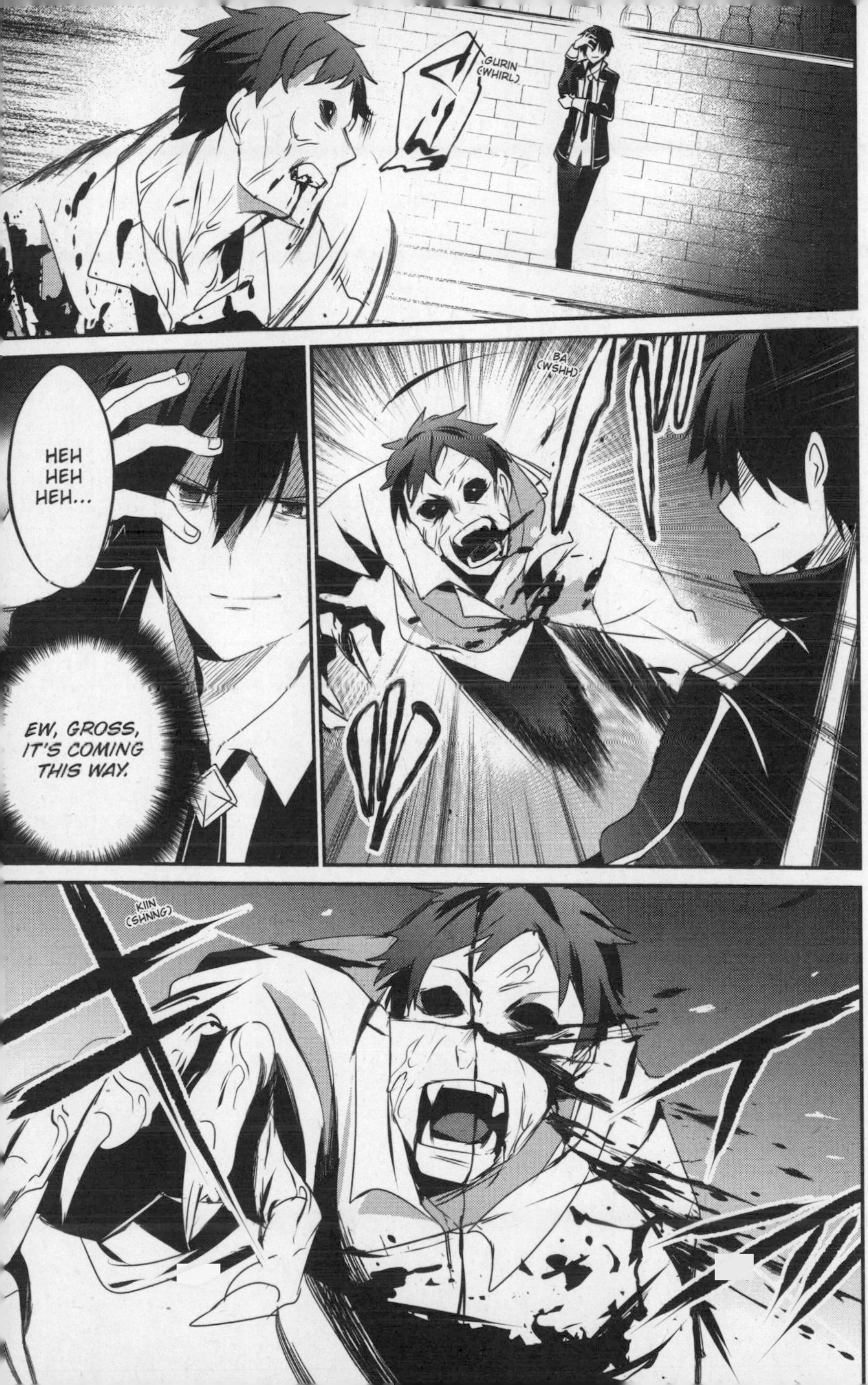
GURIN (WHIRL)
BA (WSHH)
HEH HEH HEH...
EW, GROSS, IT'S COMING THIS WAY.
KIIN (SHNNG)

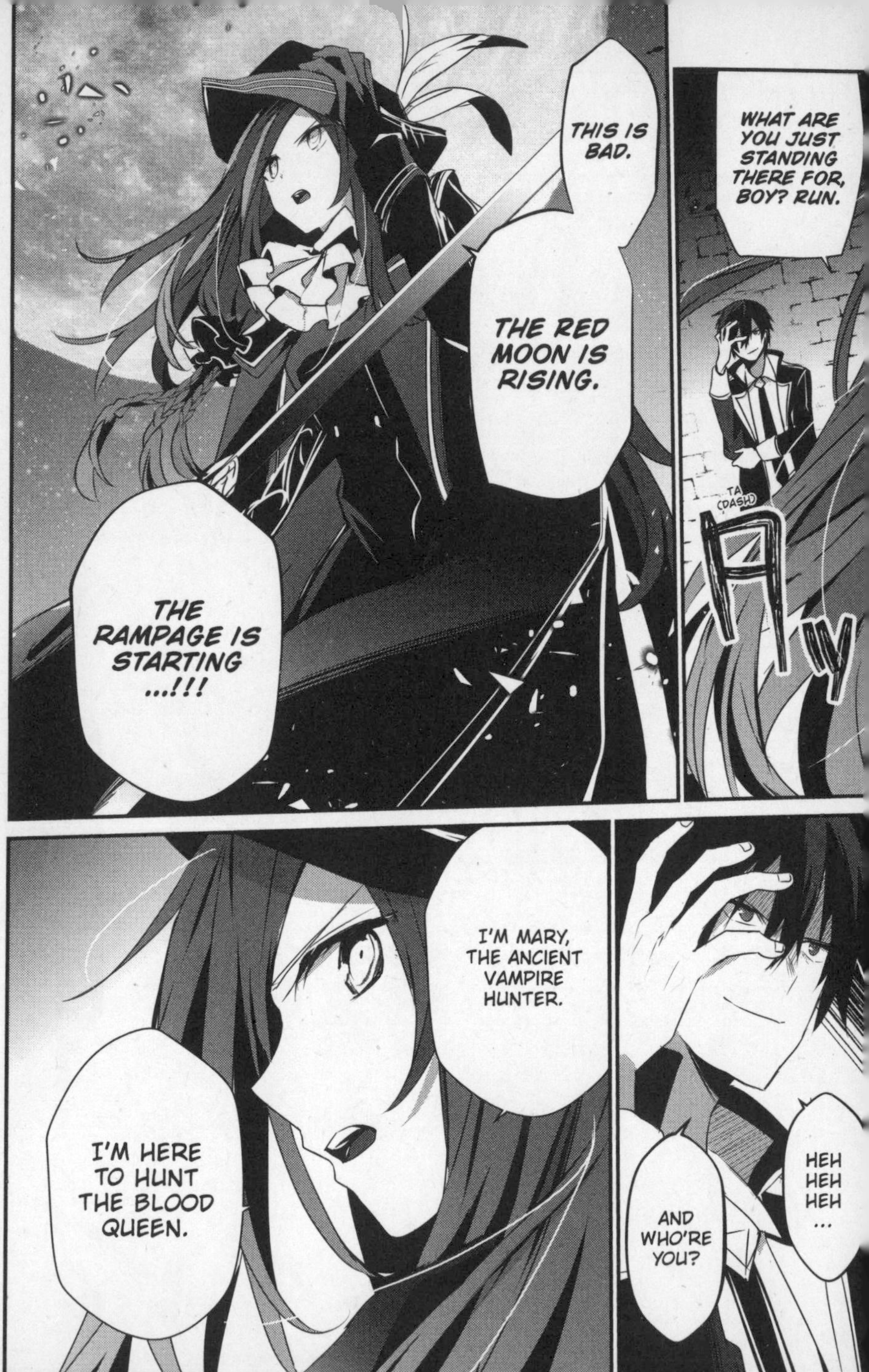
WHAT ARE YOU JUST STANDING THERE FOR, BOY? RUN.
TA (DASH)
THIS IS BAD.
THE RED MOON IS RISING.
THE RAMPAGE IS STARTING ...!!!
HEH HEH HEH ...
AND WHO'RE YOU?
I'M MARY, THE ANCIENT VAMPIRE HUNTER.
I'M HERE TO HUNT THE BLOOD QUEEN.

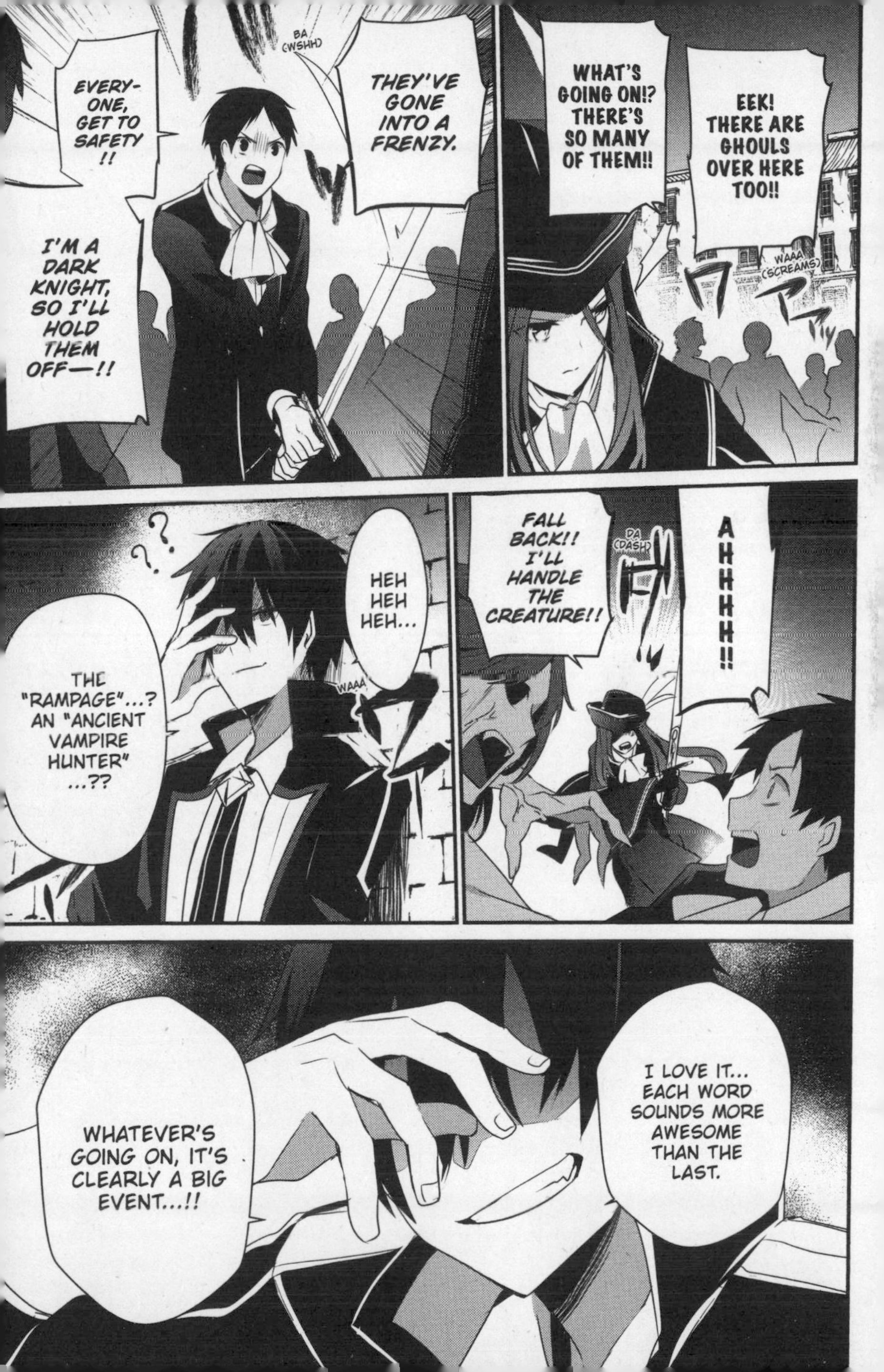
EEK! THERE ARE GHOULS OVER HERE TOO!!
WAAA (SCREAMS)
WHAT'S GOING ON!? THERE'S SO MANY OF THEM!!
THEY'VE GONE INTO A FRENZY.
BA (WSHH)
EVERY-ONE, GET TO SAFETY!!
I'M A DARK KNIGHT, SO I'LL HOLD THEM OFF—!!
AHHHHH!!
DA (DASH)
FALL BACK!! I'LL HANDLE THE CREATURE!!
HEH HEH HEH...
WAAA
THE "RAMPAGE"...? AN "ANCIENT VAMPIRE HUNTER"...??
I LOVE IT... EACH WORD SOUNDS MORE AWESOME THAN THE LAST.
WHATEVER'S GOING ON, IT'S CLEARLY A BIG EVENT...!!

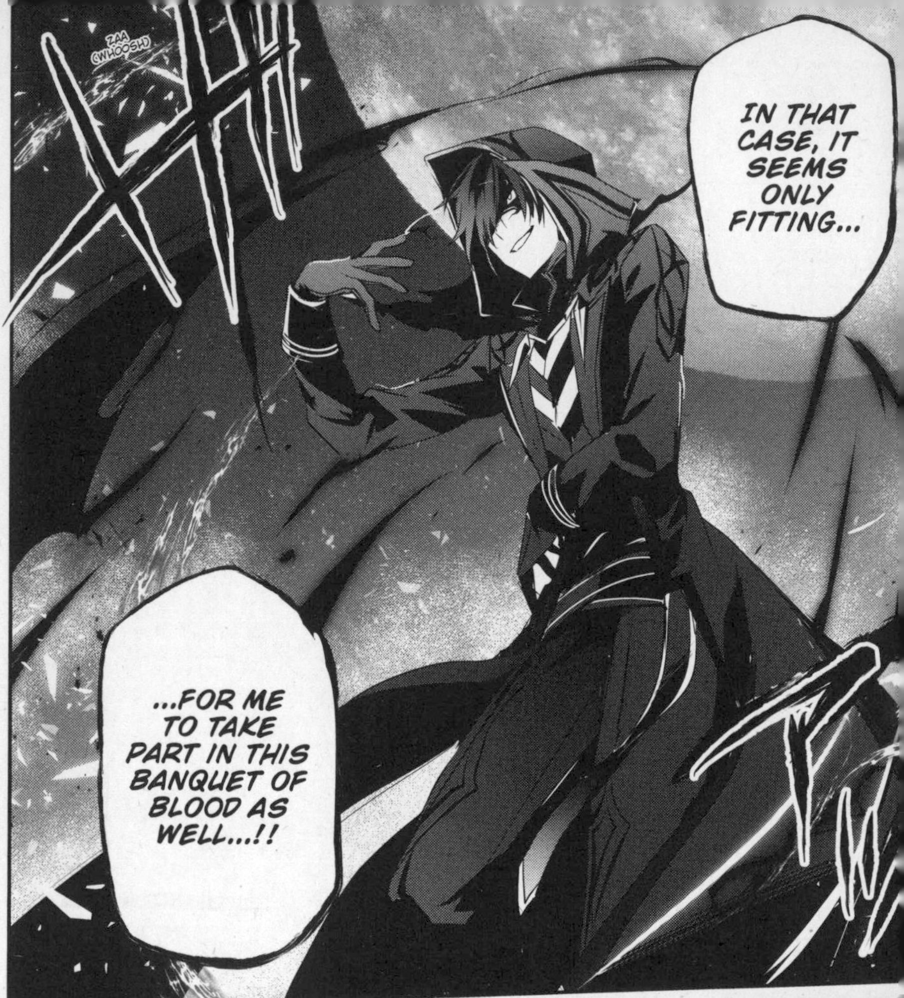
IN THAT CASE, IT SEEMS ONLY FITTING...
ZAA (WHOOSH)
...FOR ME TO TAKE PART IN THIS BANQUET OF BLOOD AS WELL...!!
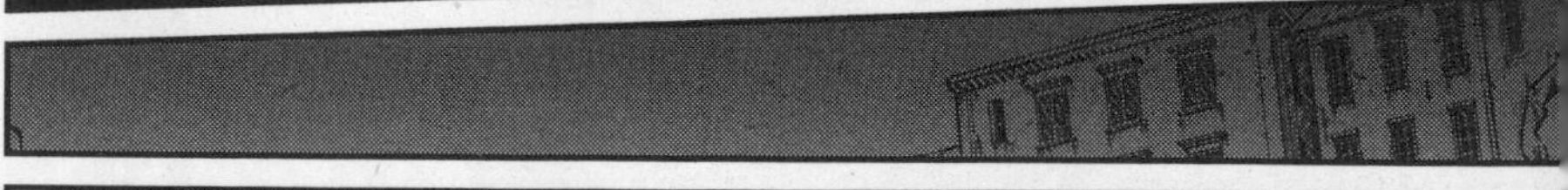
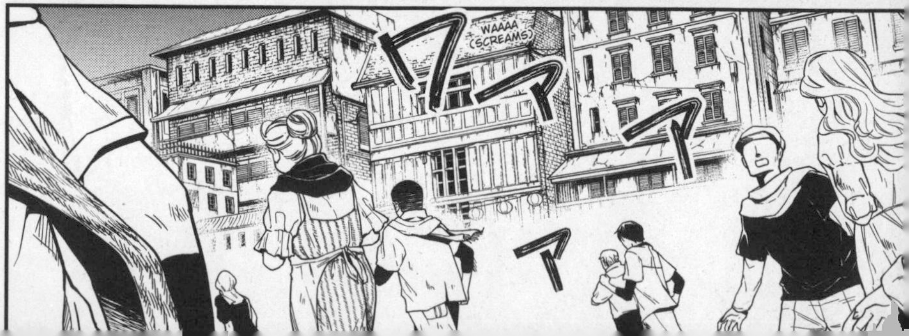
WAAAA (SCREAMS)

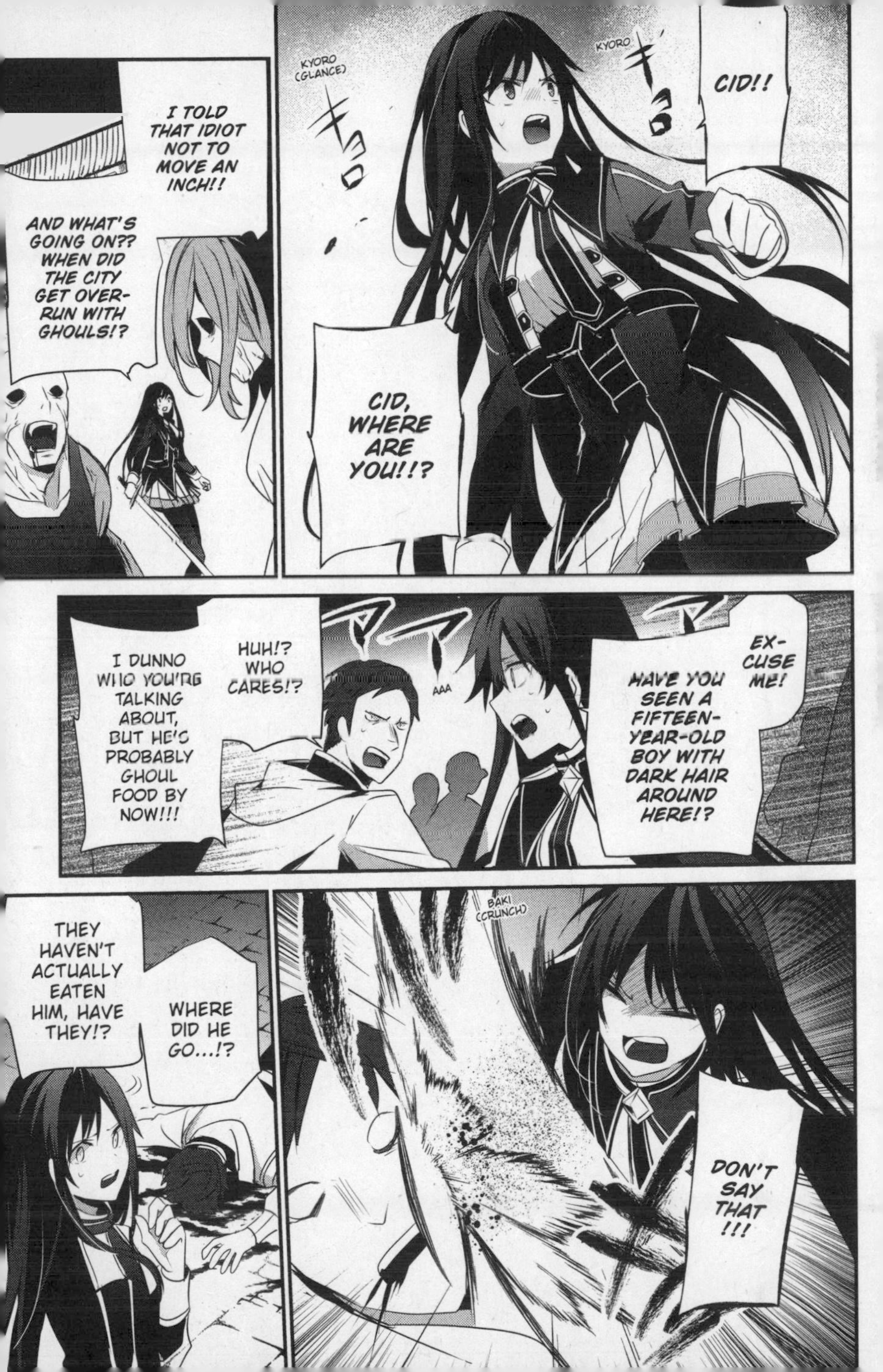
KYORO
KYORO (GLANCE)
CID!!
CID, WHERE ARE YOU!!?
I TOLD THAT IDIOT NOT TO MOVE AN INCH!!
AND WHAT'S GOING ON?? WHEN DID THE CITY GET OVER-RUN WITH GHOULS!?
EX-CUSE ME!
HAVE YOU SEEN A FIFTEEN-YEAR-OLD BOY WITH DARK HAIR AROUND HERE!?
AAA
HUH!? WHO CARES!?
I DUNNO WHO YOU'RE TALKING ABOUT, BUT HE'S PROBABLY GHOUL FOOD BY NOW!!!
BAKI (CRUNCH)
DON'T SAY THAT!!!
WHERE DID HE GO...!?
THEY HAVEN'T ACTUALLY EATEN HIM, HAVE THEY!?

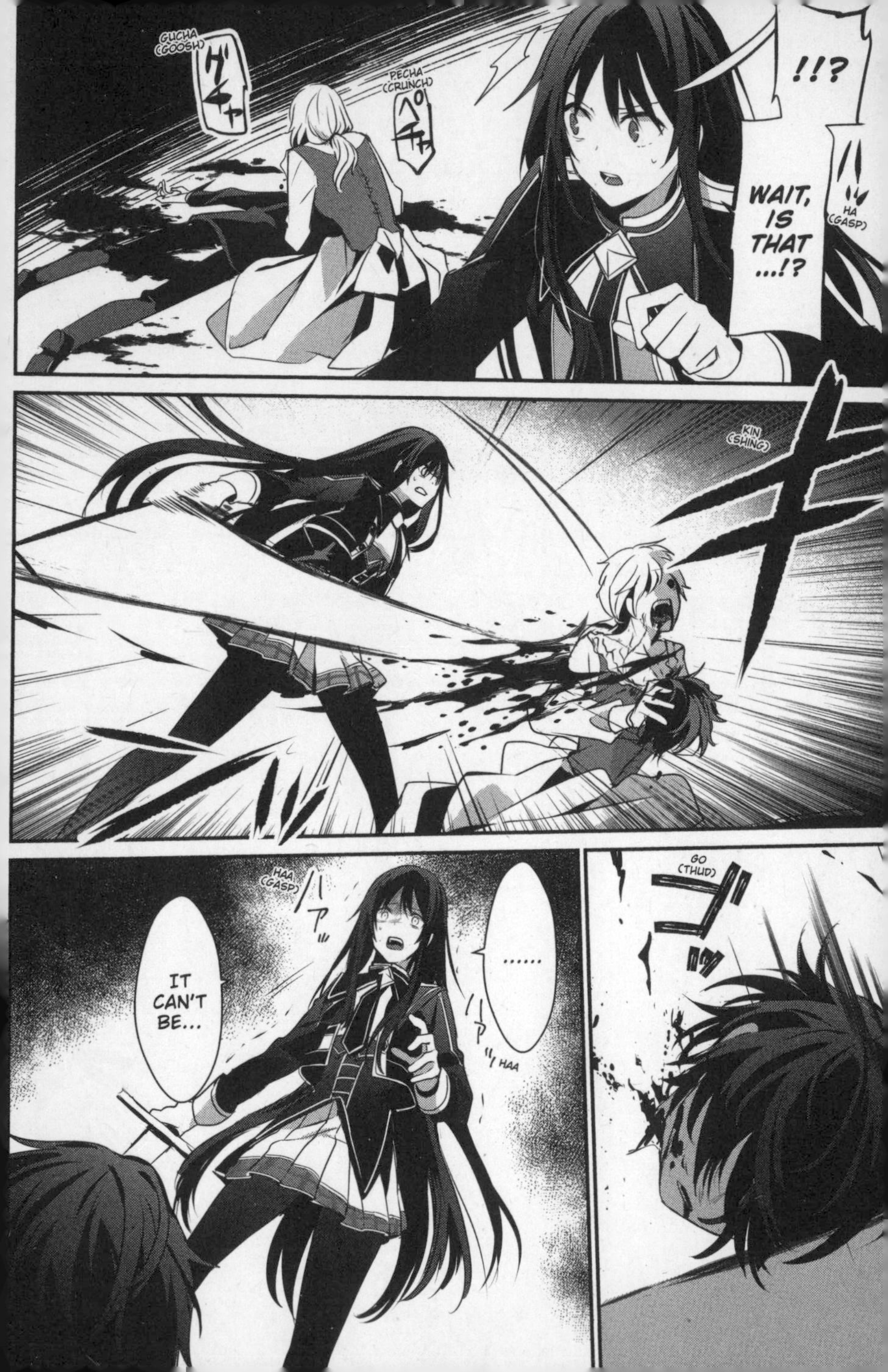

!!?
HA (GASP)
WAIT, IS THAT ...!?
PECHA (CRUNCH)
GUCHA (GOOSH)
KIN (SHING)
GO (THUD)
......
HAA (GASP)
IT CAN'T BE...
HAA

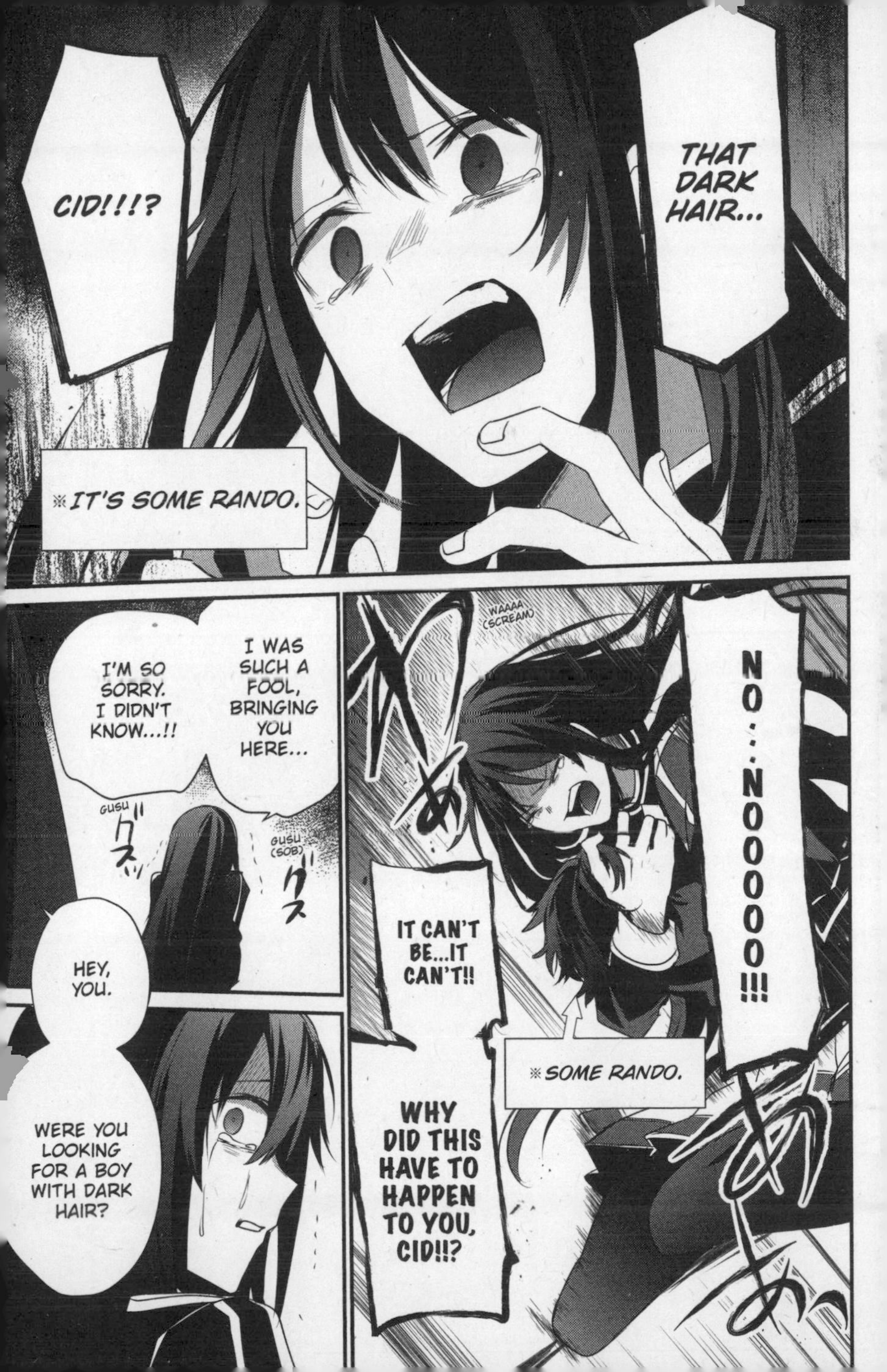
THAT DARK HAIR...
CID!!!?
※IT'S SOME RANDO.
WAAAA (SCREAM)
NO...NOOOOOO!!!
IT CAN'T BE...IT CAN'T!!
※SOME RANDO.
WHY DID THIS HAVE TO HAPPEN TO YOU, CID!!?
I WAS SUCH A FOOL, BRINGING YOU HERE...
I'M SO SORRY. I DIDN'T KNOW...!!
GUSU (SOB)
GUSU
HEY, YOU.
WERE YOU LOOKING FOR A BOY WITH DARK HAIR?

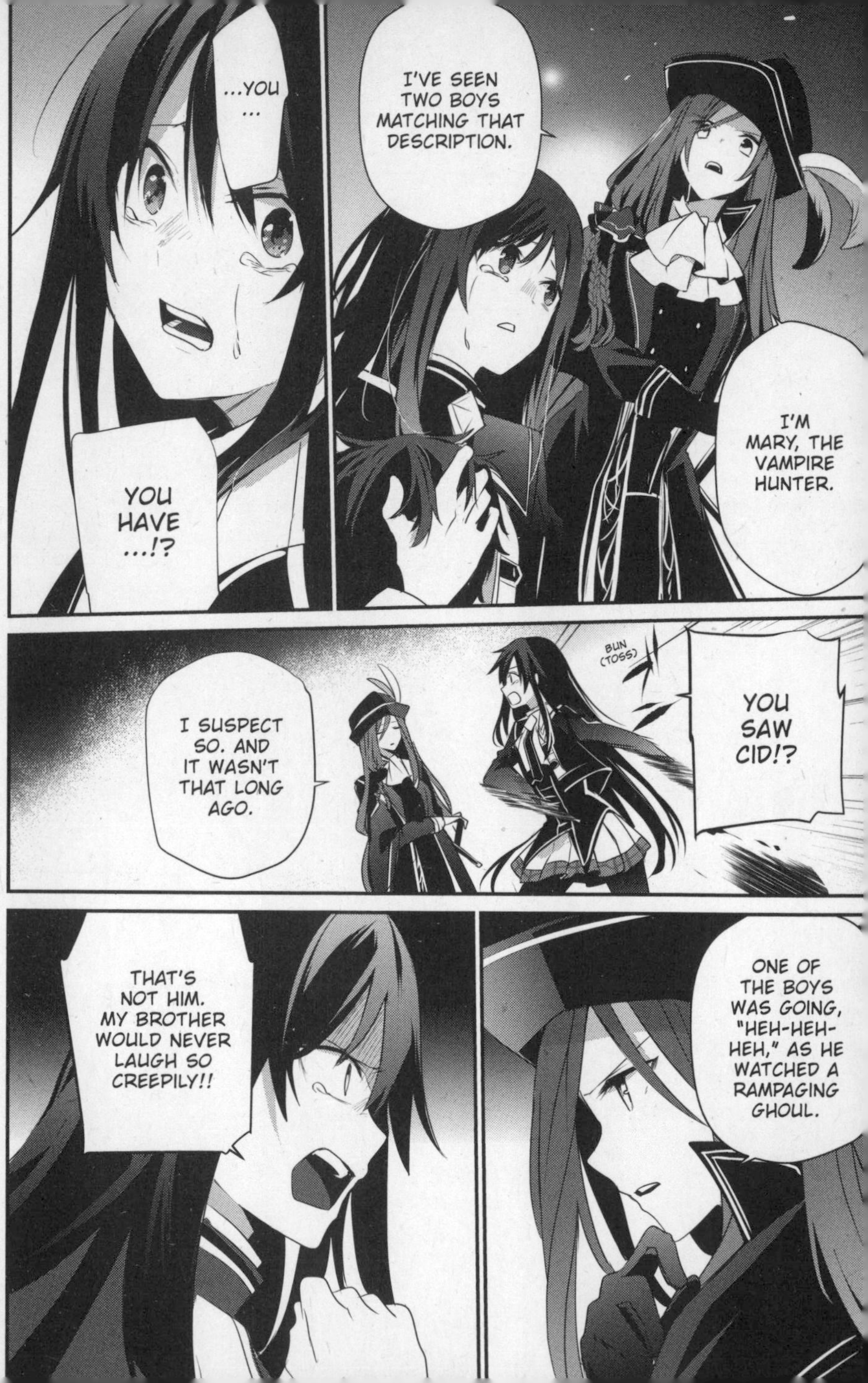

I'M MARY, THE VAMPIRE HUNTER.
I'VE SEEN TWO BOYS MATCHING THAT DESCRIPTION.
...YOU ...
YOU HAVE ...!?
BUN (TOSS)
YOU SAW CID!?
I SUSPECT SO. AND IT WASN'T THAT LONG AGO.
ONE OF THE BOYS WAS GOING, "HEH-HEH-HEH," AS HE WATCHED A RAMPAGING GHOUL.
THAT'S NOT HIM. MY BROTHER WOULD NEVER LAUGH SO CREEPILY!!

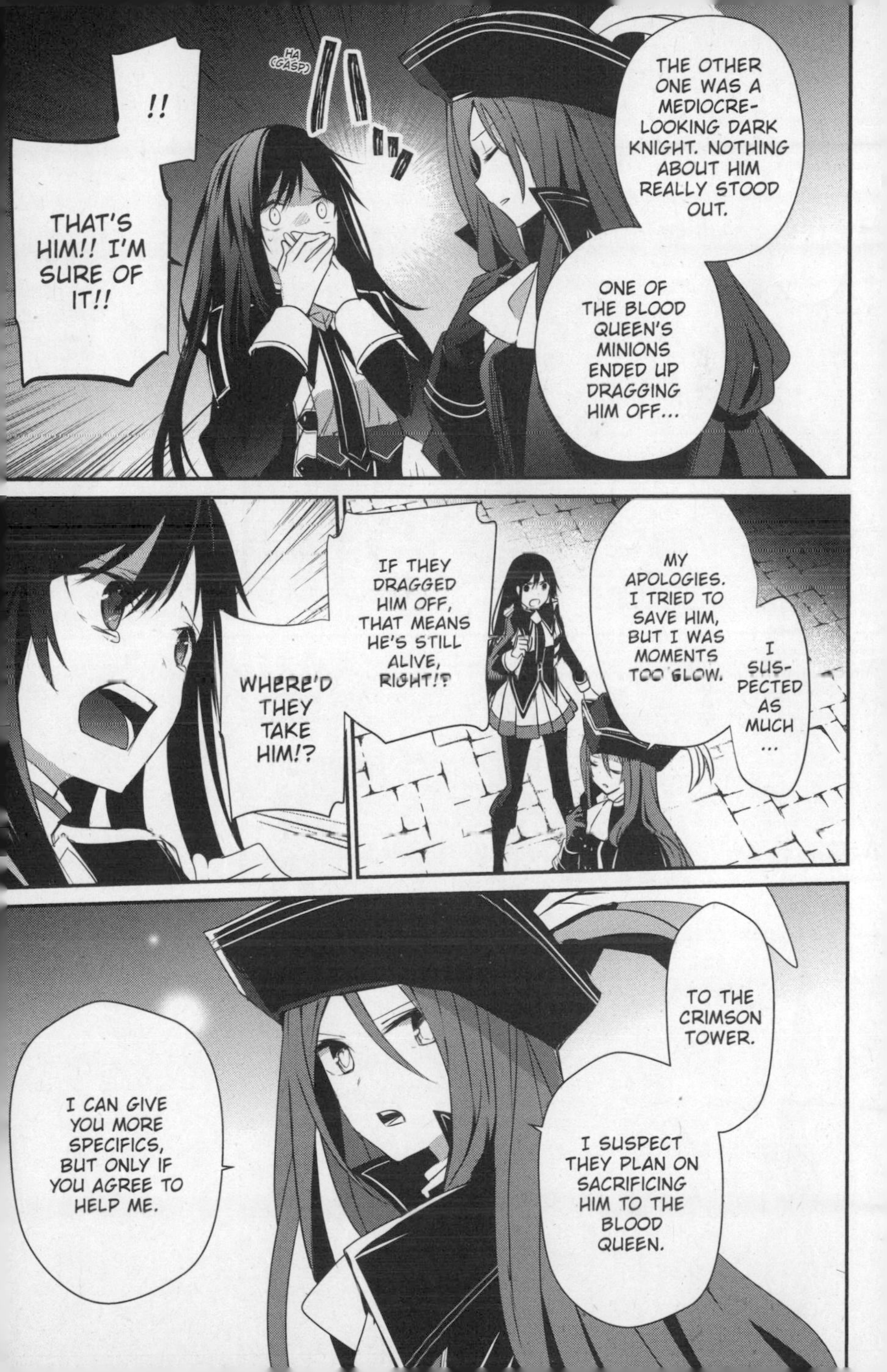
THE OTHER ONE WAS A MEDIOCRE-LOOKING DARK KNIGHT. NOTHING ABOUT HIM REALLY STOOD OUT.
ONE OF THE BLOOD QUEEN'S MINIONS ENDED UP DRAGGING HIM OFF...
HA (GASP)
!!
THAT'S HIM!! I'M SURE OF IT!!
MY APOLOGIES. I TRIED TO SAVE HIM, BUT I WAS MOMENTS TOO SLOW.
I SUSPECTED AS MUCH...
IF THEY DRAGGED HIM OFF, THAT MEANS HE'S STILL ALIVE, RIGHT!?
WHERE'D THEY TAKE HIM!?
TO THE CRIMSON TOWER.
I SUSPECT THEY PLAN ON SACRIFICING HIM TO THE BLOOD QUEEN.
I CAN GIVE YOU MORE SPECIFICS, BUT ONLY IF YOU AGREE TO HELP ME.

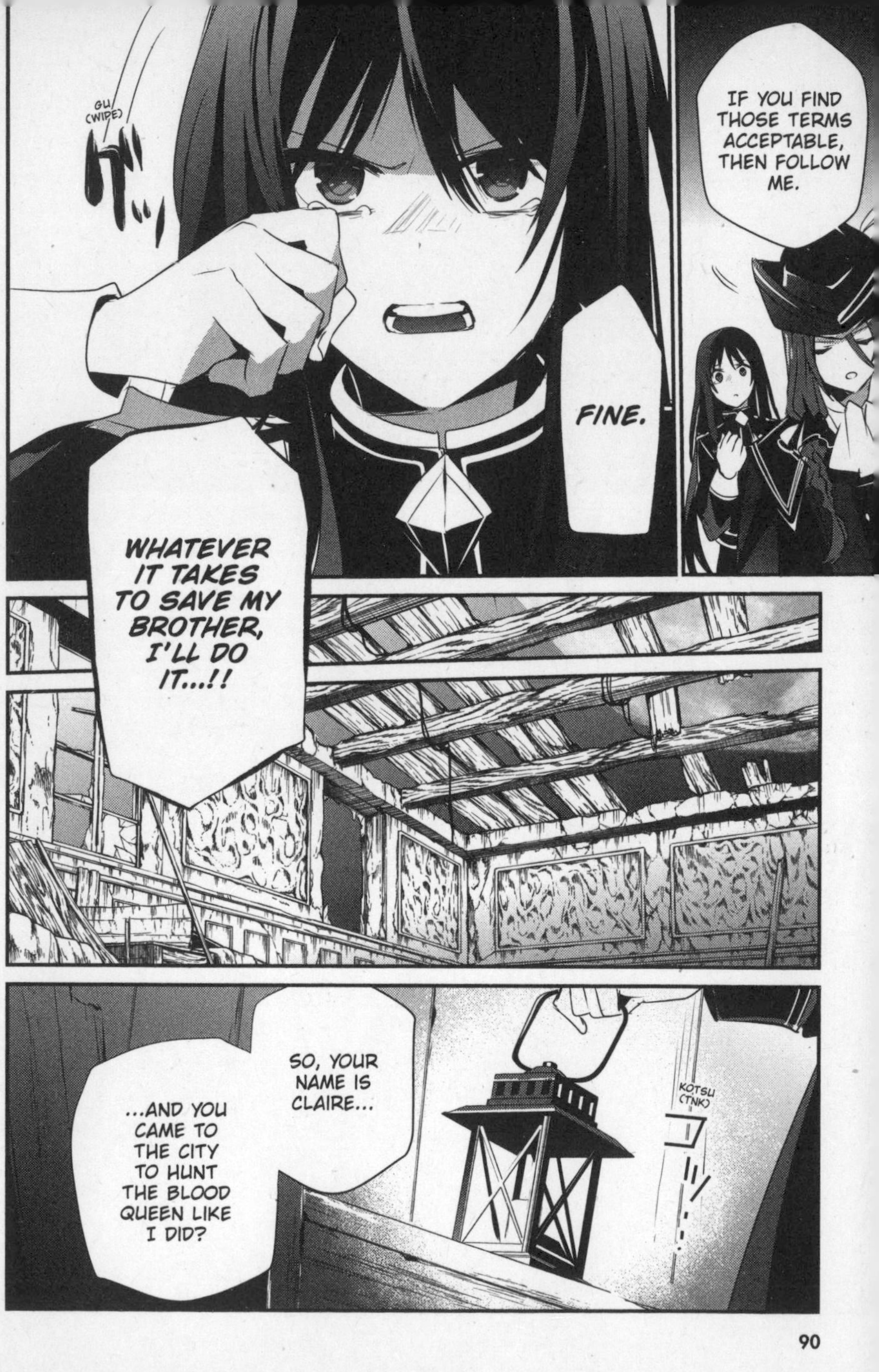
IF YOU FIND THOSE TERMS ACCEPTABLE, THEN FOLLOW ME.
GU (WIPE)
FINE.
WHATEVER IT TAKES TO SAVE MY BROTHER, I'LL DO IT...!!
KOTSU (TNK)
SO, YOUR NAME IS CLAIRE...
...AND YOU CAME TO THE CITY TO HUNT THE BLOOD QUEEN LIKE I DID?

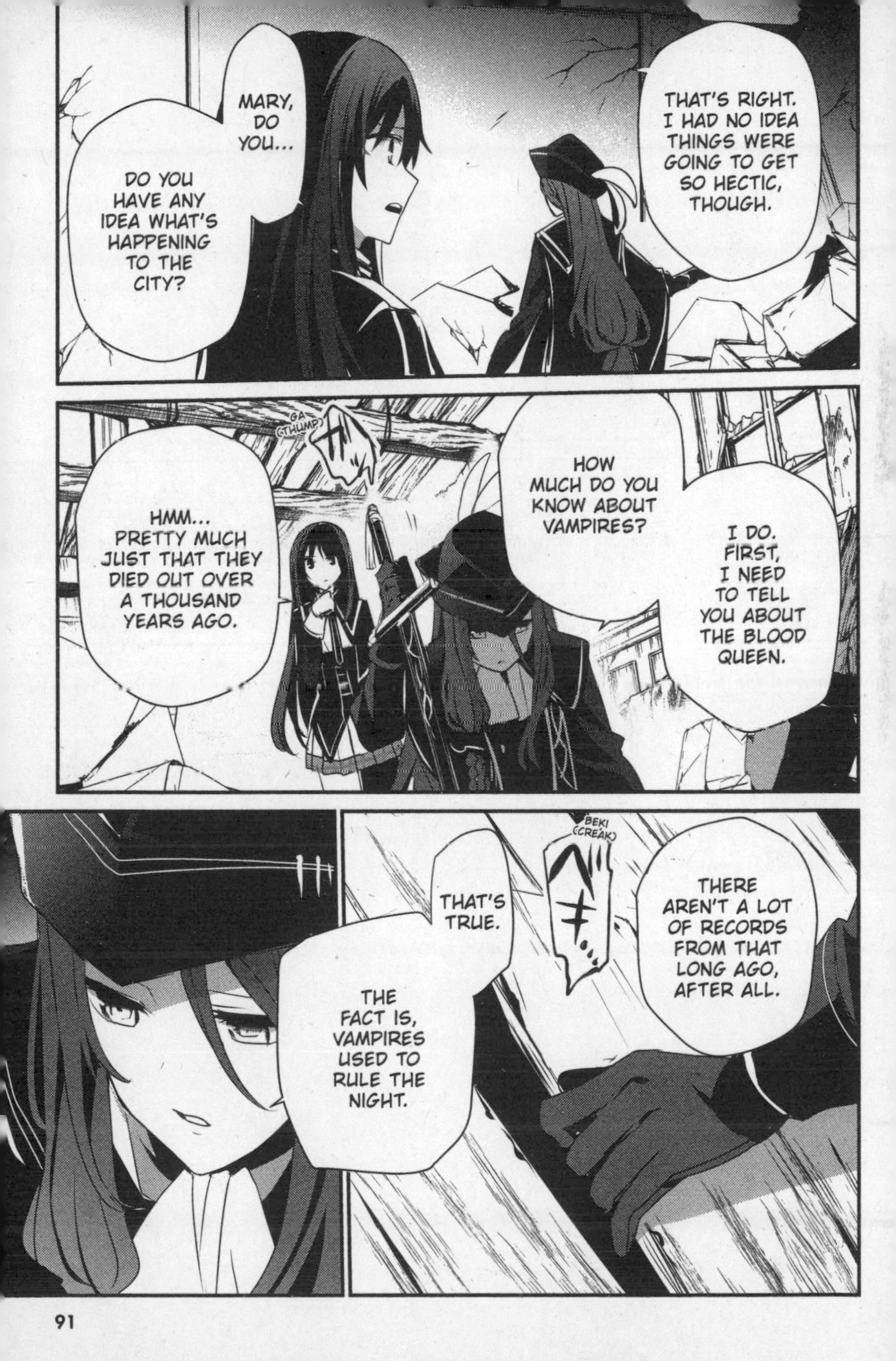
THAT'S RIGHT. I HAD NO IDEA THINGS WERE GOING TO GET SO HECTIC, THOUGH.
MARY, DO YOU...
DO YOU HAVE ANY IDEA WHAT'S HAPPENING TO THE CITY?
I DO. FIRST, I NEED TO TELL YOU ABOUT THE BLOOD QUEEN.
HOW MUCH DO YOU KNOW ABOUT VAMPIRES?
GA (THUMP)
HMM... PRETTY MUCH JUST THAT THEY DIED OUT OVER A THOUSAND YEARS AGO.
BEKI (CREAK)
THAT'S TRUE.
THERE AREN'T A LOT OF RECORDS FROM THAT LONG AGO, AFTER ALL.
THE FACT IS, VAMPIRES USED TO RULE THE NIGHT.

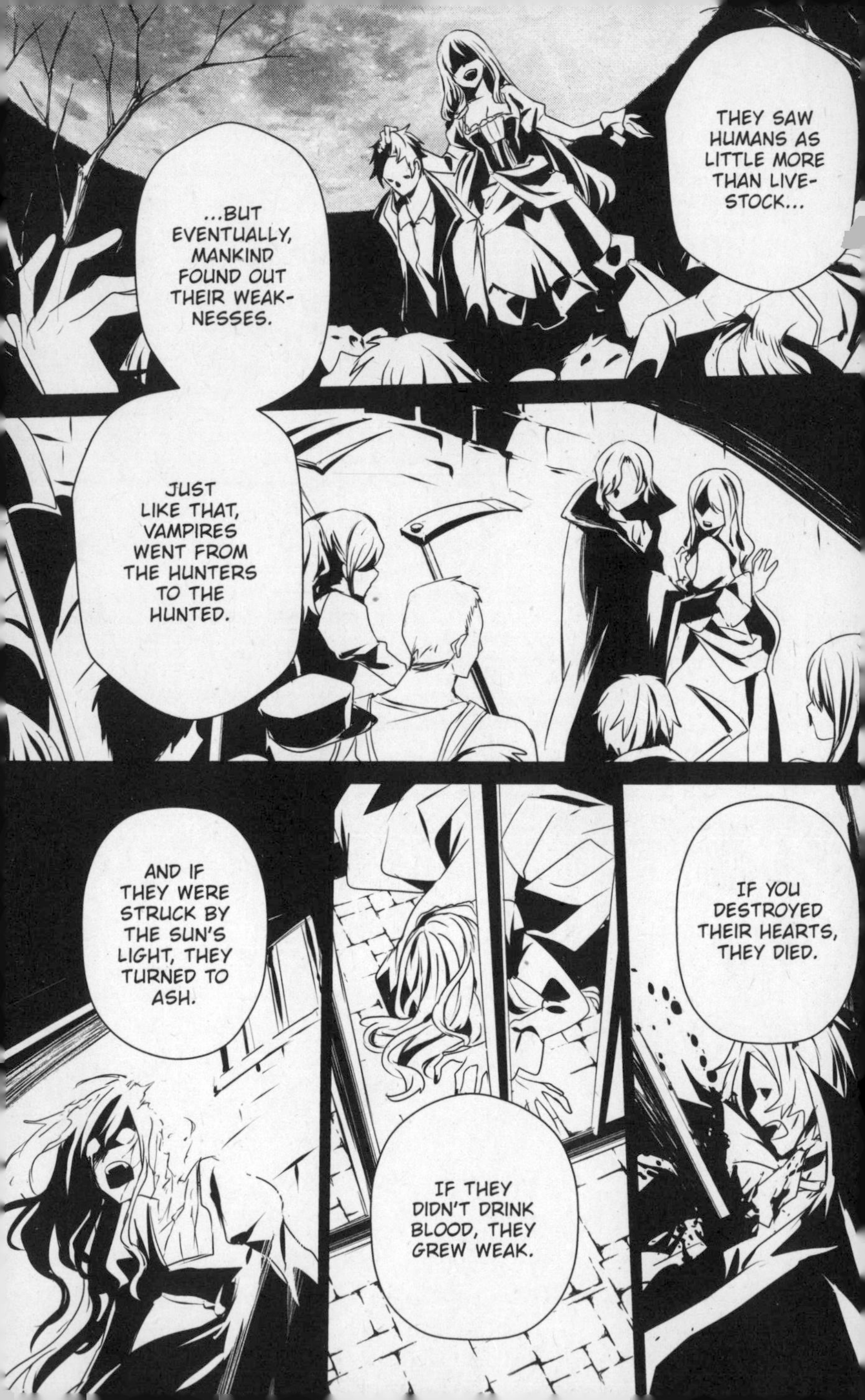
THEY SAW HUMANS AS LITTLE MORE THAN LIVE-STOCK...
...BUT EVENTUALLY, MANKIND FOUND OUT THEIR WEAK-NESSES.
JUST LIKE THAT, VAMPIRES WENT FROM THE HUNTERS TO THE HUNTED.
IF YOU DESTROYED THEIR HEARTS, THEY DIED.
IF THEY DIDN'T DRINK BLOOD, THEY GREW WEAK.
AND IF THEY WERE STRUCK BY THE SUN'S LIGHT, THEY TURNED TO ASH.

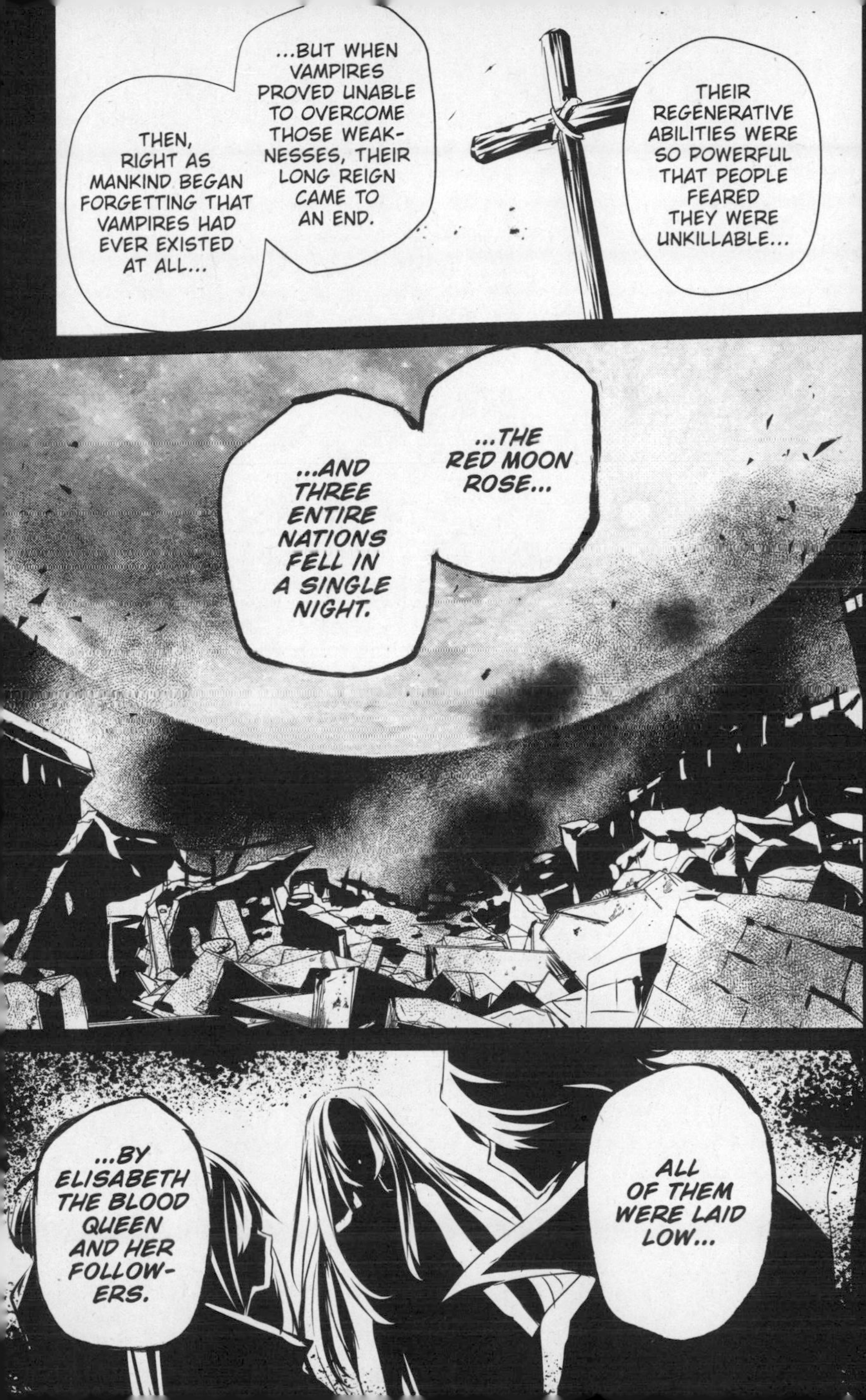
THEIR REGENERATIVE ABILITIES WERE SO POWERFUL THAT PEOPLE FEARED THEY WERE UNKILLABLE...
...BUT WHEN VAMPIRES PROVED UNABLE TO OVERCOME THOSE WEAKNESSES, THEIR LONG REIGN CAME TO AN END.
THEN, RIGHT AS MANKIND BEGAN FORGETTING THAT VAMPIRES HAD EVER EXISTED AT ALL...
...THE RED MOON ROSE...
...AND THREE ENTIRE NATIONS FELL IN A SINGLE NIGHT.
ALL OF THEM WERE LAID LOW...
...BY ELISABETH THE BLOOD QUEEN AND HER FOLLOWERS.

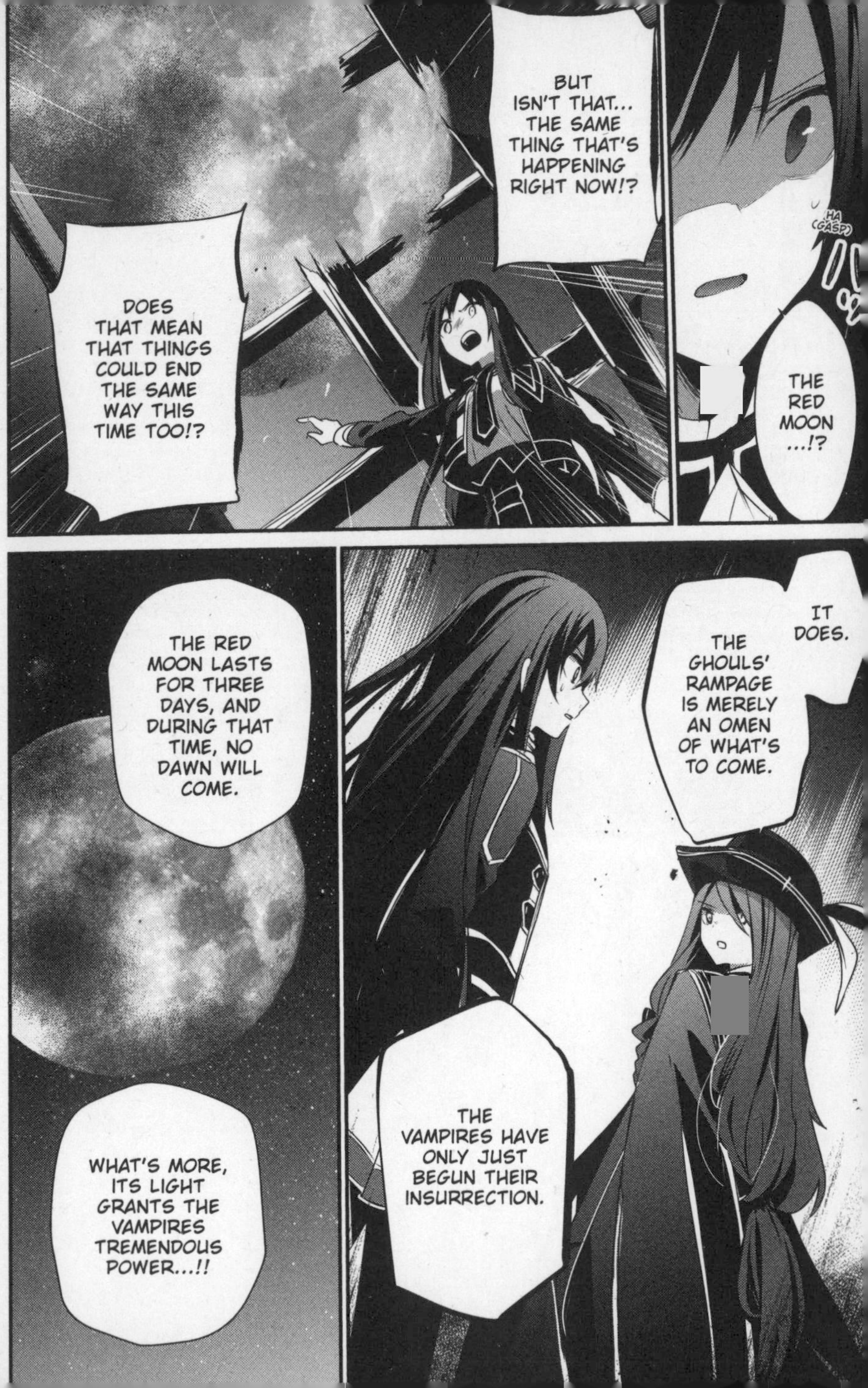

HA (GASP)
THE RED MOON ...!?
BUT ISN'T THAT... THE SAME THING THAT'S HAPPENING RIGHT NOW!?
DOES THAT MEAN THAT THINGS COULD END THE SAME WAY THIS TIME TOO!?
IT DOES.
THE GHOULS' RAMPAGE IS MERELY AN OMEN OF WHAT'S TO COME.
THE VAMPIRES HAVE ONLY JUST BEGUN THEIR INSURRECTION.
THE RED MOON LASTS FOR THREE DAYS, AND DURING THAT TIME, NO DAWN WILL COME.
WHAT'S MORE, ITS LIGHT GRANTS THE VAMPIRES TREMENDOUS POWER...!!

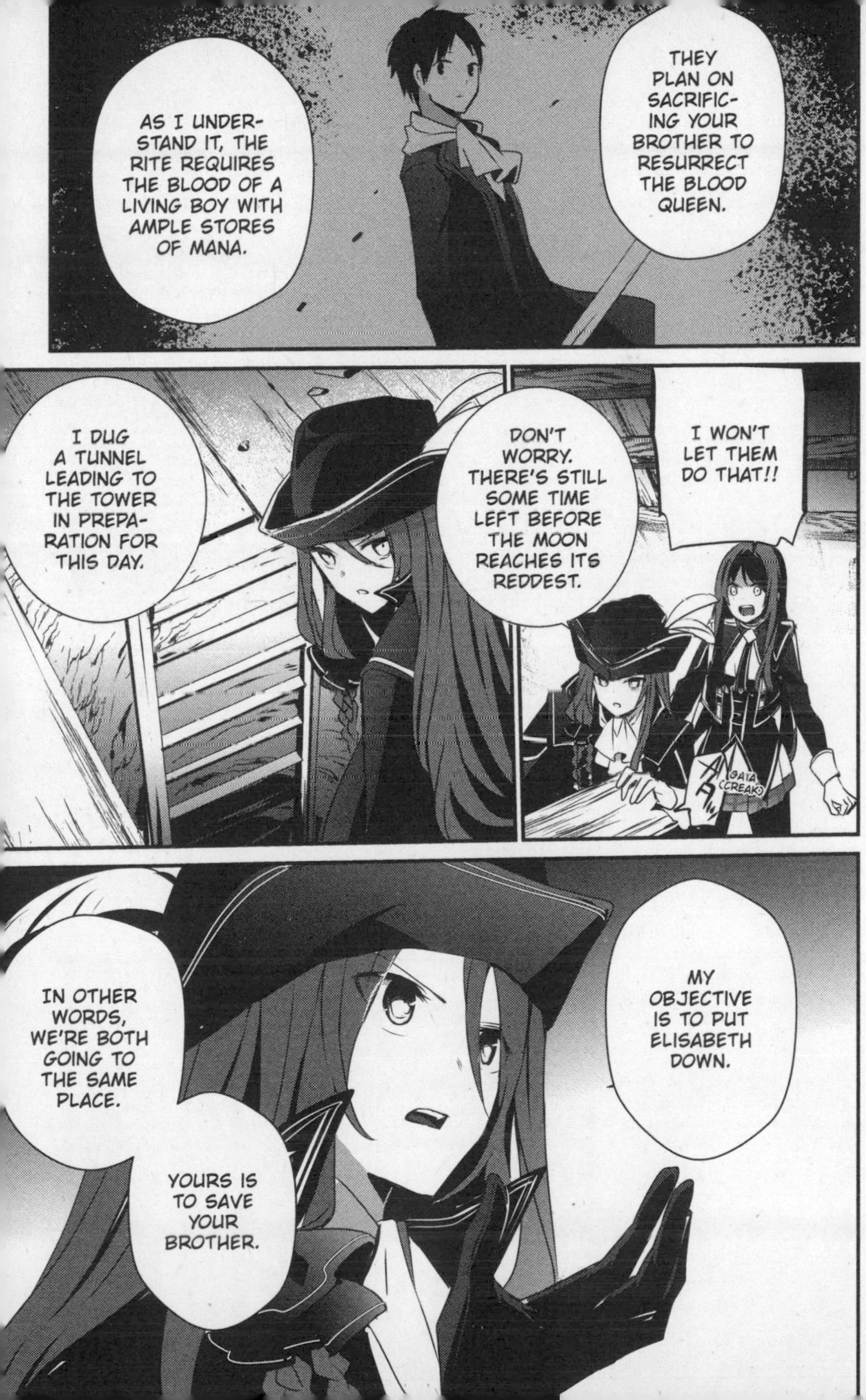

THEY PLAN ON SACRIFICING YOUR BROTHER TO RESURRECT THE BLOOD QUEEN.
AS I UNDERSTAND IT, THE RITE REQUIRES THE BLOOD OF A LIVING BOY WITH AMPLE STORES OF MANA.
I WON'T LET THEM DO THAT!!
GATA (CREAK)
DON'T WORRY. THERE'S STILL SOME TIME LEFT BEFORE THE MOON REACHES ITS REDDEST.
I DUG A TUNNEL LEADING TO THE TOWER IN PREPARATION FOR THIS DAY.
MY OBJECTIVE IS TO PUT ELISABETH DOWN.
YOURS IS TO SAVE YOUR BROTHER.
IN OTHER WORDS, WE'RE BOTH GOING TO THE SAME PLACE.

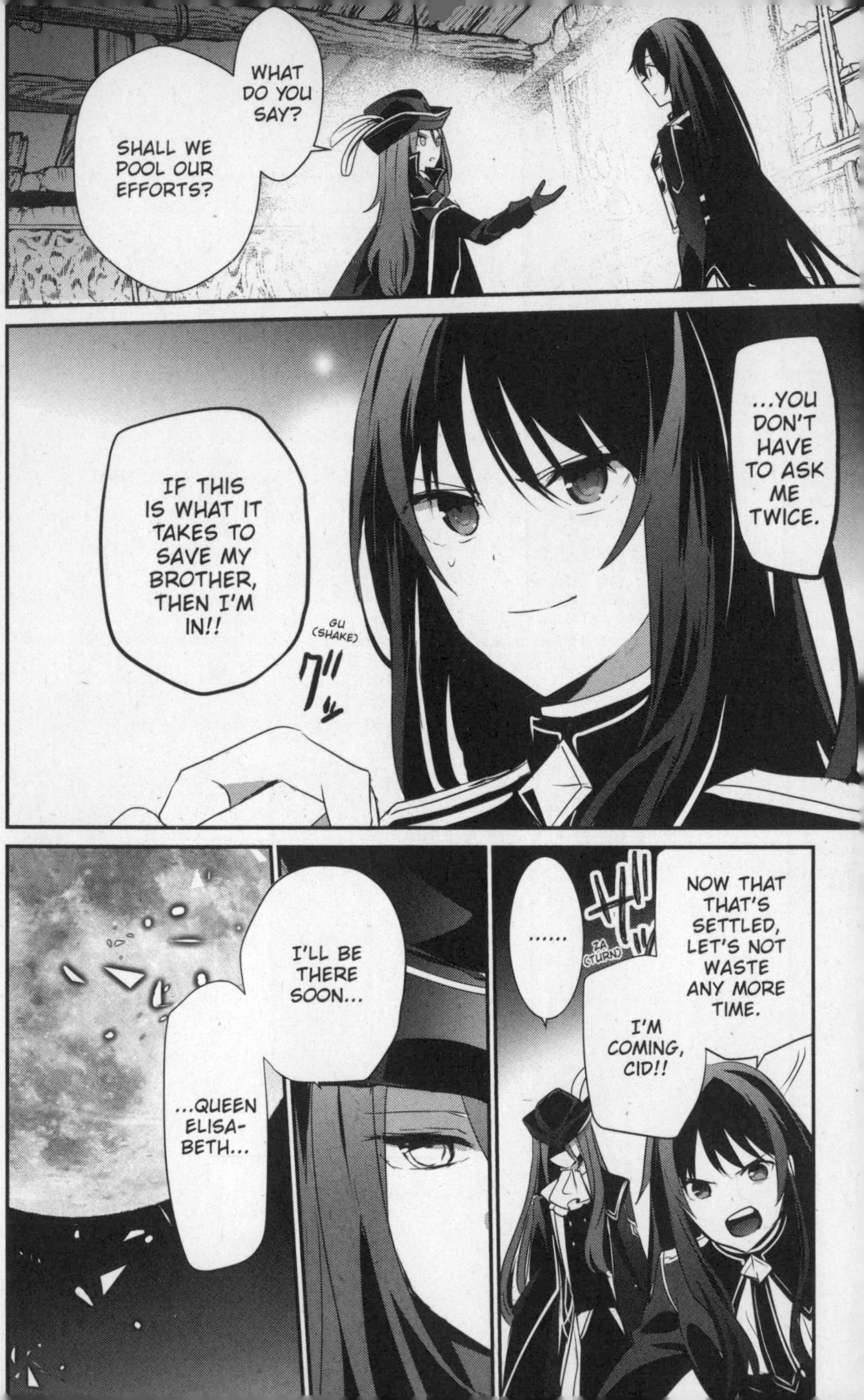
WHAT DO YOU SAY?
SHALL WE POOL OUR EFFORTS?
...YOU DON'T HAVE TO ASK ME TWICE.
IF THIS IS WHAT IT TAKES TO SAVE MY BROTHER, THEN I'M IN!!
GU (SHAKE)
NOW THAT THAT'S SETTLED, LET'S NOT WASTE ANY MORE TIME.
ZA (TURN)
......
I'M COMING, CID!!
I'LL BE THERE SOON...
...QUEEN ELISA-BETH...

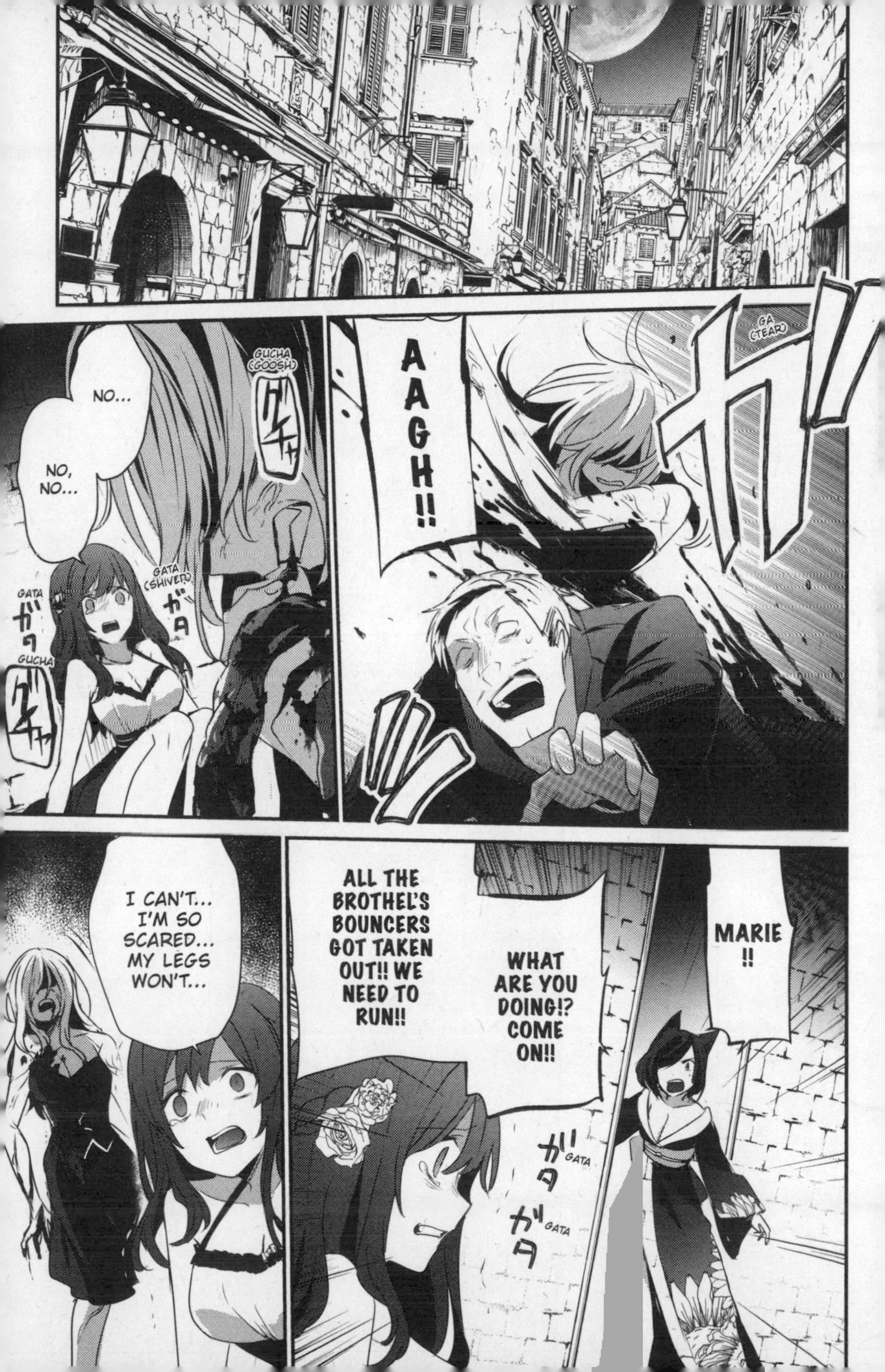
GA (TEAR)
ガッ
AAGH!!
GUCHA (GOOSH)
グチャ
NO...
NO, NO...
GATA (SHIVER)
ガタ
GATA
ガタ
GUCHA
グチャ
MARIE!!
WHAT ARE YOU DOING!? COME ON!!
ALL THE BROTHEL'S BOUNCERS GOT TAKEN OUT!! WE NEED TO RUN!!
ガタ GATA
ガタ GATA
I CAN'T... I'M SO SCARED... MY LEGS WON'T...

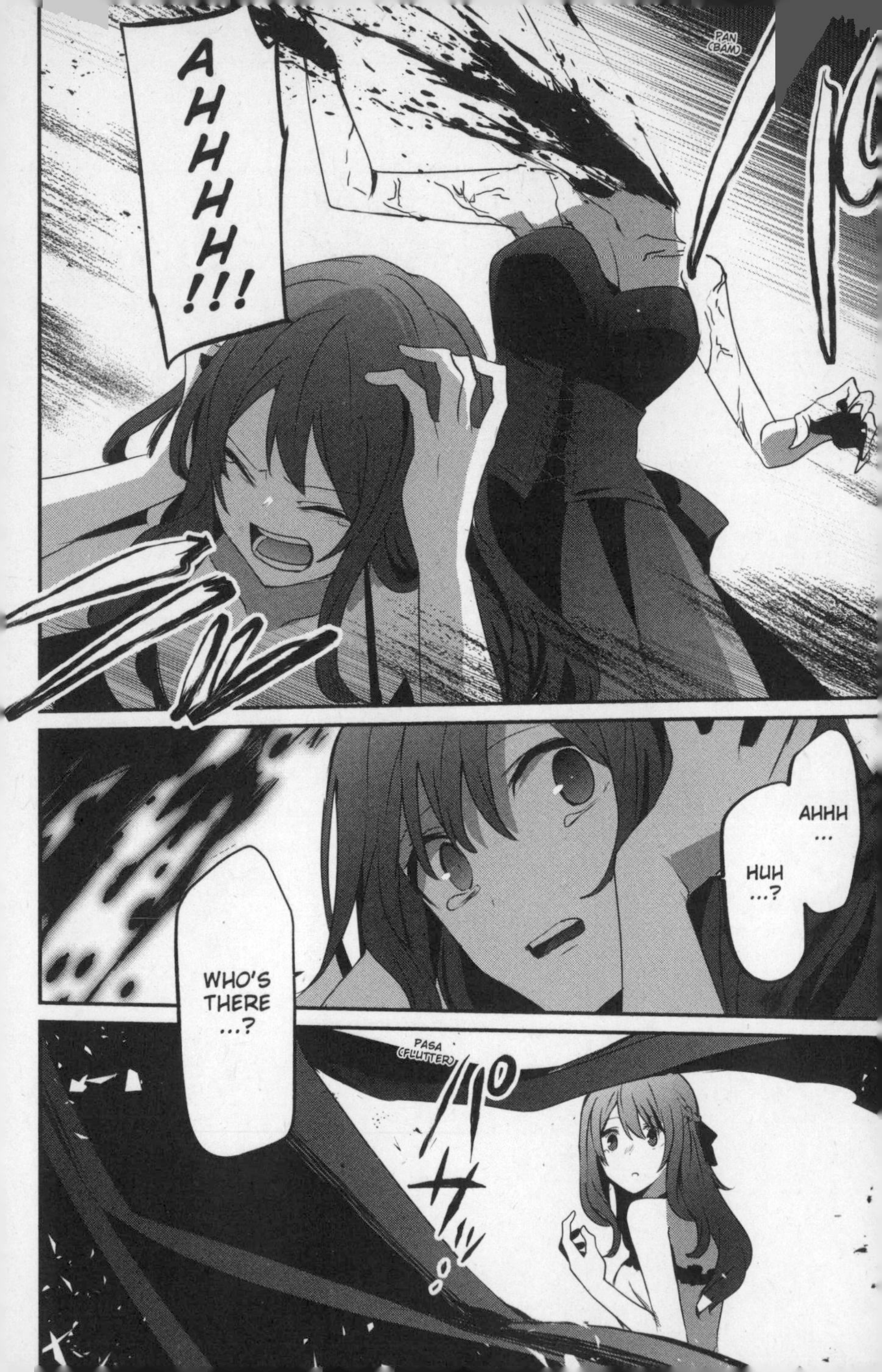
PAN (BAN)
AHHHH!!!
AHHH ... HUH ...?
WHO'S THERE ...?
PASA (FLUTTER)

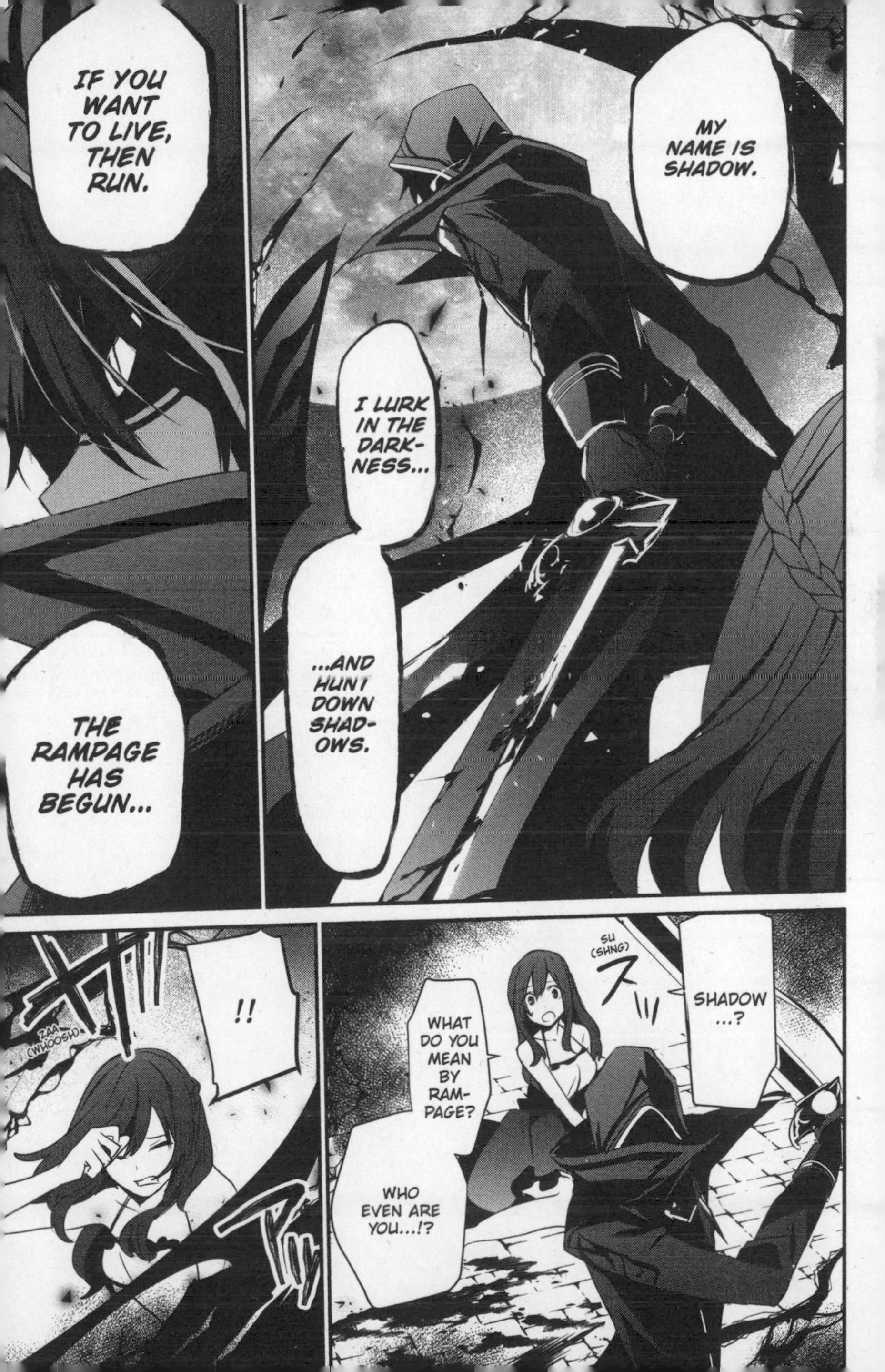
MY NAME IS SHADOW.
I LURK IN THE DARK-NESS...
...AND HUNT DOWN SHAD-OWS.
IF YOU WANT TO LIVE, THEN RUN.
THE RAMPAGE HAS BEGUN...
SU (SHNG)
SHADOW...?
WHAT DO YOU MEAN BY RAM-PAGE?
WHO EVEN ARE YOU...!?
ZAA (WHOOSH)
!!

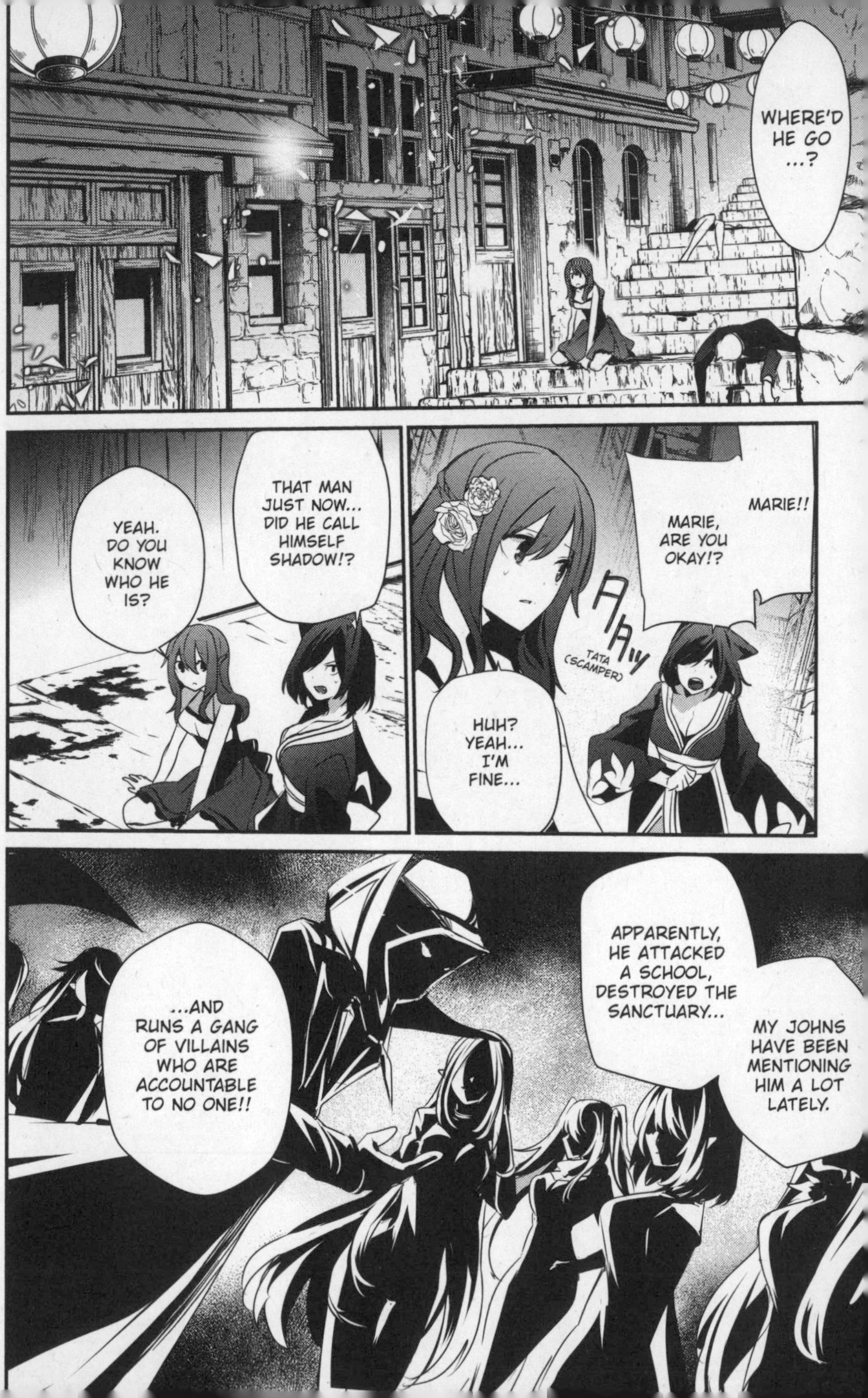
WHERE'D HE GO ...?
MARIE!!
MARIE, ARE YOU OKAY!?
TATA (SCAMPER)
HUH? YEAH... I'M FINE...
THAT MAN JUST NOW... DID HE CALL HIMSELF SHADOW!?
YEAH. DO YOU KNOW WHO HE IS?
MY JOHNS HAVE BEEN MENTIONING HIM A LOT LATELY.
APPARENTLY, HE ATTACKED A SCHOOL, DESTROYED THE SANCTUARY...
...AND RUNS A GANG OF VILLAINS WHO ARE ACCOUNTABLE TO NO ONE!!

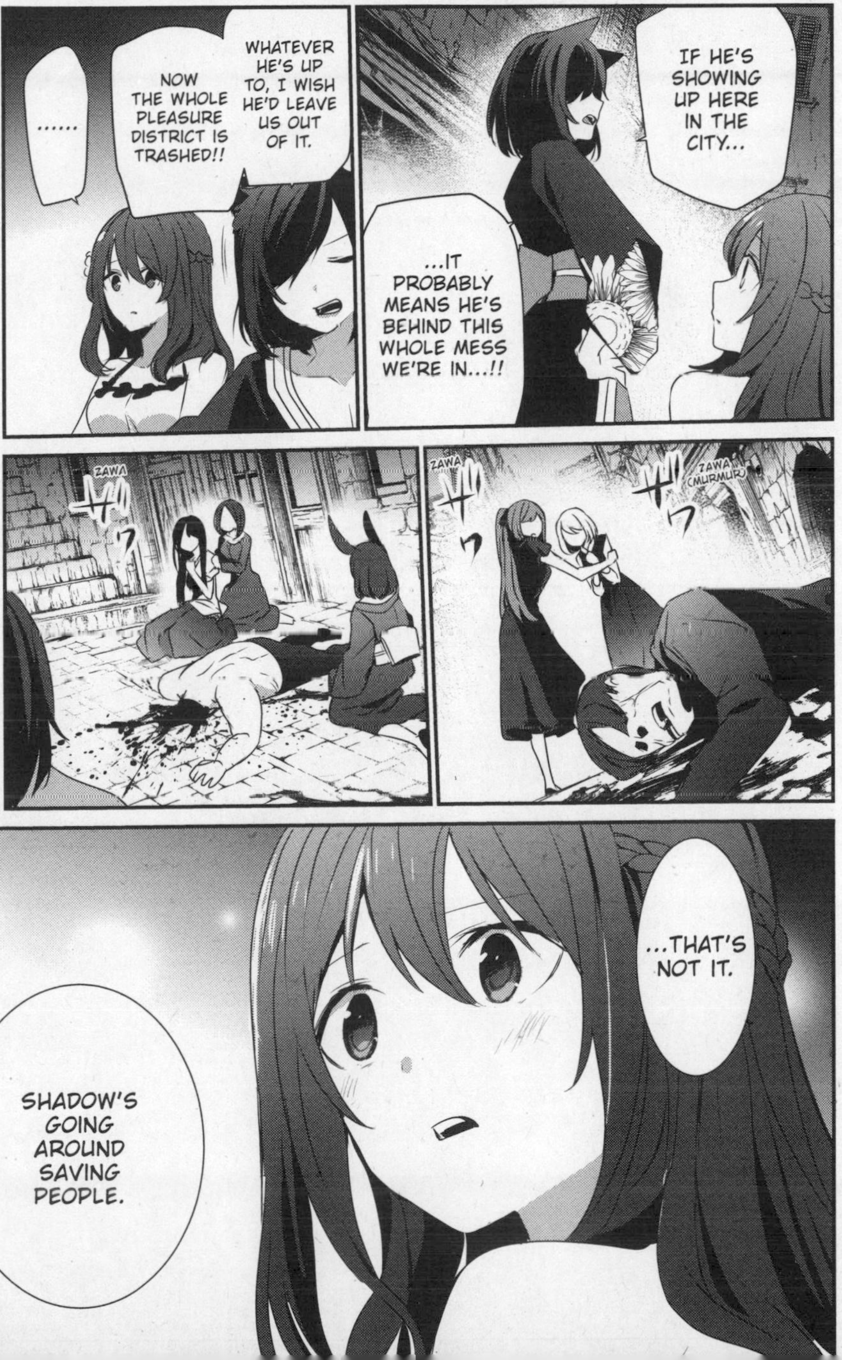
IF HE'S SHOWING UP HERE IN THE CITY...
...IT PROBABLY MEANS HE'S BEHIND THIS WHOLE MESS WE'RE IN...!!
WHATEVER HE'S UP TO, I WISH HE'D LEAVE US OUT OF IT.
NOW THE WHOLE PLEASURE DISTRICT IS TRASHED!!
......
ZAWA (MURMUR)
ZAWA
ZAWA
...THAT'S NOT IT.
SHADOW'S GOING AROUND SAVING PEOPLE.

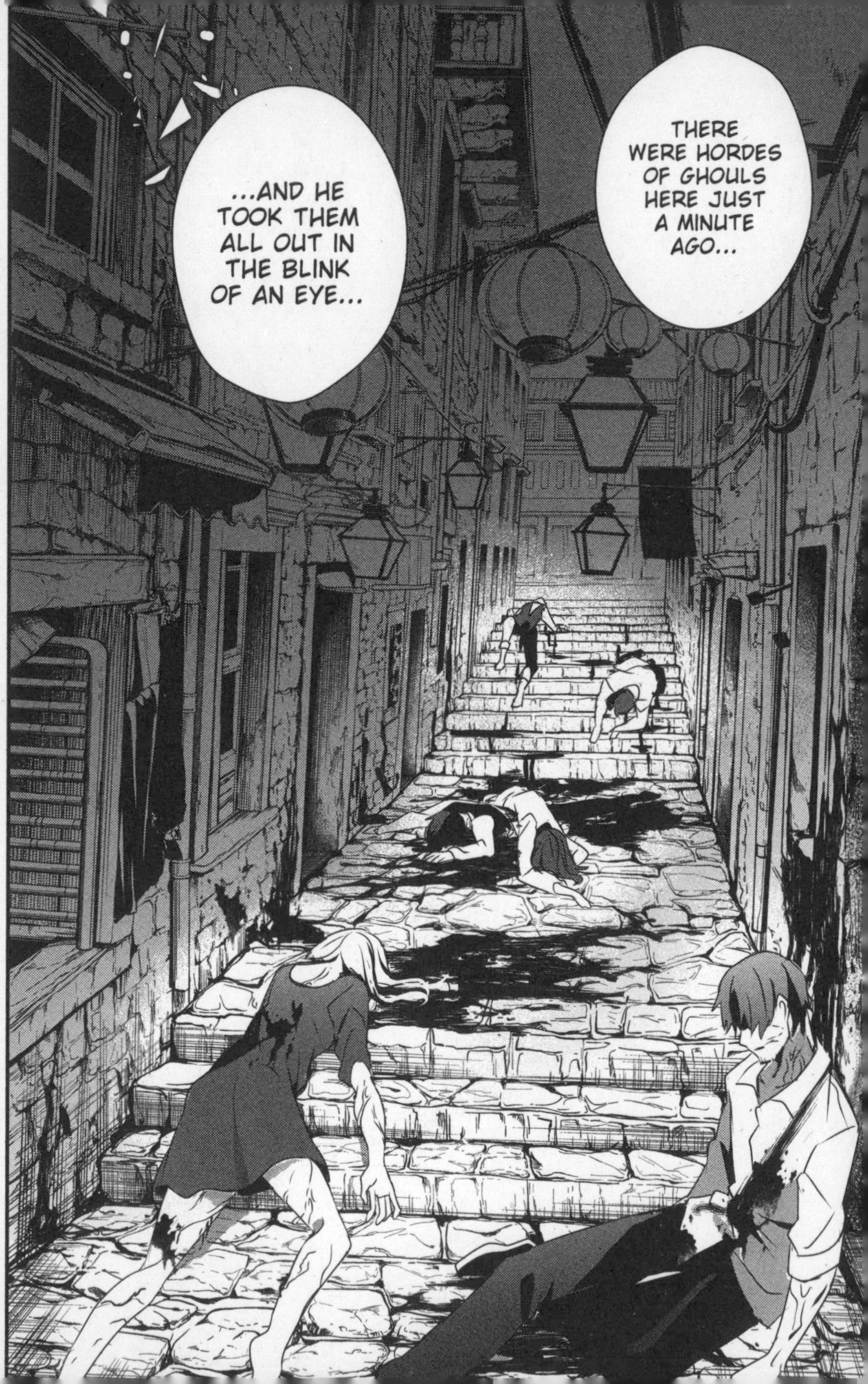
THERE WERE HORDES OF GHOULS HERE JUST A MINUTE AGO...
...AND HE TOOK THEM ALL OUT IN THE BLINK OF AN EYE...

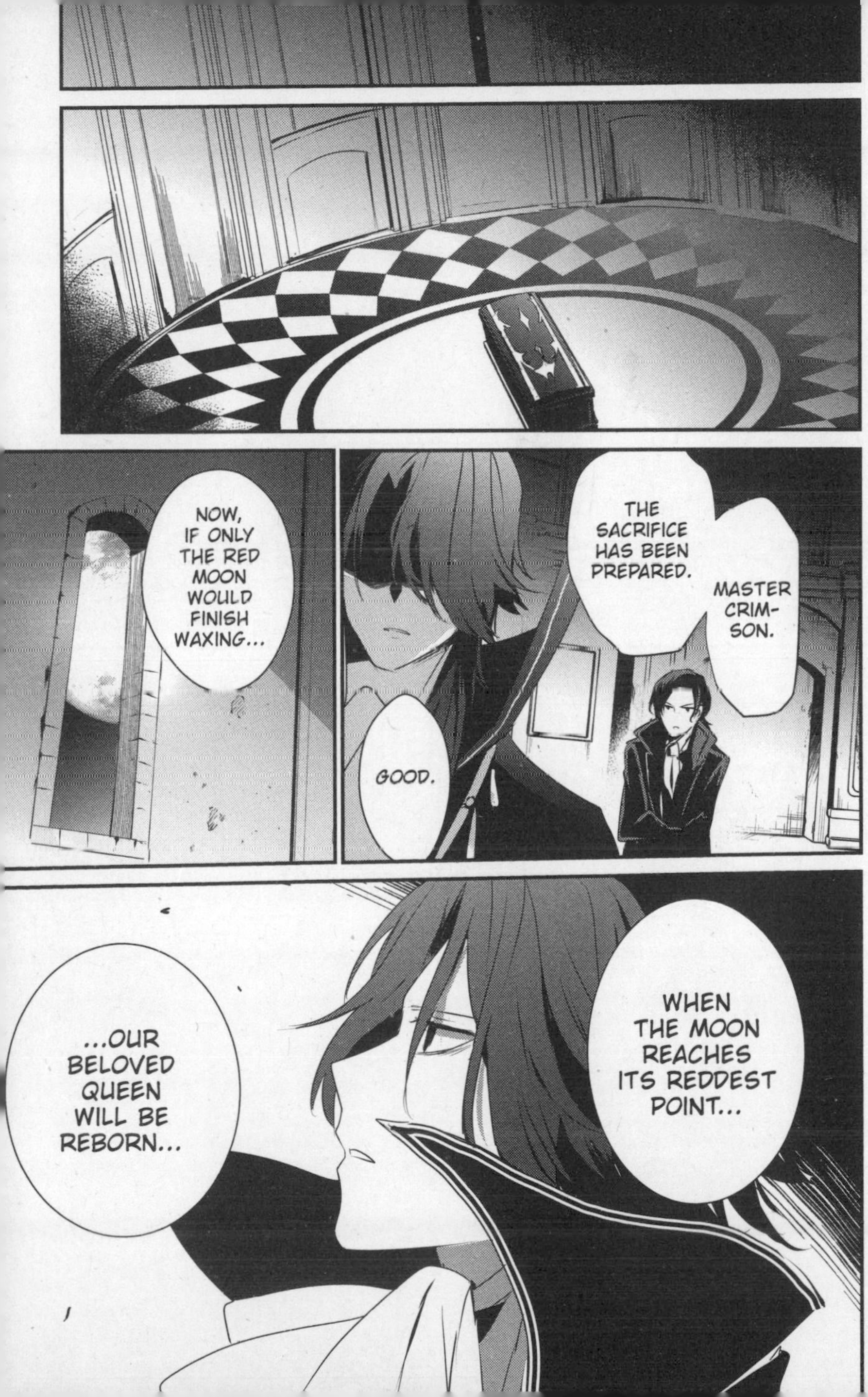
THE SACRIFICE HAS BEEN PREPARED.
MASTER CRIMSON.
GOOD.
NOW, IF ONLY THE RED MOON WOULD FINISH WAXING...
WHEN THE MOON REACHES ITS REDDEST POINT...
...OUR BELOVED QUEEN WILL BE REBORN...

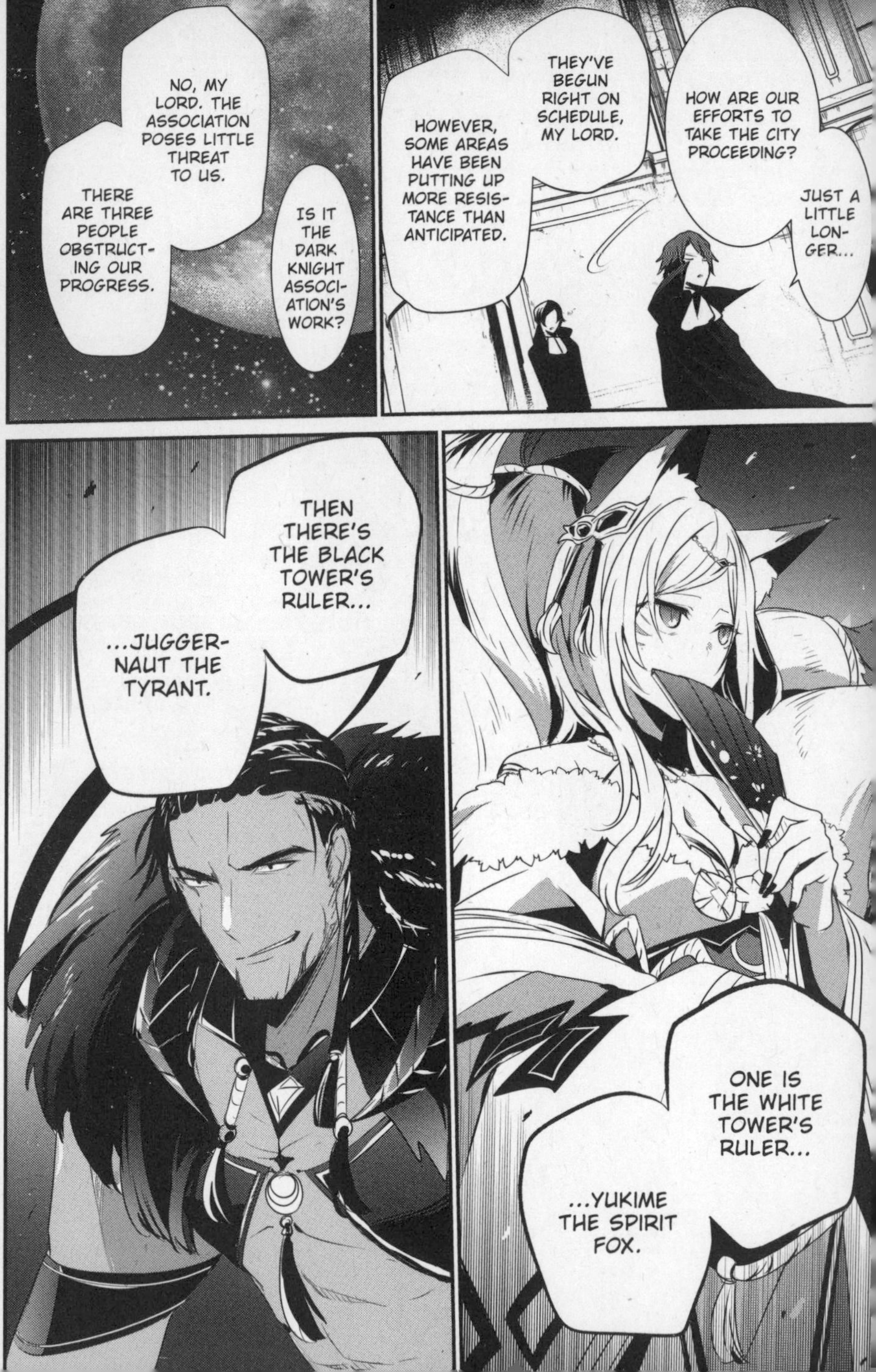
HOW ARE OUR EFFORTS TO TAKE THE CITY PROCEEDING?
JUST A LITTLE LONGER...
THEY'VE BEGUN RIGHT ON SCHEDULE, MY LORD.
HOWEVER, SOME AREAS HAVE BEEN PUTTING UP MORE RESISTANCE THAN ANTICIPATED.
IS IT THE DARK KNIGHT ASSOCIATION'S WORK?
NO, MY LORD. THE ASSOCIATION POSES LITTLE THREAT TO US.
THERE ARE THREE PEOPLE OBSTRUCTING OUR PROGRESS.
ONE IS THE WHITE TOWER'S RULER...
...YUKIME THE SPIRIT FOX.
THEN THERE'S THE BLACK TOWER'S RULER...
...JUGGERNAUT THE TYRANT.

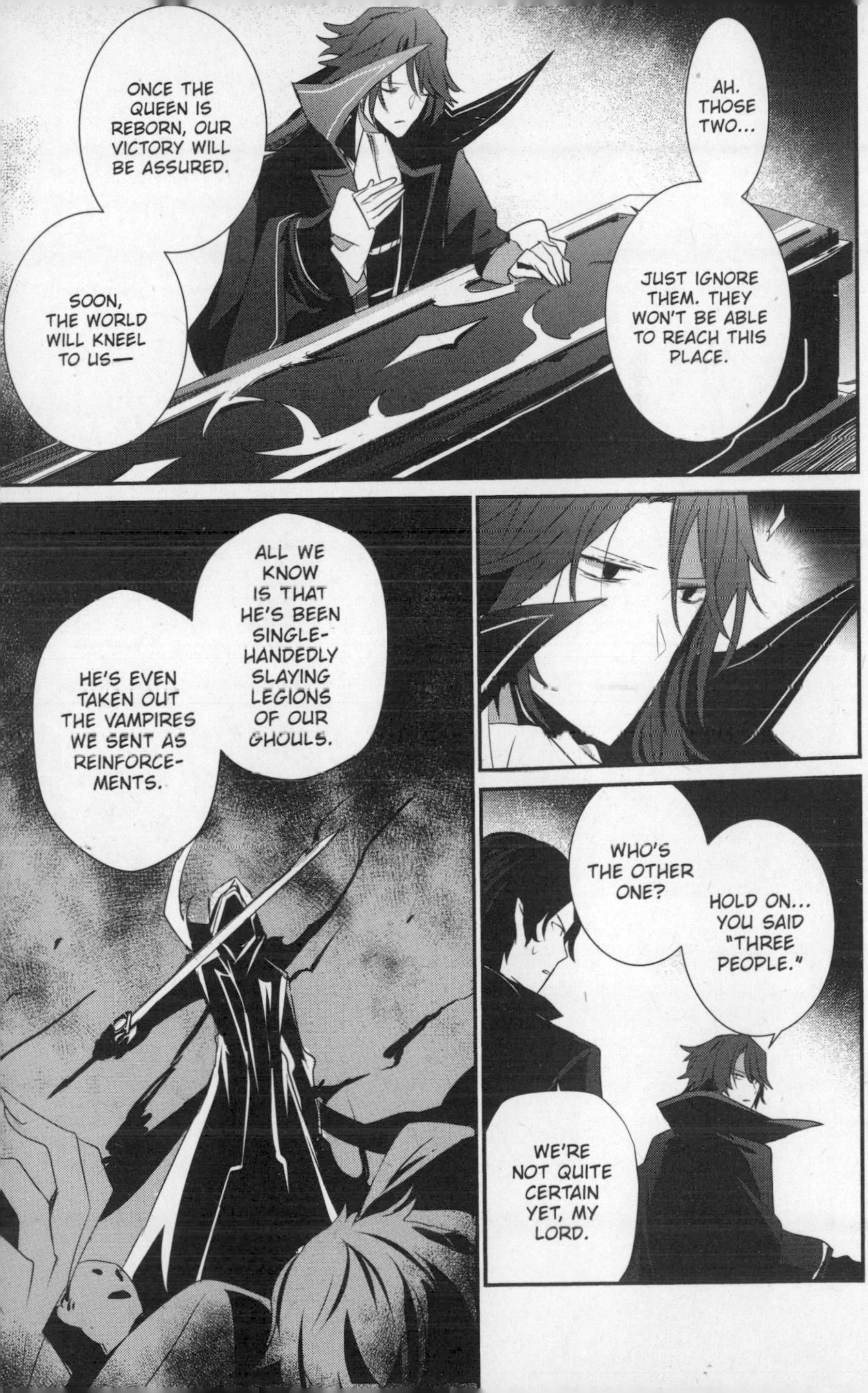
AH. THOSE TWO...
JUST IGNORE THEM. THEY WON'T BE ABLE TO REACH THIS PLACE.
ONCE THE QUEEN IS REBORN, OUR VICTORY WILL BE ASSURED.
SOON, THE WORLD WILL KNEEL TO US—
HOLD ON... YOU SAID "THREE PEOPLE."
WHO'S THE OTHER ONE?
WE'RE NOT QUITE CERTAIN YET, MY LORD.
ALL WE KNOW IS THAT HE'S BEEN SINGLE-HANDEDLY SLAYING LEGIONS OF OUR GHOULS.
HE'S EVEN TAKEN OUT THE VAMPIRES WE SENT AS REINFORCE-MENTS.

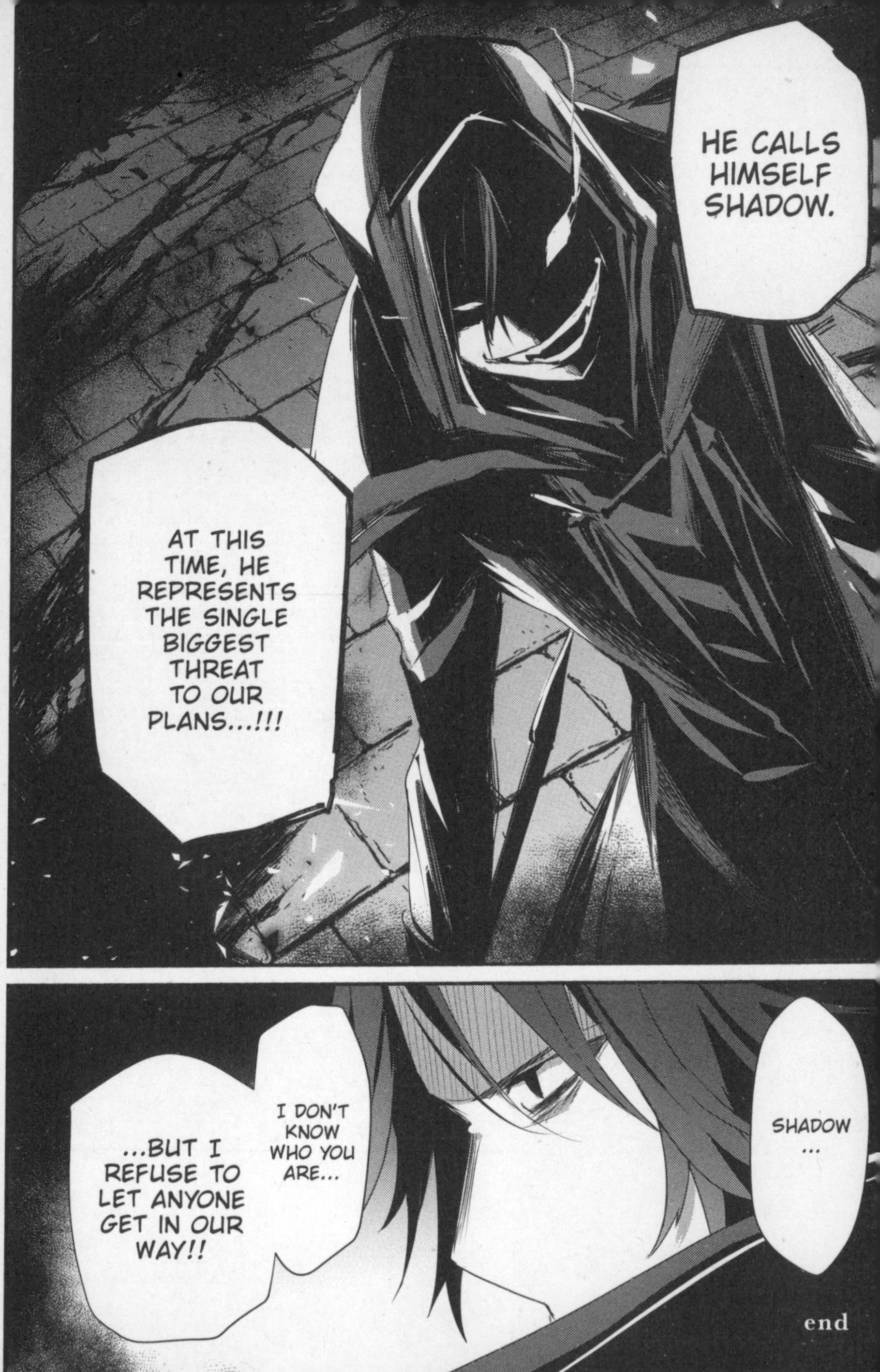
HE CALLS HIMSELF SHADOW.
AT THIS TIME, HE REPRESENTS THE SINGLE BIGGEST THREAT TO OUR PLANS...!!!
SHADOW...
I DON'T KNOW WHO YOU ARE...
...BUT I REFUSE TO LET ANYONE GET IN OUR WAY!!
end

Episode. 29

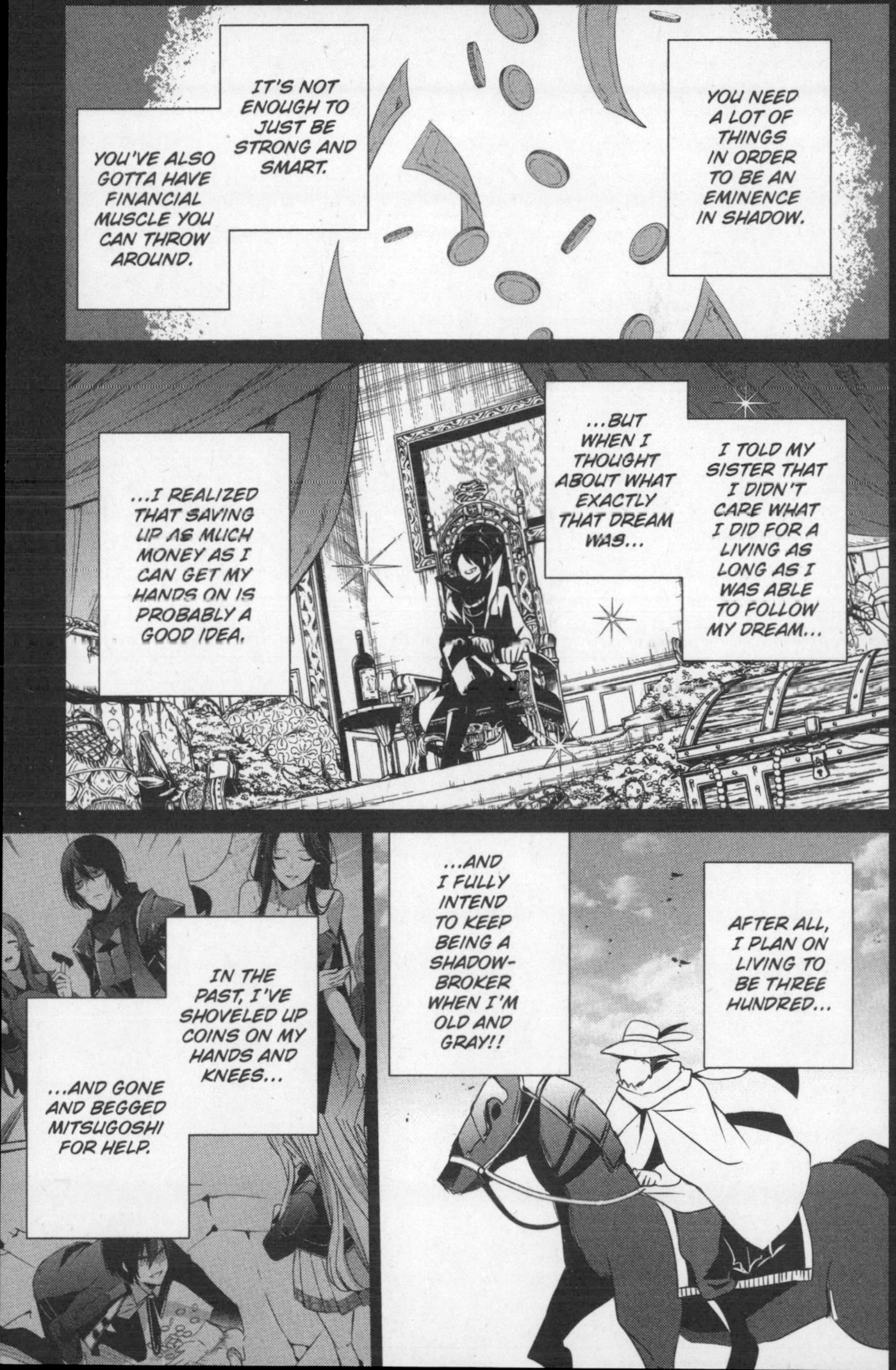
YOU NEED A LOT OF THINGS IN ORDER TO BE AN EMINENCE IN SHADOW.
IT'S NOT ENOUGH TO JUST BE STRONG AND SMART.
YOU'VE ALSO GOTTA HAVE FINANCIAL MUSCLE YOU CAN THROW AROUND.
I TOLD MY SISTER THAT I DIDN'T CARE WHAT I DID FOR A LIVING AS LONG AS I WAS ABLE TO FOLLOW MY DREAM...
...BUT WHEN I THOUGHT ABOUT WHAT EXACTLY THAT DREAM WAS...
...I REALIZED THAT SAVING UP AS MUCH MONEY AS I CAN GET MY HANDS ON IS PROBABLY A GOOD IDEA.
AFTER ALL, I PLAN ON LIVING TO BE THREE HUNDRED...
...AND I FULLY INTEND TO KEEP BEING A SHADOW-BROKER WHEN I'M OLD AND GRAY!!
IN THE PAST, I'VE SHOVELED UP COINS ON MY HANDS AND KNEES...
...AND GONE AND BEGGED MITSUGOSHI FOR HELP.

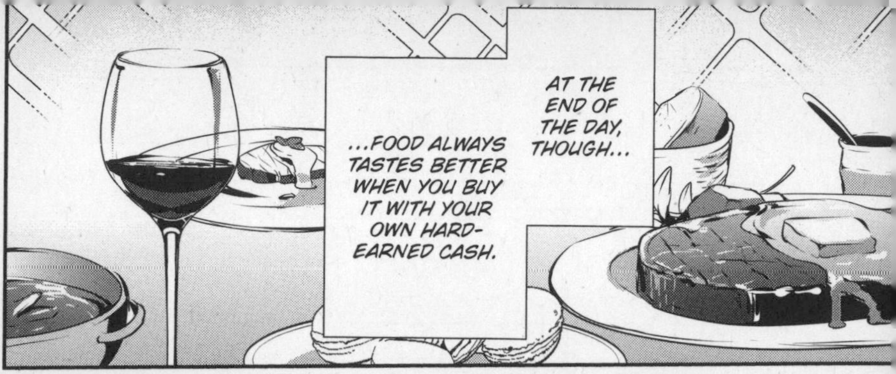
AT THE END OF THE DAY, THOUGH...
...FOOD ALWAYS TASTES BETTER WHEN YOU BUY IT WITH YOUR OWN HARD-EARNED CASH.

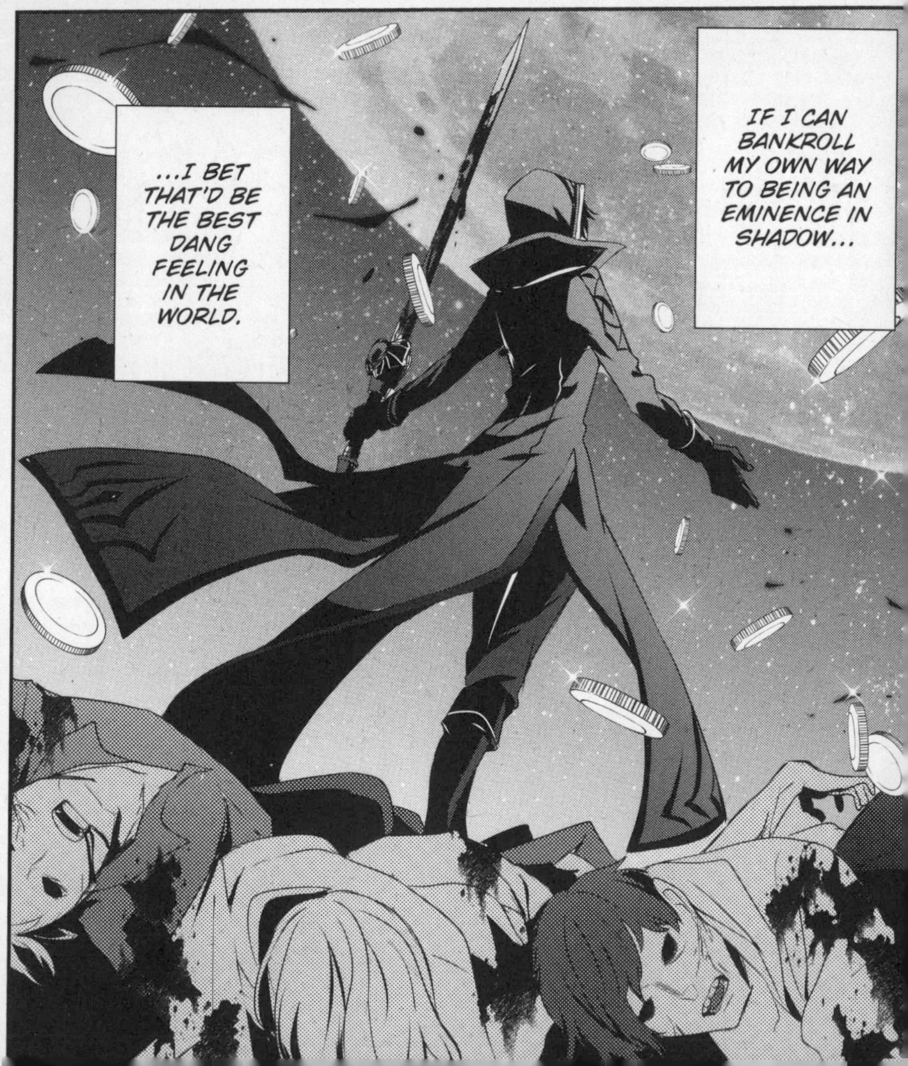
IF I CAN BANKROLL MY OWN WAY TO BEING AN EMINENCE IN SHADOW...
...I BET THAT'D BE THE BEST DANG FEELING IN THE WORLD.

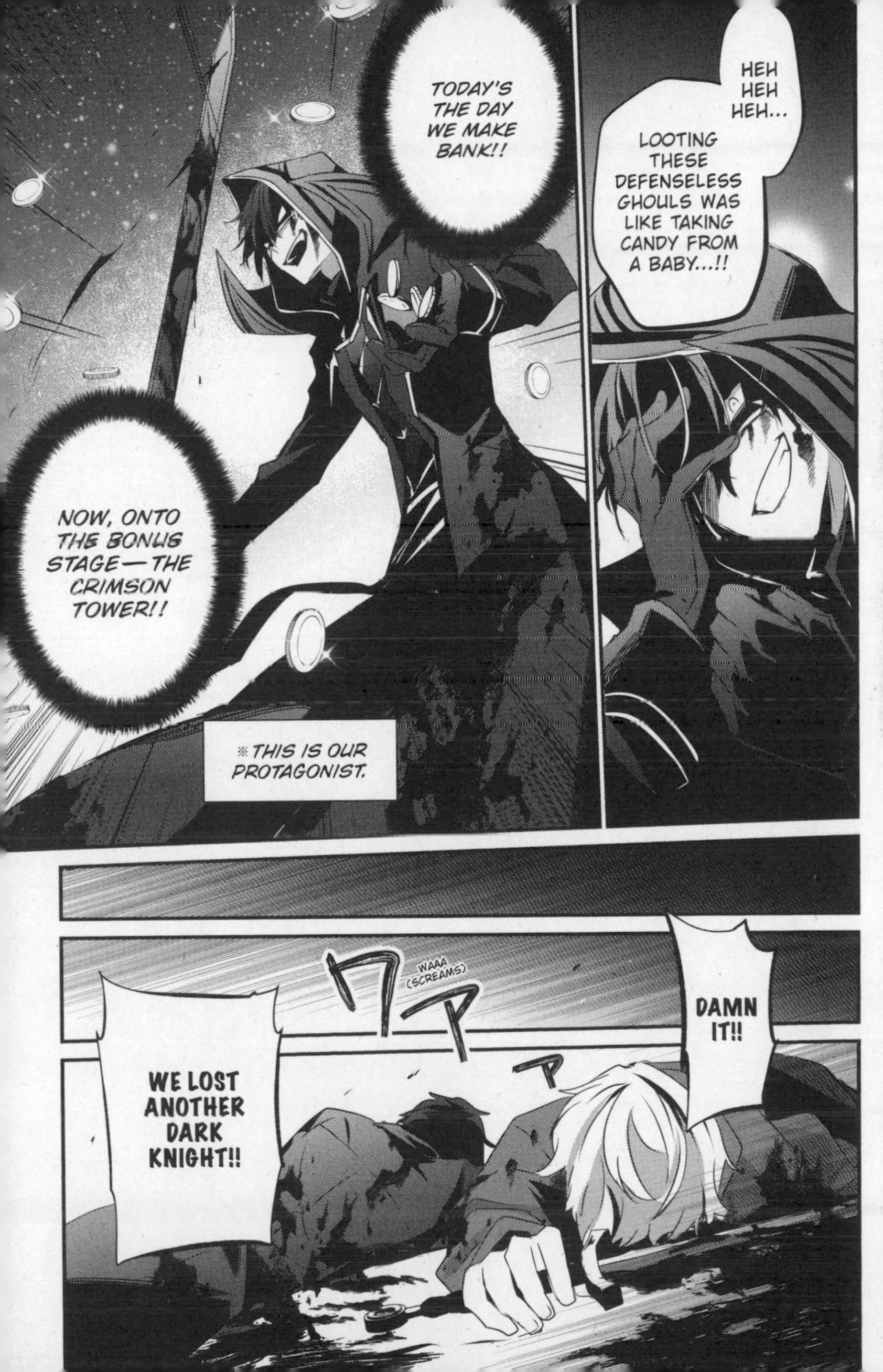
HEH HEH HEH...
LOOTING THESE DEFENSELESS GHOULS WAS LIKE TAKING CANDY FROM A BABY...!!
TODAY'S THE DAY WE MAKE BANK!!
NOW, ONTO THE BONUS STAGE—THE CRIMSON TOWER!!
※THIS IS OUR PROTAGONIST.
DAMN IT!!
WAAA (SCREAMS)
WE LOST ANOTHER DARK KNIGHT!!

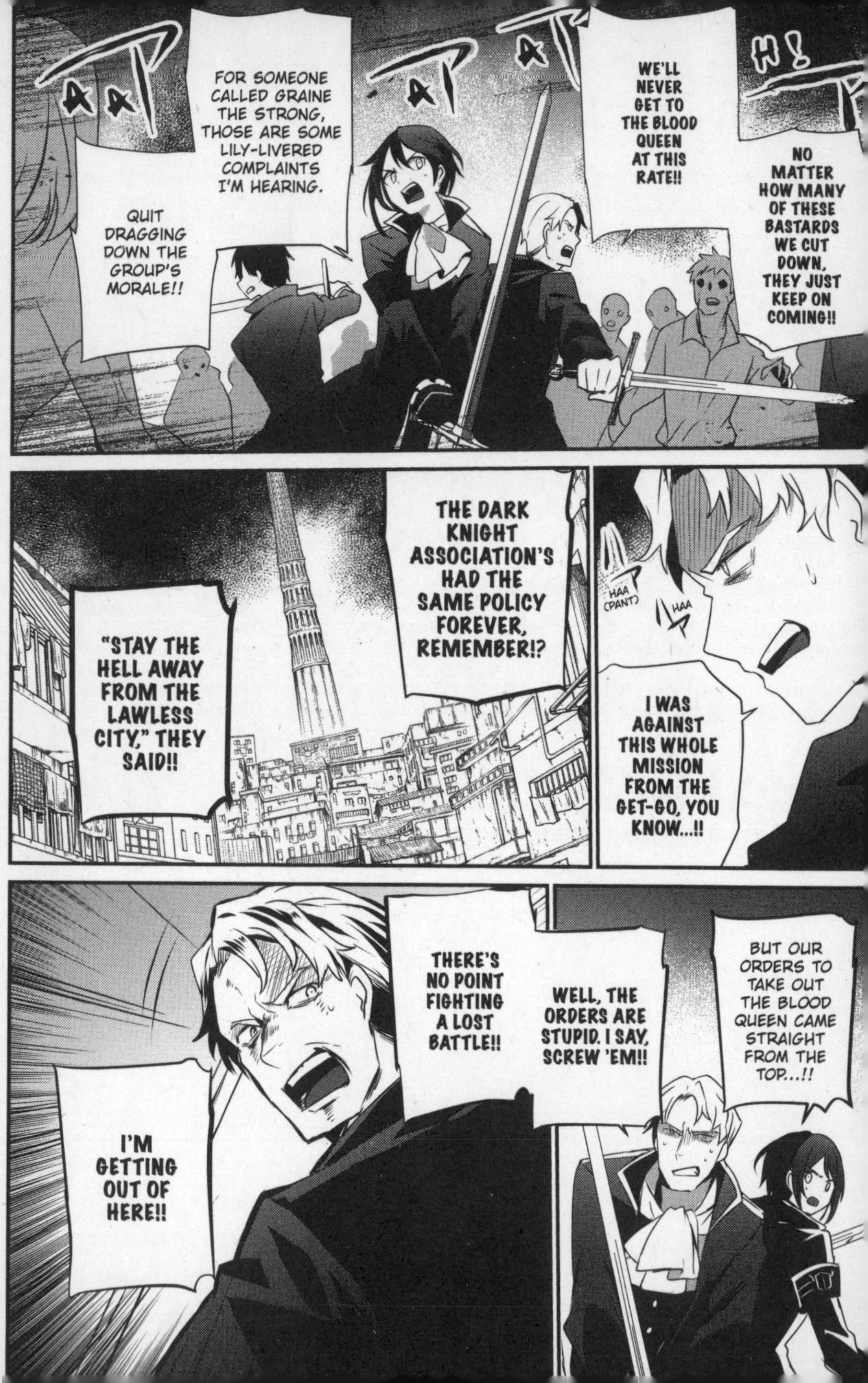
NO MATTER HOW MANY OF THESE BASTARDS WE CUT DOWN, THEY JUST KEEP ON COMING!!
WE'LL NEVER GET TO THE BLOOD QUEEN AT THIS RATE!!
FOR SOMEONE CALLED GRAINE THE STRONG, THOSE ARE SOME LILY-LIVERED COMPLAINTS I'M HEARING.
QUIT DRAGGING DOWN THE GROUP'S MORALE!!
HAA (PANT)
HAA
I WAS AGAINST THIS WHOLE MISSION FROM THE GET-GO, YOU KNOW...!!
THE DARK KNIGHT ASSOCIATION'S HAD THE SAME POLICY FOREVER, REMEMBER!?
"STAY THE HELL AWAY FROM THE LAWLESS CITY," THEY SAID!!
BUT OUR ORDERS TO TAKE OUT THE BLOOD QUEEN CAME STRAIGHT FROM THE TOP...!!
WELL, THE ORDERS ARE STUPID. I SAY, SCREW 'EM!!
THERE'S NO POINT FIGHTING A LOST BATTLE!!
I'M GETTING OUT OF HERE!!

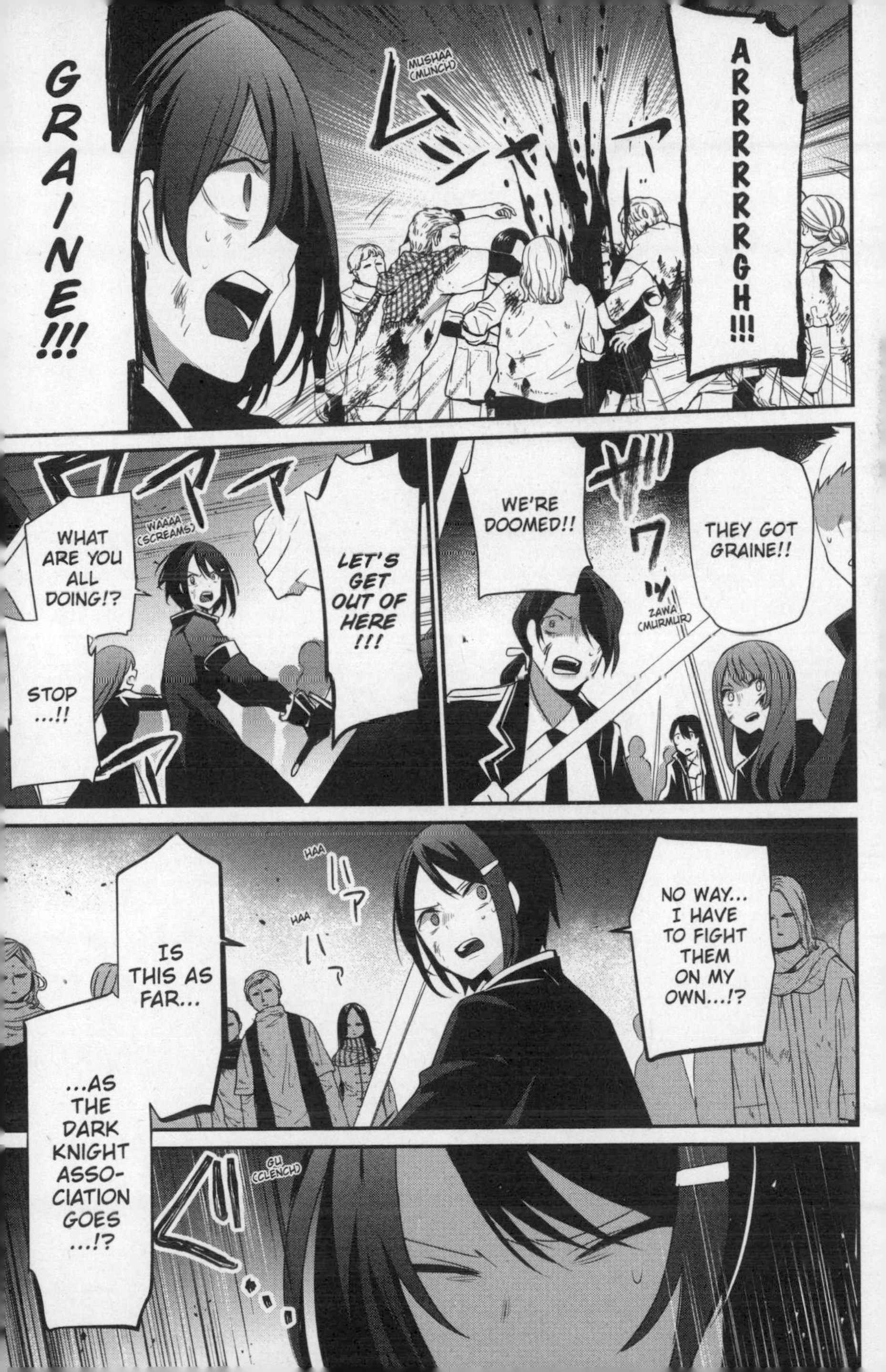

ARRRRRRGH!!!
MUSHAA (MUNCH)
GRAINE!!!
THEY GOT GRAINE!!
ZAWA (MURMUR)
WE'RE DOOMED!!
LET'S GET OUT OF HERE!!!
WAAAA (SCREAMS)
WHAT ARE YOU ALL DOING!?
STOP...!!
NO WAY... I HAVE TO FIGHT THEM ON MY OWN...!?
HAA
HAA
IS THIS AS FAR...
GU (CLENCH)
...AS THE DARK KNIGHT ASSOCIATION GOES...!?

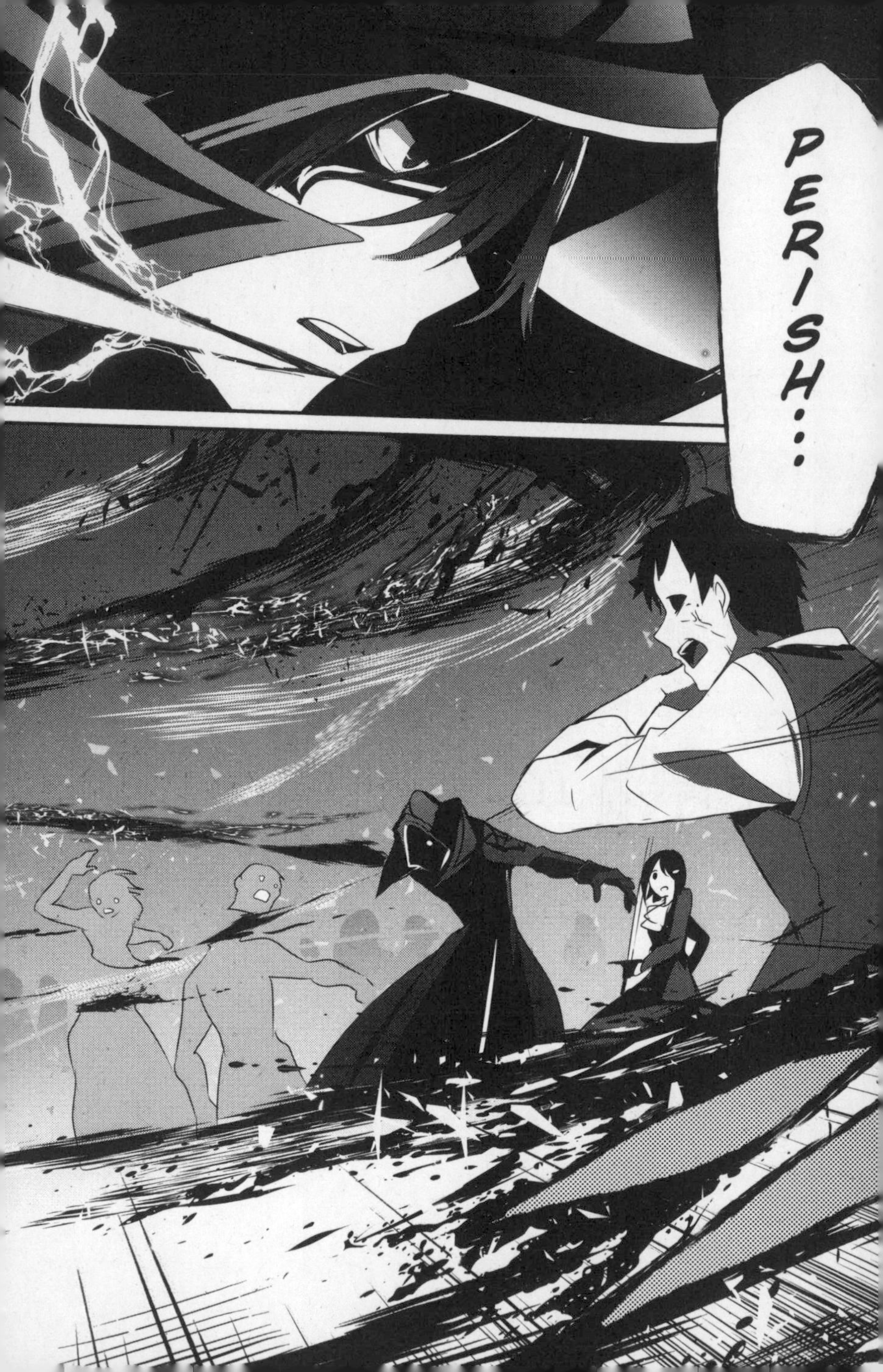
PERISH...

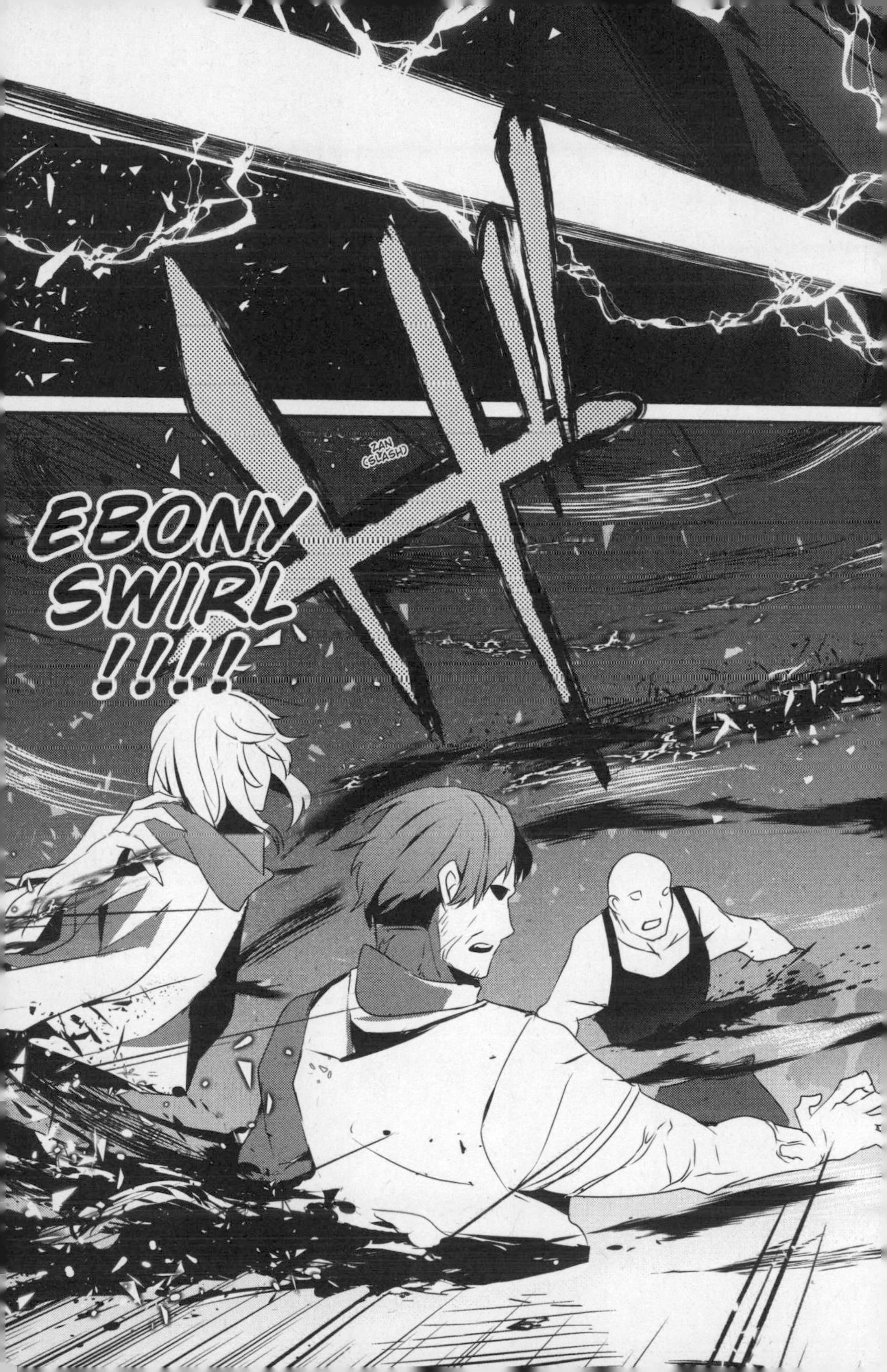
ZAN (SLASH)
EBONY SWIRL !!!!

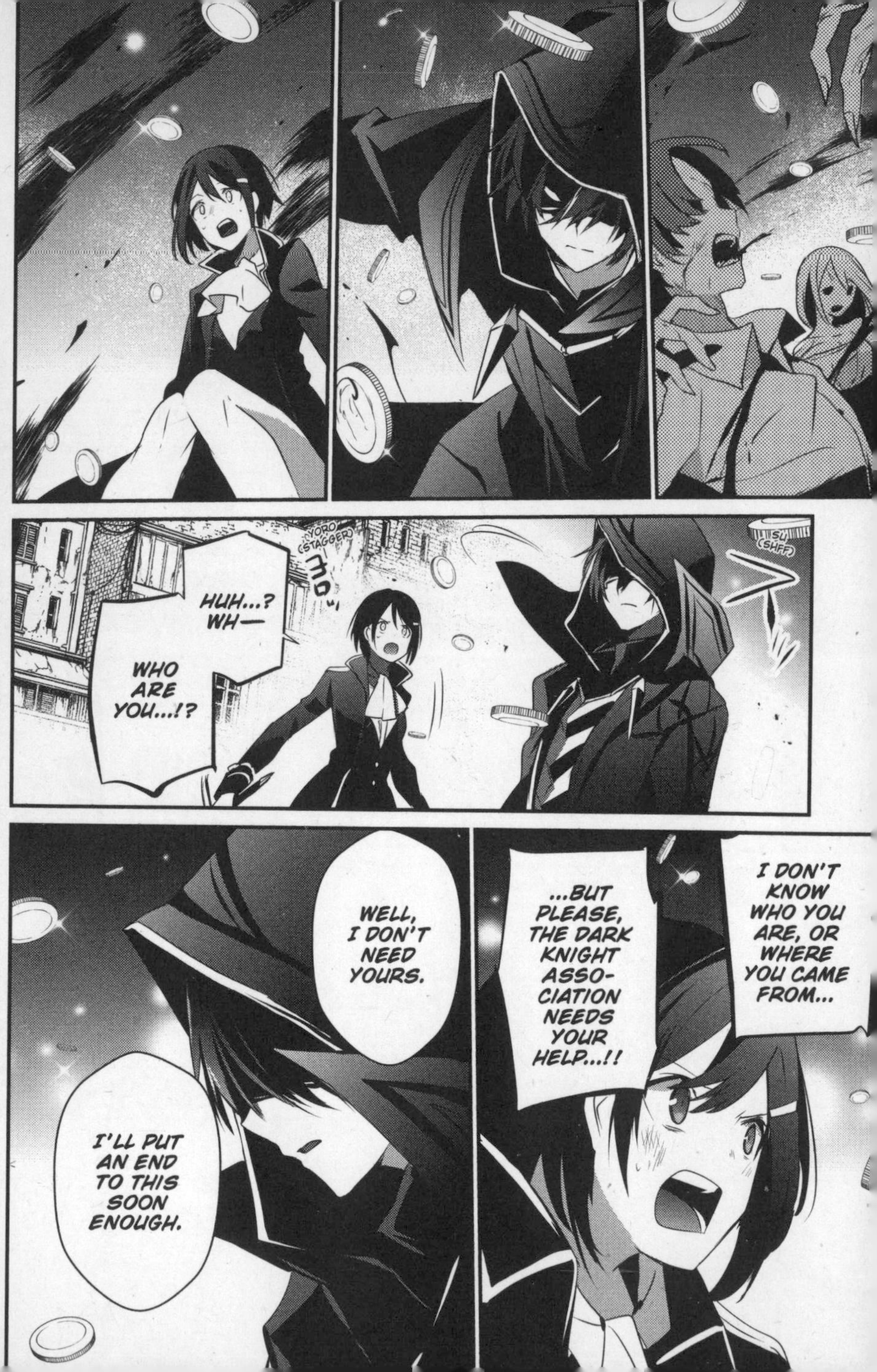
SU (SHFF)
YORO (STAGGER)
HUH...? WH—
WHO ARE YOU...!?
I DON'T KNOW WHO YOU ARE, OR WHERE YOU CAME FROM...
...BUT PLEASE, THE DARK KNIGHT ASSO-CIATION NEEDS YOUR HELP...!!
WELL, I DON'T NEED YOURS.
I'LL PUT AN END TO THIS SOON ENOUGH.

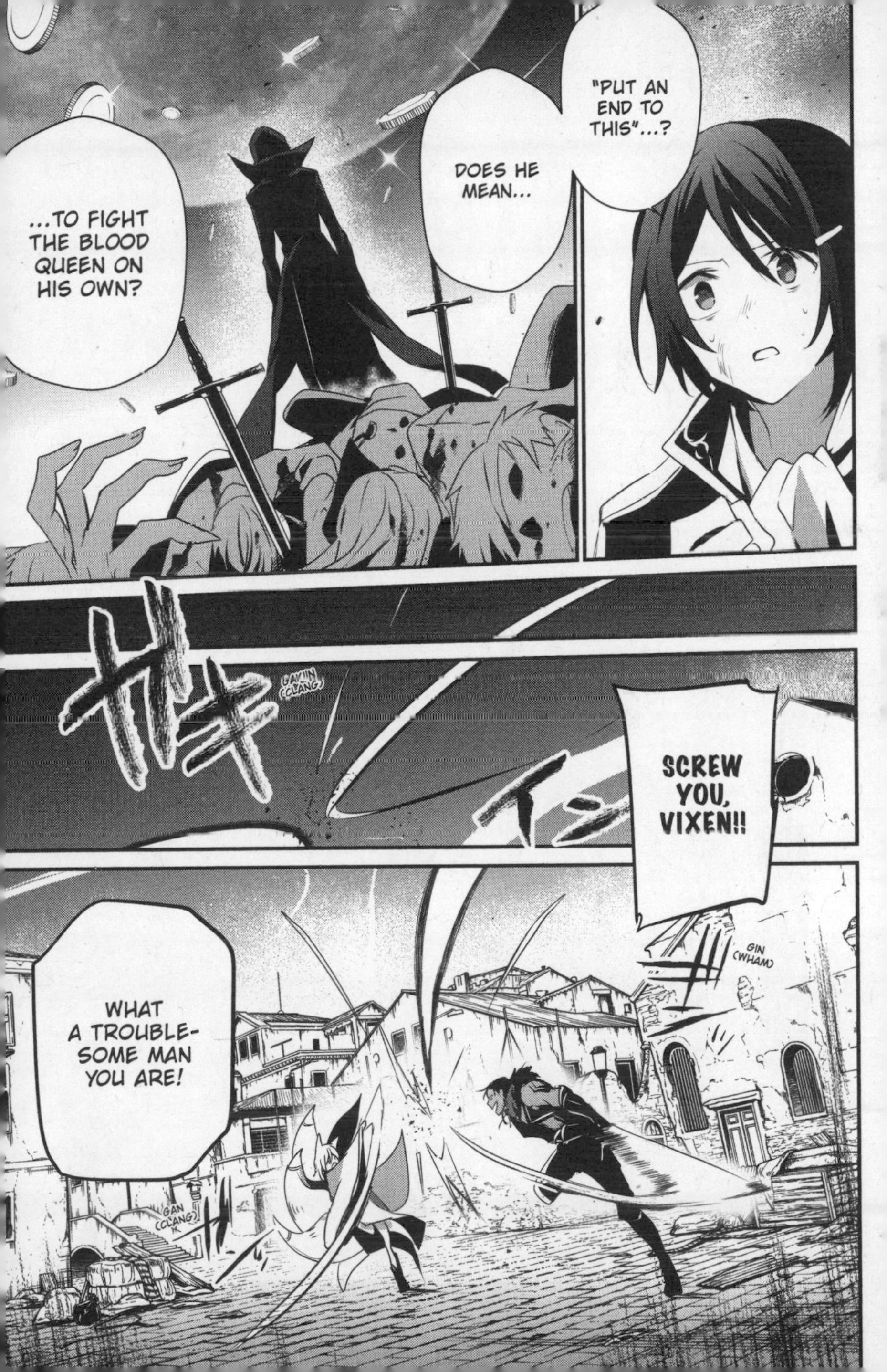

"PUT AN END TO THIS"...?
DOES HE MEAN...
...TO FIGHT THE BLOOD QUEEN ON HIS OWN?
(CLANG)
SCREW YOU, VIXEN!!
GIN (WHAM)
WHAT A TROUBLE-SOME MAN YOU ARE!
GAN (CLANG)

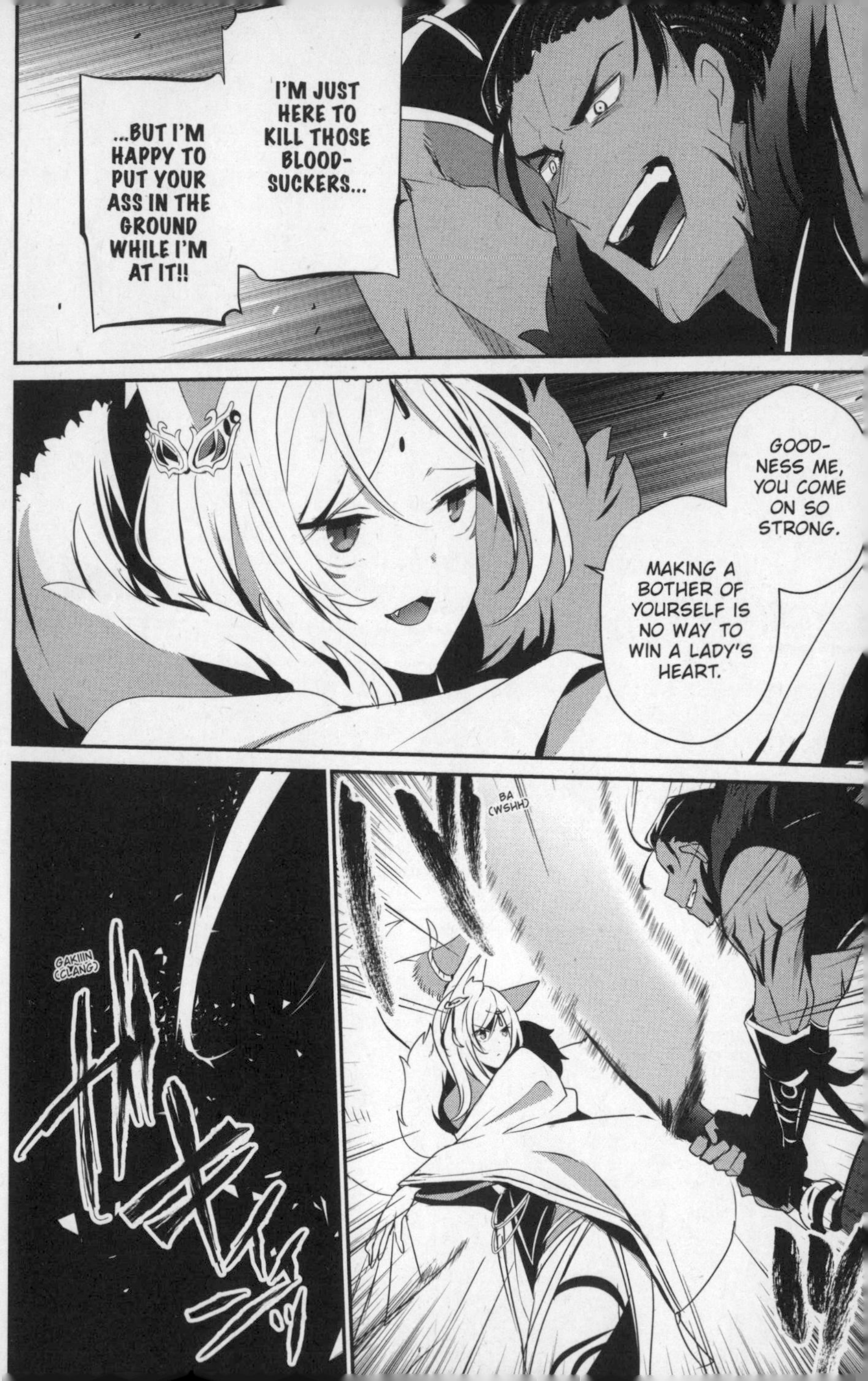
I'M JUST HERE TO KILL THOSE BLOOD-SUCKERS...
...BUT I'M HAPPY TO PUT YOUR ASS IN THE GROUND WHILE I'M AT IT!!
GOOD-NESS ME, YOU COME ON SO STRONG.
MAKING A BOTHER OF YOURSELF IS NO WAY TO WIN A LADY'S HEART.
BA (WSHH)
GAKIIIN (CLANG)

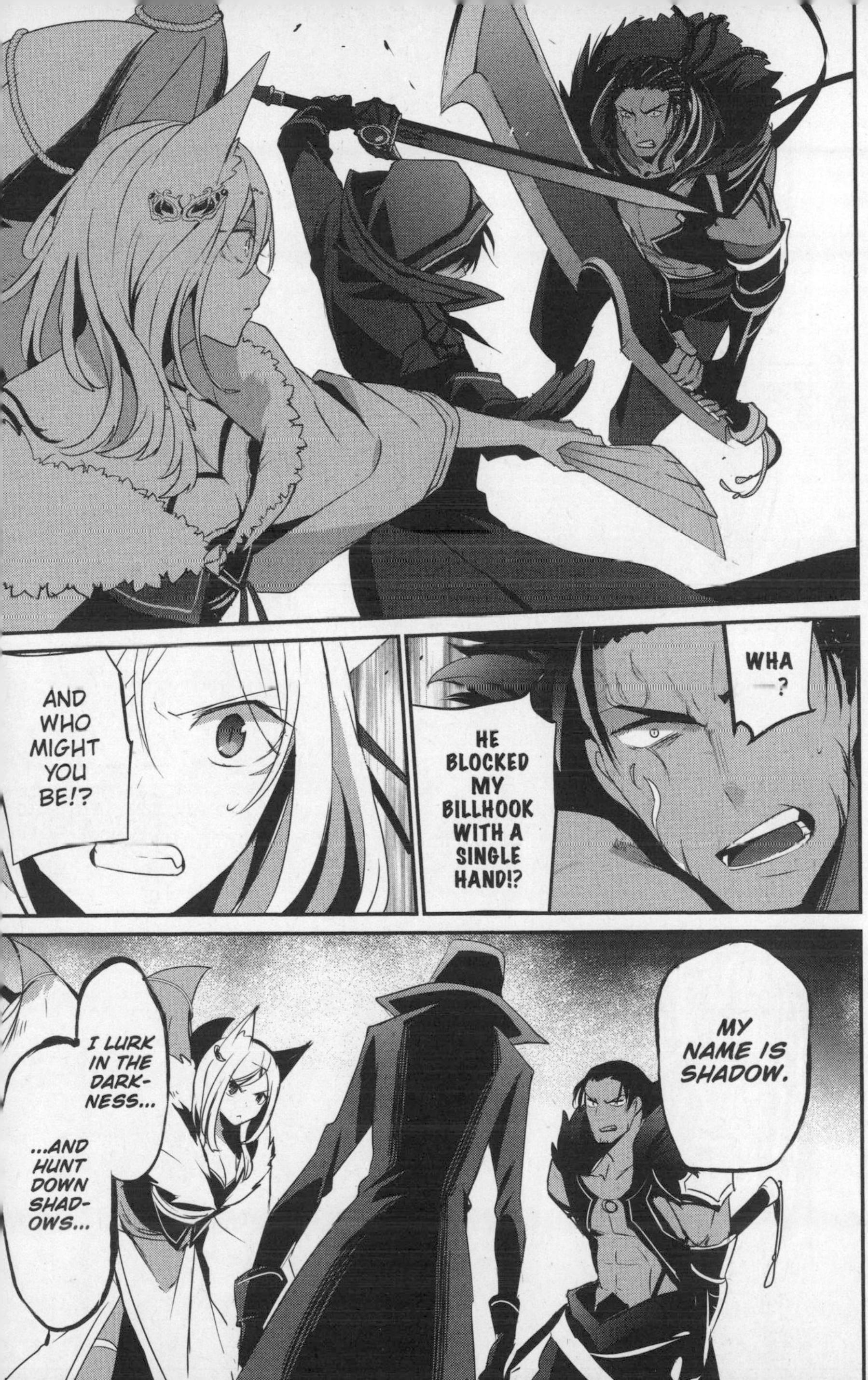
WHA—?
HE BLOCKED MY BILLHOOK WITH A SINGLE HAND!?
AND WHO MIGHT YOU BE!?
MY NAME IS SHADOW.
I LURK IN THE DARKNESS...
...AND HUNT DOWN SHADOWS...

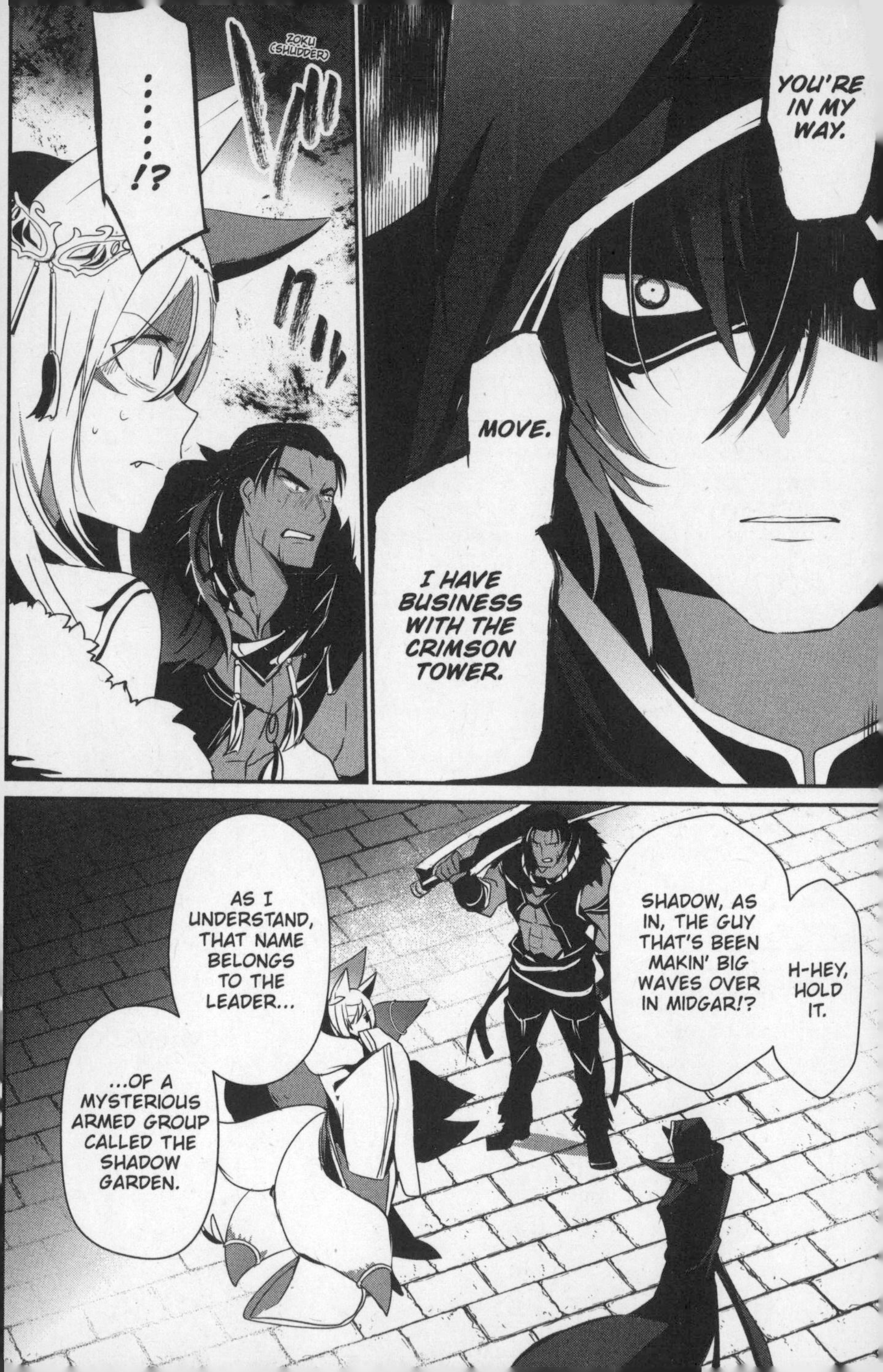
YOU'RE IN MY WAY.
MOVE.
I HAVE BUSINESS WITH THE CRIMSON TOWER.
ZOKU (SHUDDER)
......!?
H-HEY, HOLD IT.
SHADOW, AS IN, THE GUY THAT'S BEEN MAKIN' BIG WAVES OVER IN MIDGAR!?
AS I UNDERSTAND, THAT NAME BELONGS TO THE LEADER...
...OF A MYSTERIOUS ARMED GROUP CALLED THE SHADOW GARDEN.

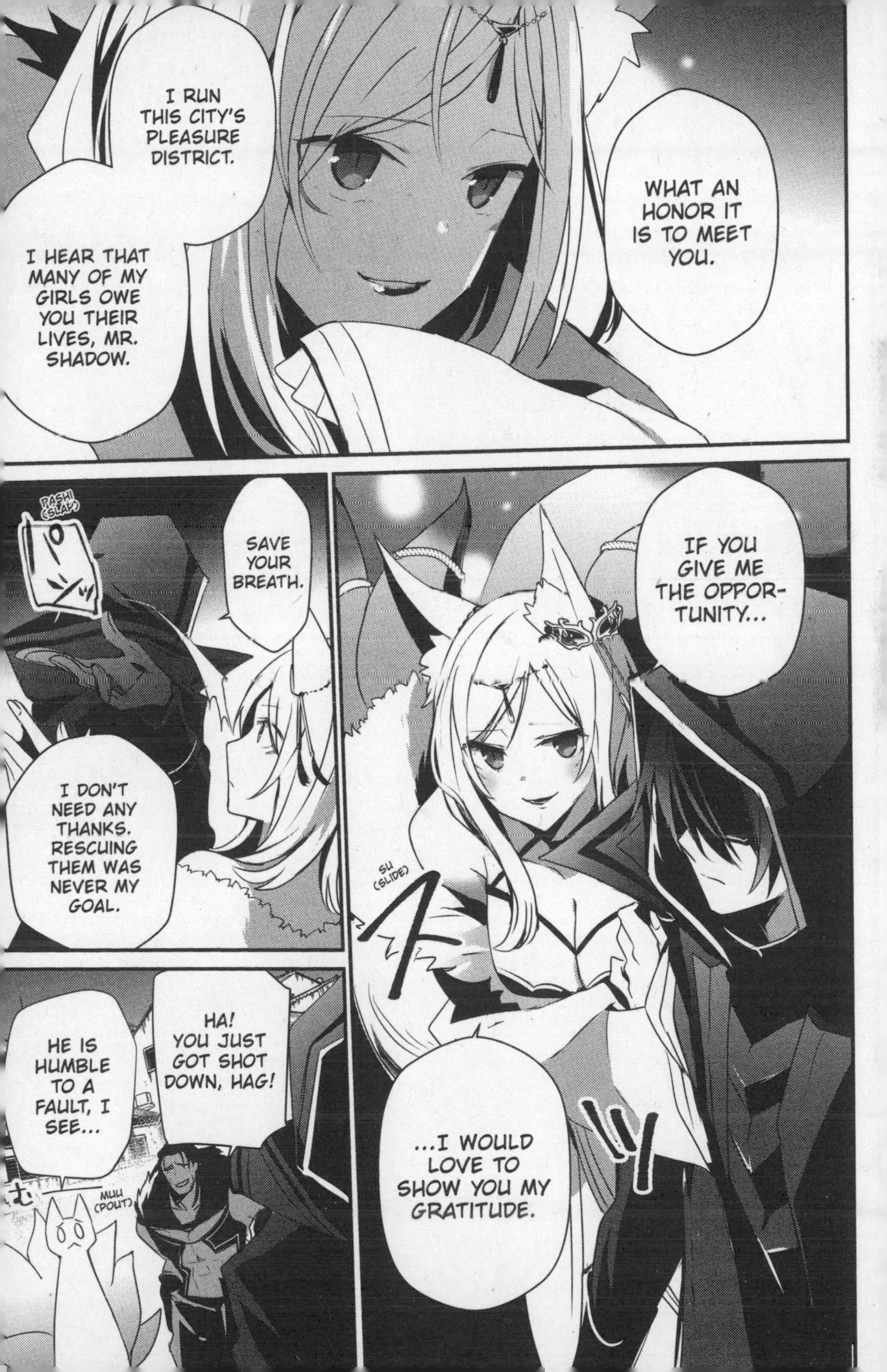
WHAT AN HONOR IT IS TO MEET YOU.
I RUN THIS CITY'S PLEASURE DISTRICT.
I HEAR THAT MANY OF MY GIRLS OWE YOU THEIR LIVES, MR. SHADOW.
IF YOU GIVE ME THE OPPOR-TUNITY...
SU (SLIDE)
...I WOULD LOVE TO SHOW YOU MY GRATITUDE.
PASHI (SLAP)
SAVE YOUR BREATH.
I DON'T NEED ANY THANKS. RESCUING THEM WAS NEVER MY GOAL.
HA! YOU JUST GOT SHOT DOWN, HAG!
HE IS HUMBLE TO A FAULT, I SEE...
MUU (POUT)

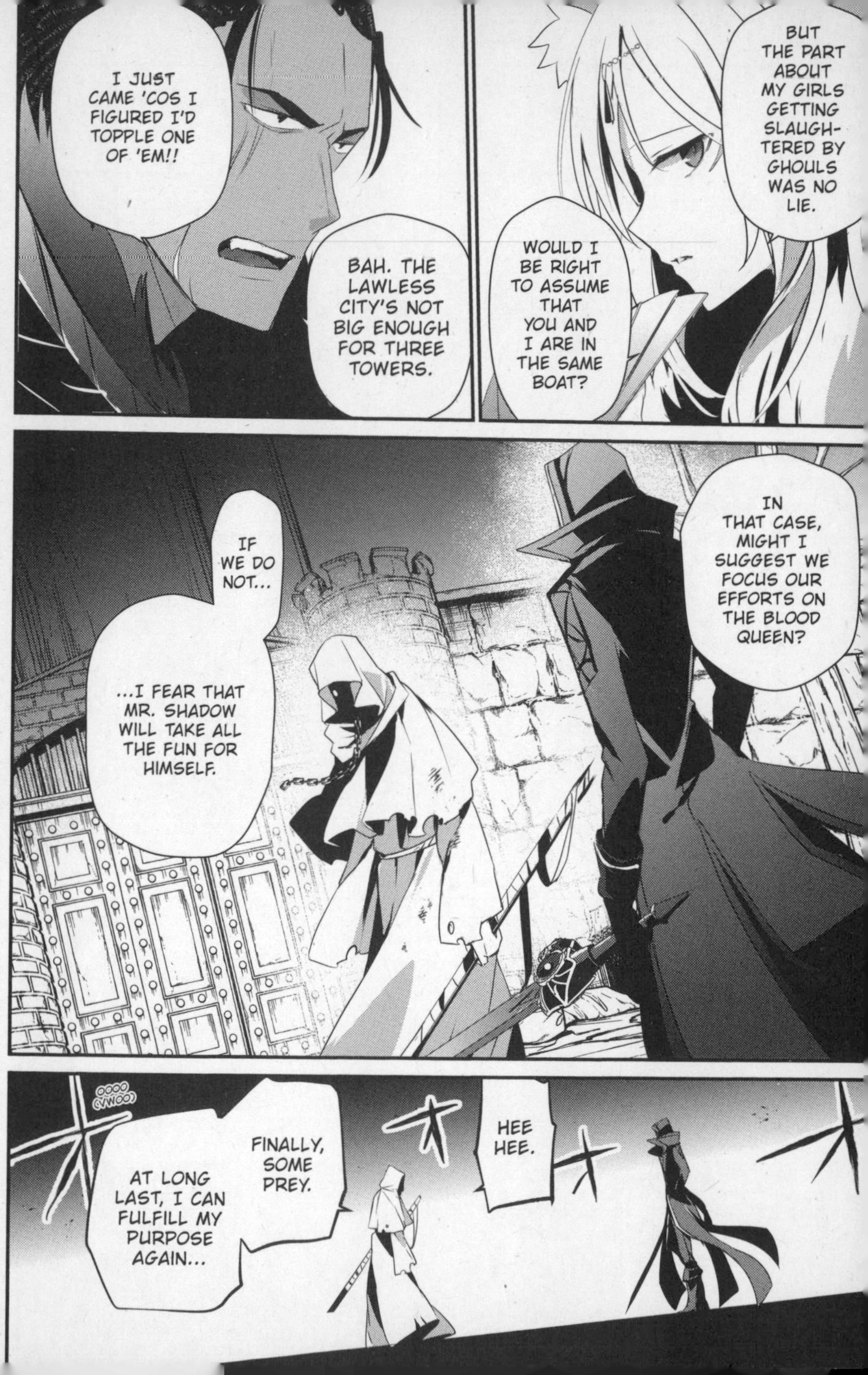
BUT THE PART ABOUT MY GIRLS GETTING SLAUGHTERED BY GHOULS WAS NO LIE.
WOULD I BE RIGHT TO ASSUME THAT YOU AND I ARE IN THE SAME BOAT?
BAH. THE LAWLESS CITY'S NOT BIG ENOUGH FOR THREE TOWERS.
I JUST CAME 'COS I FIGURED I'D TOPPLE ONE OF 'EM!!
IN THAT CASE, MIGHT I SUGGEST WE FOCUS OUR EFFORTS ON THE BLOOD QUEEN?
IF WE DO NOT...
...I FEAR THAT MR. SHADOW WILL TAKE ALL THE FUN FOR HIMSELF.
HEE HEE.
FINALLY, SOME PREY.
AT LONG LAST, I CAN FULFILL MY PURPOSE AGAIN...
OOOO (VWOO)

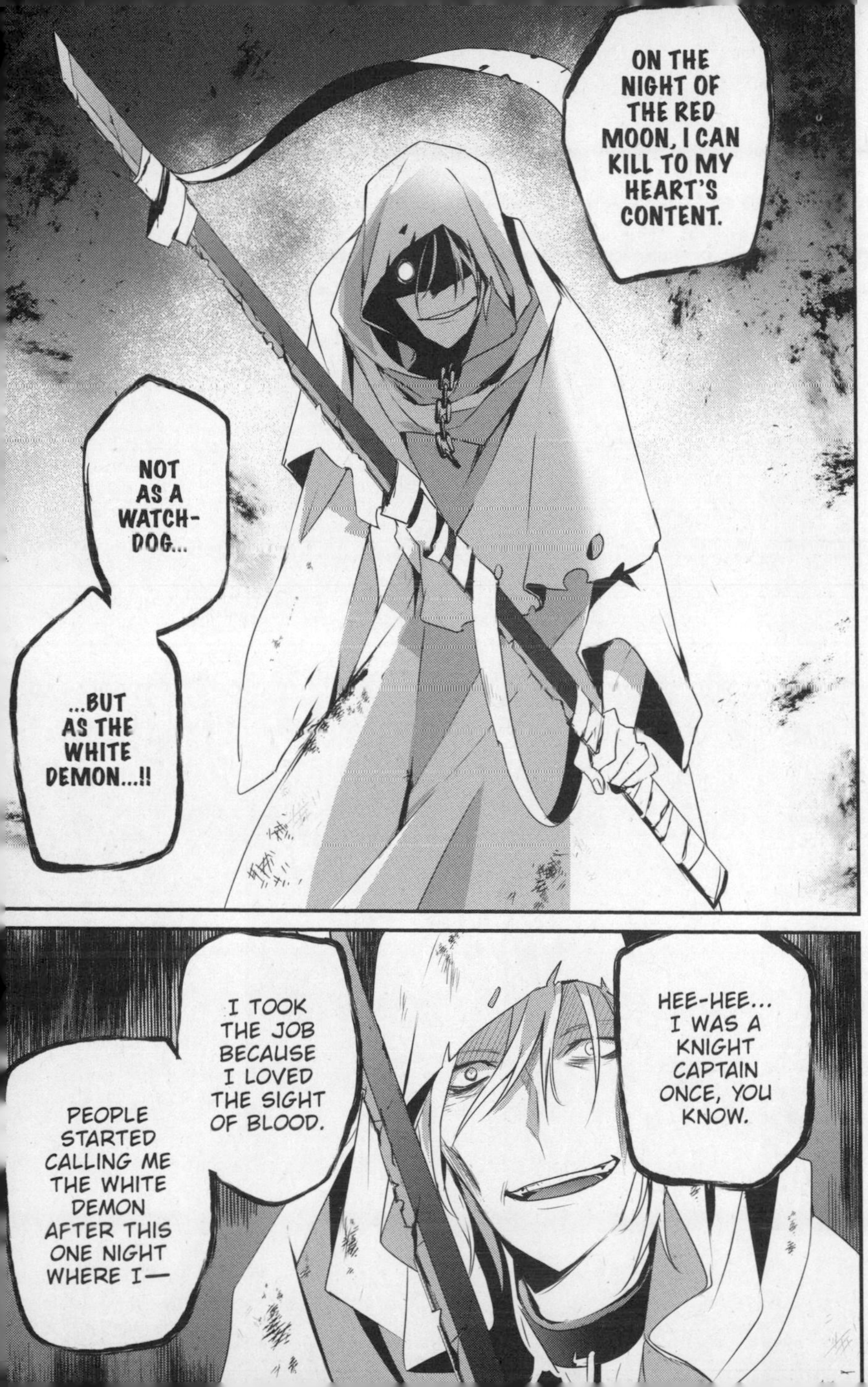
ON THE NIGHT OF THE RED MOON, I CAN KILL TO MY HEART'S CONTENT.
NOT AS A WATCH-DOG...
...BUT AS THE WHITE DEMON...!!
HEE-HEE... I WAS A KNIGHT CAPTAIN ONCE, YOU KNOW.
I TOOK THE JOB BECAUSE I LOVED THE SIGHT OF BLOOD.
PEOPLE STARTED CALLING ME THE WHITE DEMON AFTER THIS ONE NIGHT WHERE I—

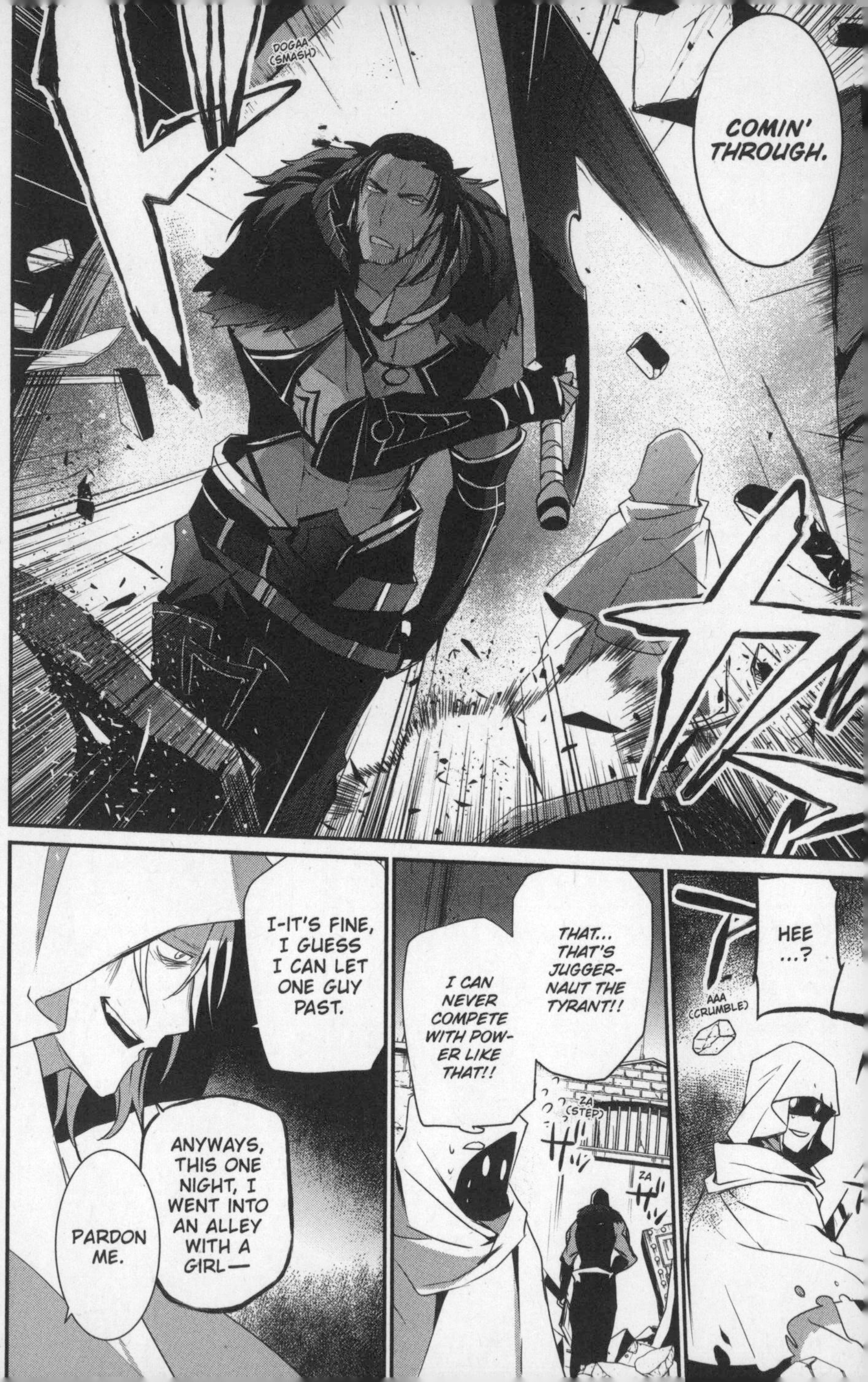
COMIN' THROUGH.
DOGAA (SMASH)
HEE ...?
AAA (CRUMBLE)
THAT... THAT'S JUGGER-NAUT THE TYRANT!!
I CAN NEVER COMPETE WITH POW-ER LIKE THAT!!
ZA (STEP)
ZA
I-IT'S FINE, I GUESS I CAN LET ONE GUY PAST.
ANYWAYS, THIS ONE NIGHT, I WENT INTO AN ALLEY WITH A GIRL—
PARDON ME.

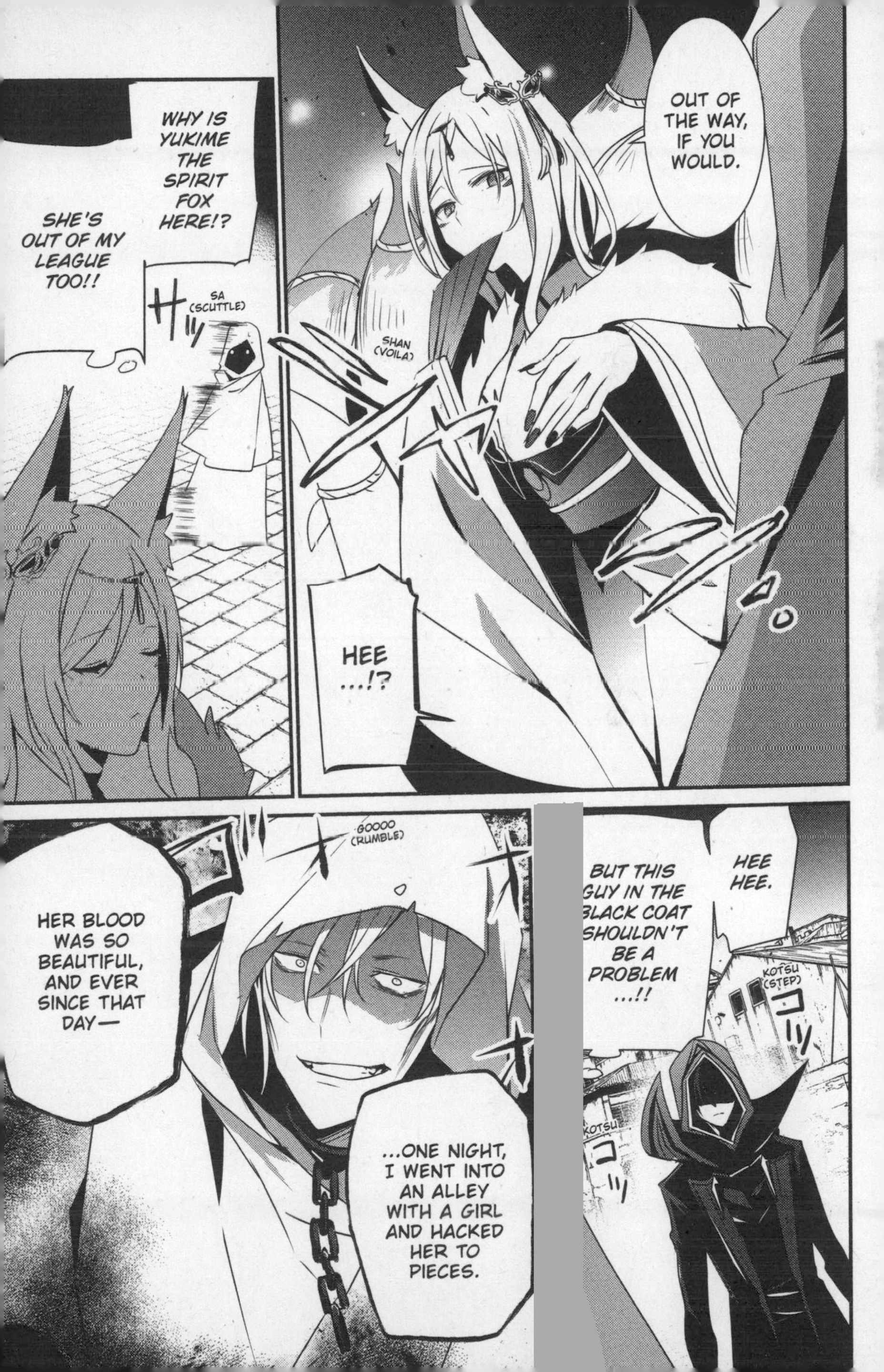
OUT OF THE WAY, IF YOU WOULD.
SHAN (VOILA)
HEE ...!?
WHY IS YUKIME THE SPIRIT FOX HERE!?
SHE'S OUT OF MY LEAGUE TOO!!
SA (SCUTTLE)
HEE HEE.
BUT THIS GUY IN THE BLACK COAT SHOULDN'T BE A PROBLEM ...!!
KOTSU (STEP)
KOTSU
GOOOO (RUMBLE)
HER BLOOD WAS SO BEAUTIFUL, AND EVER SINCE THAT DAY—
...ONE NIGHT, I WENT INTO AN ALLEY WITH A GIRL AND HACKED HER TO PIECES.

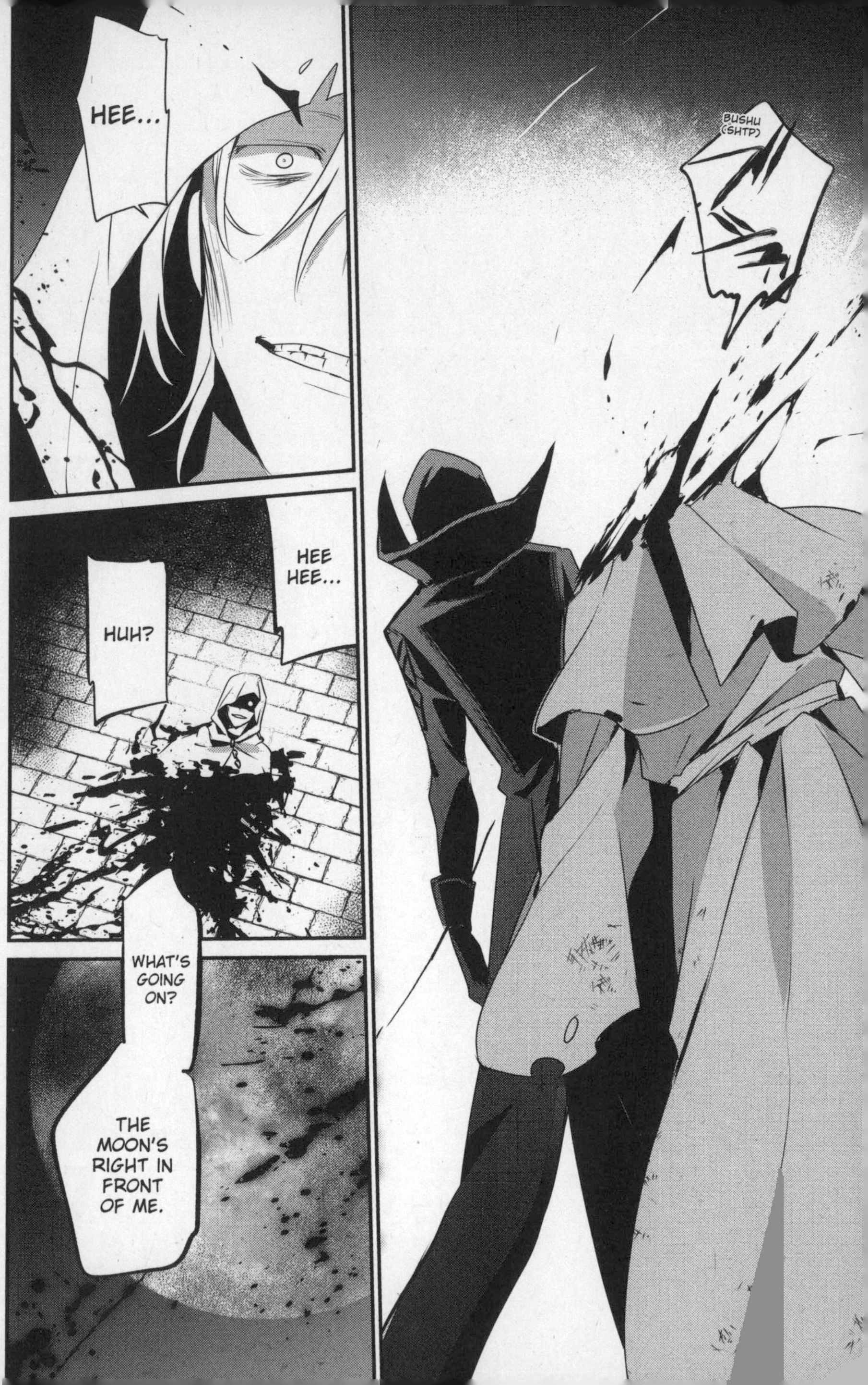
BUSHU
(SHTP)
HEE...
HEE HEE...
HUH?
WHAT'S GOING ON?
THE MOON'S RIGHT IN FRONT OF ME.

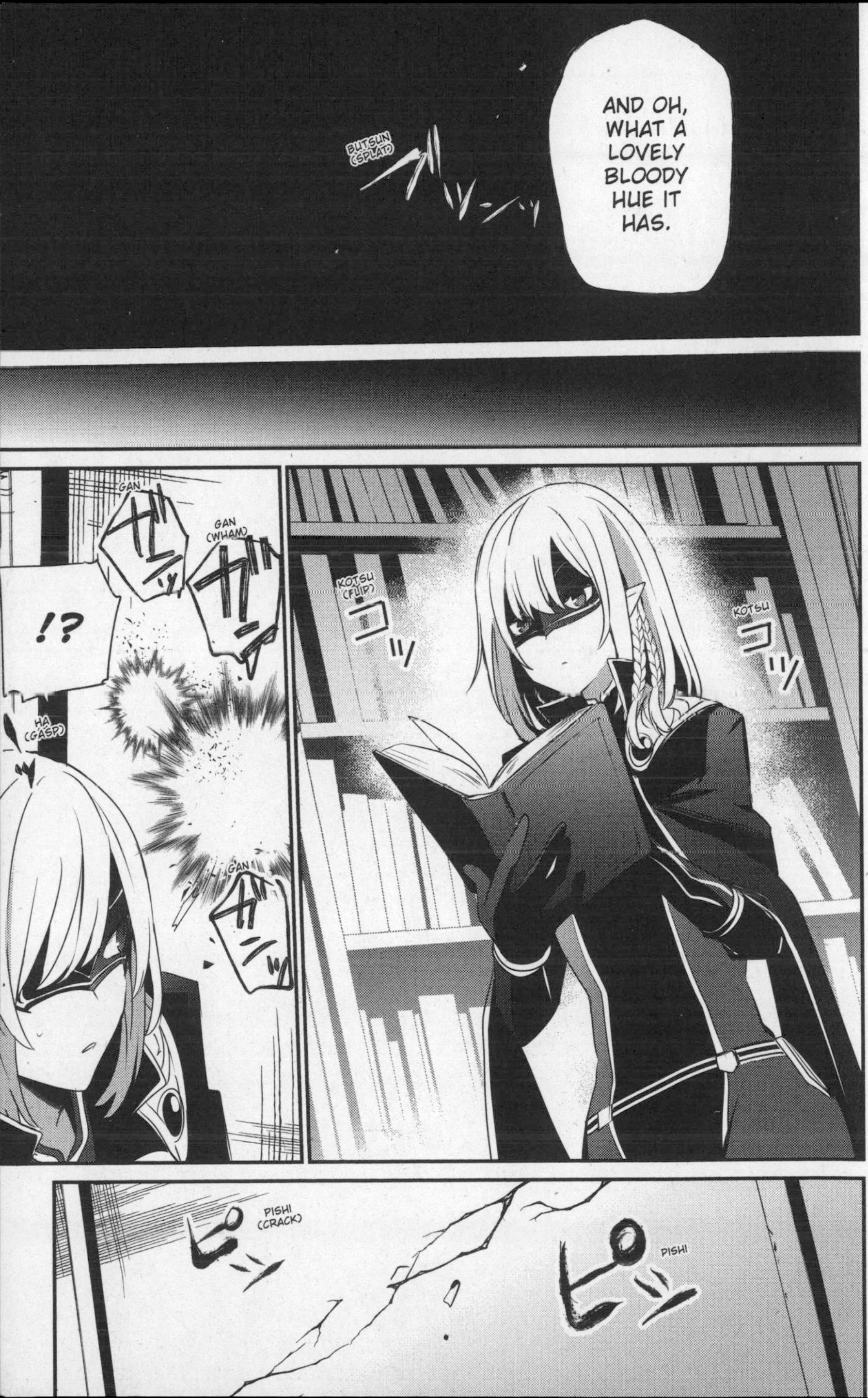
AND OH, WHAT A LOVELY BLOODY HUE IT HAS.
BUTSUN (SPLAT)
KOTSU
KOTSU (FLIP)
GAN (WHAM)
GAN
!?
HA (GASP)
GAN
PISHI
PISHI (CRACK)

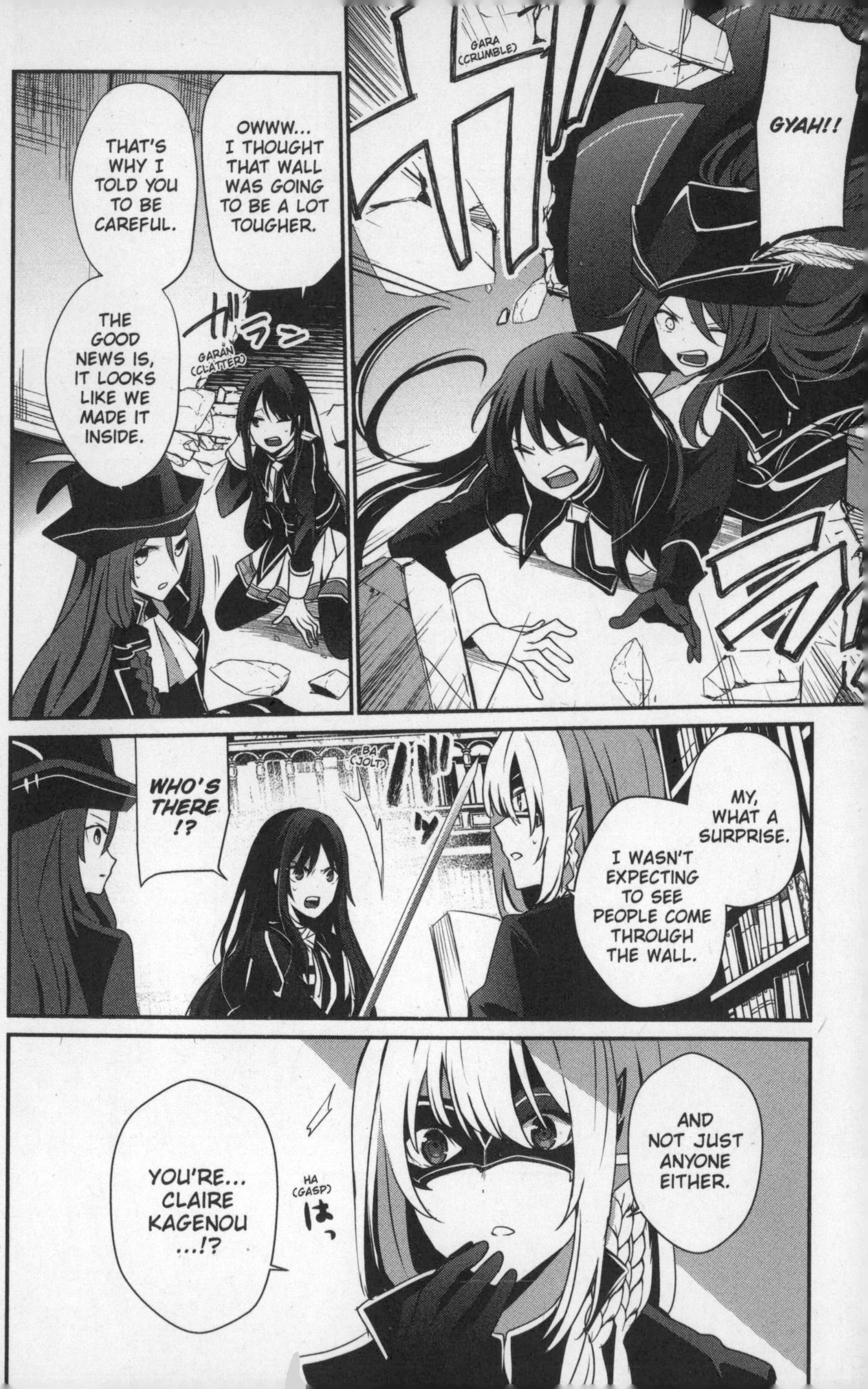
GARA (CRUMBLE)
GYAH!!
OWWW... I THOUGHT THAT WALL WAS GOING TO BE A LOT TOUGHER.
THAT'S WHY I TOLD YOU TO BE CAREFUL.
GARAN (CLATTER)
THE GOOD NEWS IS, IT LOOKS LIKE WE MADE IT INSIDE.
MY, WHAT A SURPRISE.
I WASN'T EXPECTING TO SEE PEOPLE COME THROUGH THE WALL.
BA (JOLT)
WHO'S THERE!?
AND NOT JUST ANYONE EITHER.
HA (GASP)
YOU'RE... CLAIRE KAGENOU...!?

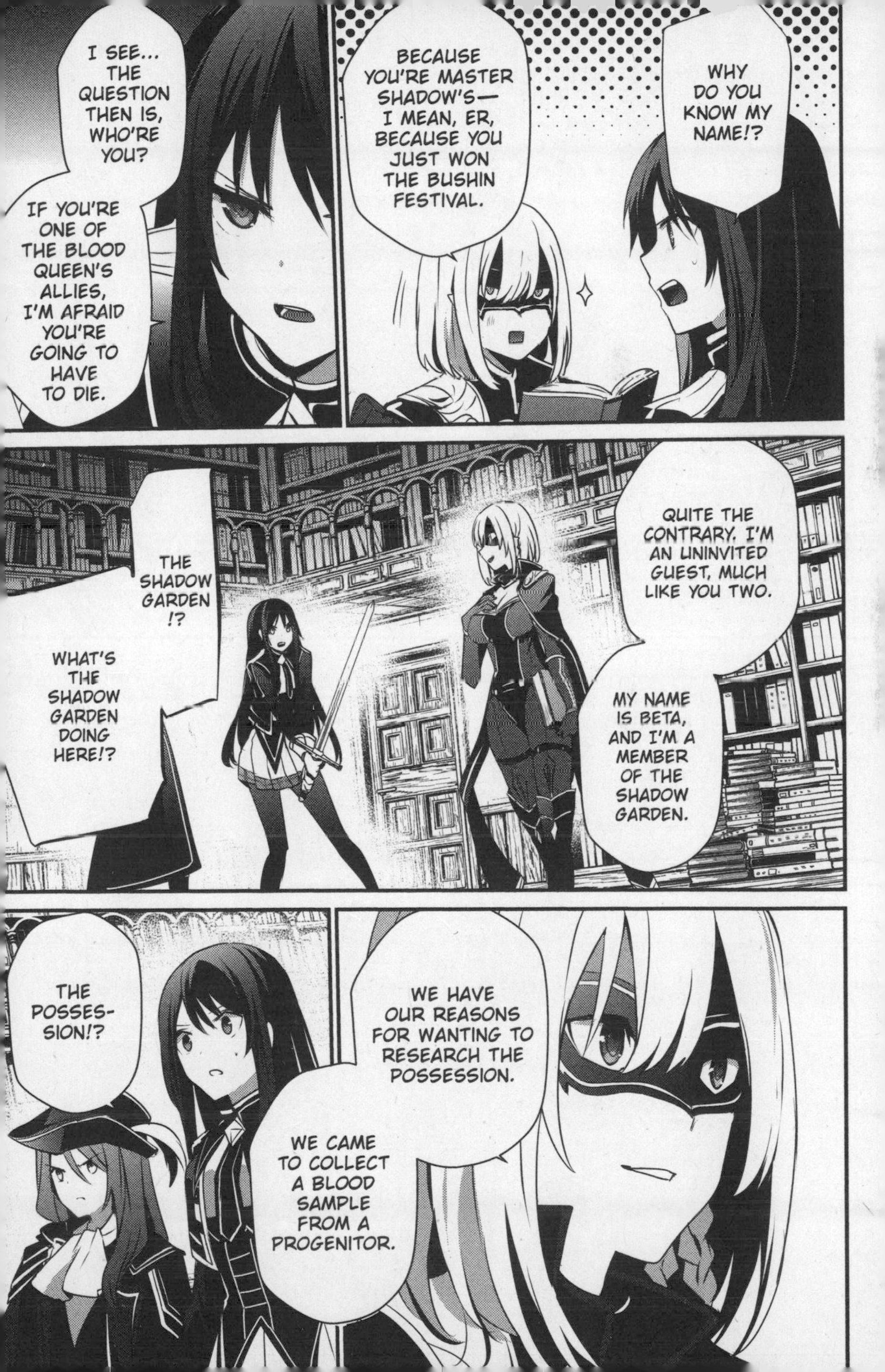
WHY DO YOU KNOW MY NAME!?
BECAUSE YOU'RE MASTER SHADOW'S— I MEAN, ER, BECAUSE YOU JUST WON THE BUSHIN FESTIVAL.
I SEE... THE QUESTION THEN IS, WHO'RE YOU?
IF YOU'RE ONE OF THE BLOOD QUEEN'S ALLIES, I'M AFRAID YOU'RE GOING TO HAVE TO DIE.
QUITE THE CONTRARY. I'M AN UNINVITED GUEST, MUCH LIKE YOU TWO.
MY NAME IS BETA, AND I'M A MEMBER OF THE SHADOW GARDEN.
THE SHADOW GARDEN!?
WHAT'S THE SHADOW GARDEN DOING HERE!?
WE HAVE OUR REASONS FOR WANTING TO RESEARCH THE POSSESSION.
WE CAME TO COLLECT A BLOOD SAMPLE FROM A PROGENITOR.
THE POSSES-SION!?

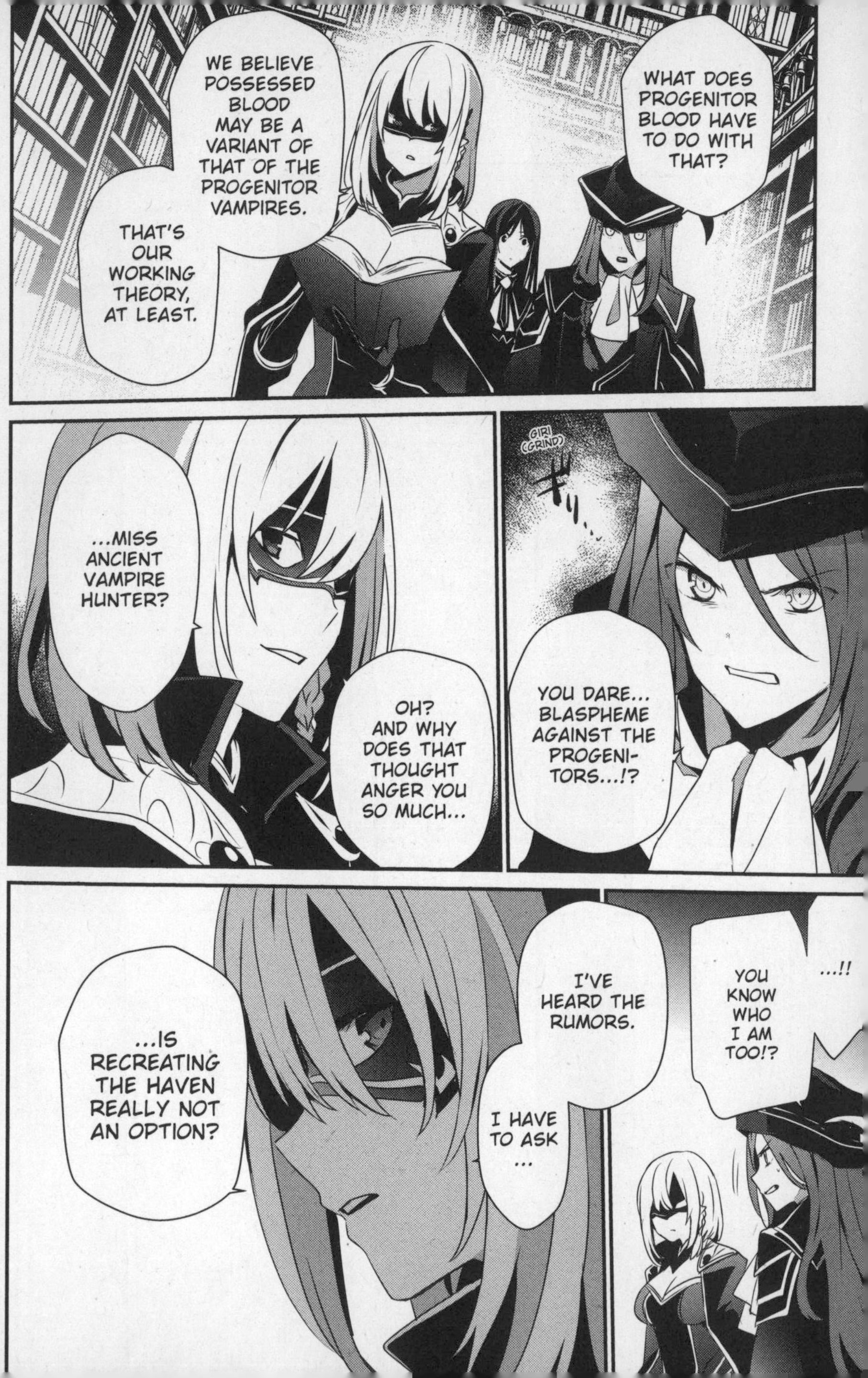
WHAT DOES PROGENITOR BLOOD HAVE TO DO WITH THAT?
WE BELIEVE POSSESSED BLOOD MAY BE A VARIANT OF THAT OF THE PROGENITOR VAMPIRES.
THAT'S OUR WORKING THEORY, AT LEAST.
GIRI (GRIND)
YOU DARE... BLASPHEME AGAINST THE PROGENITORS...!?
OH? AND WHY DOES THAT THOUGHT ANGER YOU SO MUCH...
...MISS ANCIENT VAMPIRE HUNTER?
...!!
YOU KNOW WHO I AM TOO!?
I'VE HEARD THE RUMORS.
I HAVE TO ASK ...
...IS RECREATING THE HAVEN REALLY NOT AN OPTION?

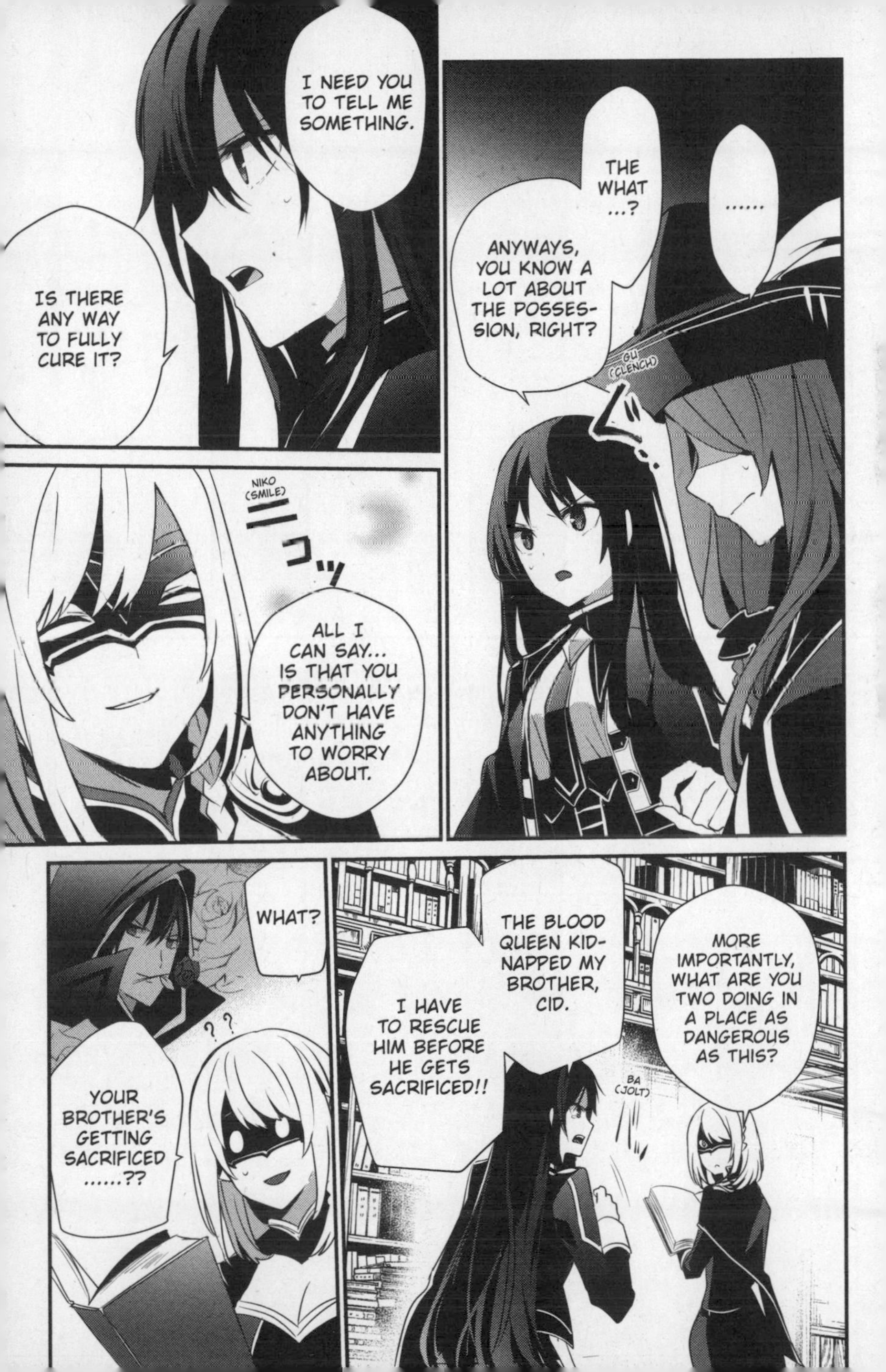
......
THE WHAT ...?
ANYWAYS, YOU KNOW A LOT ABOUT THE POSSES-SION, RIGHT?
GU (CLENCH)
I NEED YOU TO TELL ME SOMETHING.
IS THERE ANY WAY TO FULLY CURE IT?
NIKO (SMILE)
ALL I CAN SAY... IS THAT YOU PERSONALLY DON'T HAVE ANYTHING TO WORRY ABOUT.
MORE IMPORTANTLY, WHAT ARE YOU TWO DOING IN A PLACE AS DANGEROUS AS THIS?
BA (JOLT)
THE BLOOD QUEEN KID-NAPPED MY BROTHER, CID.
I HAVE TO RESCUE HIM BEFORE HE GETS SACRIFICED!!
WHAT?
??
YOUR BROTHER'S GETTING SACRIFICED ......??

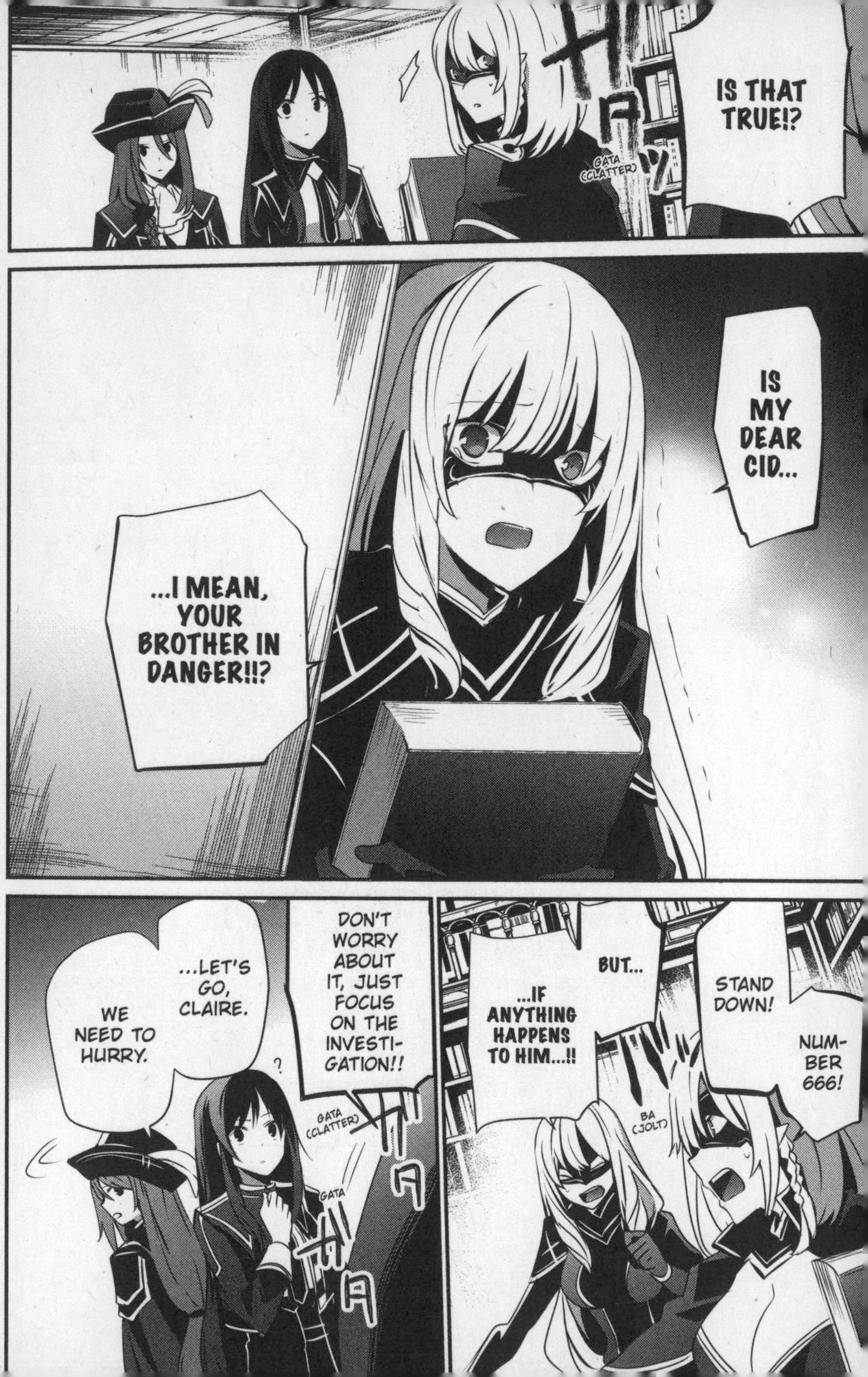
IS THAT TRUE!?
GATA (CLATTER)
IS MY DEAR CID...
...I MEAN, YOUR BROTHER IN DANGER!!?
NUM-BER 666!
STAND DOWN!
BUT...
...IF ANYTHING HAPPENS TO HIM...!!
BA (JOLT)
DON'T WORRY ABOUT IT, JUST FOCUS ON THE INVESTI-GATION!!
GATA (CLATTER)
GATA
...LET'S GO, CLAIRE.
WE NEED TO HURRY.

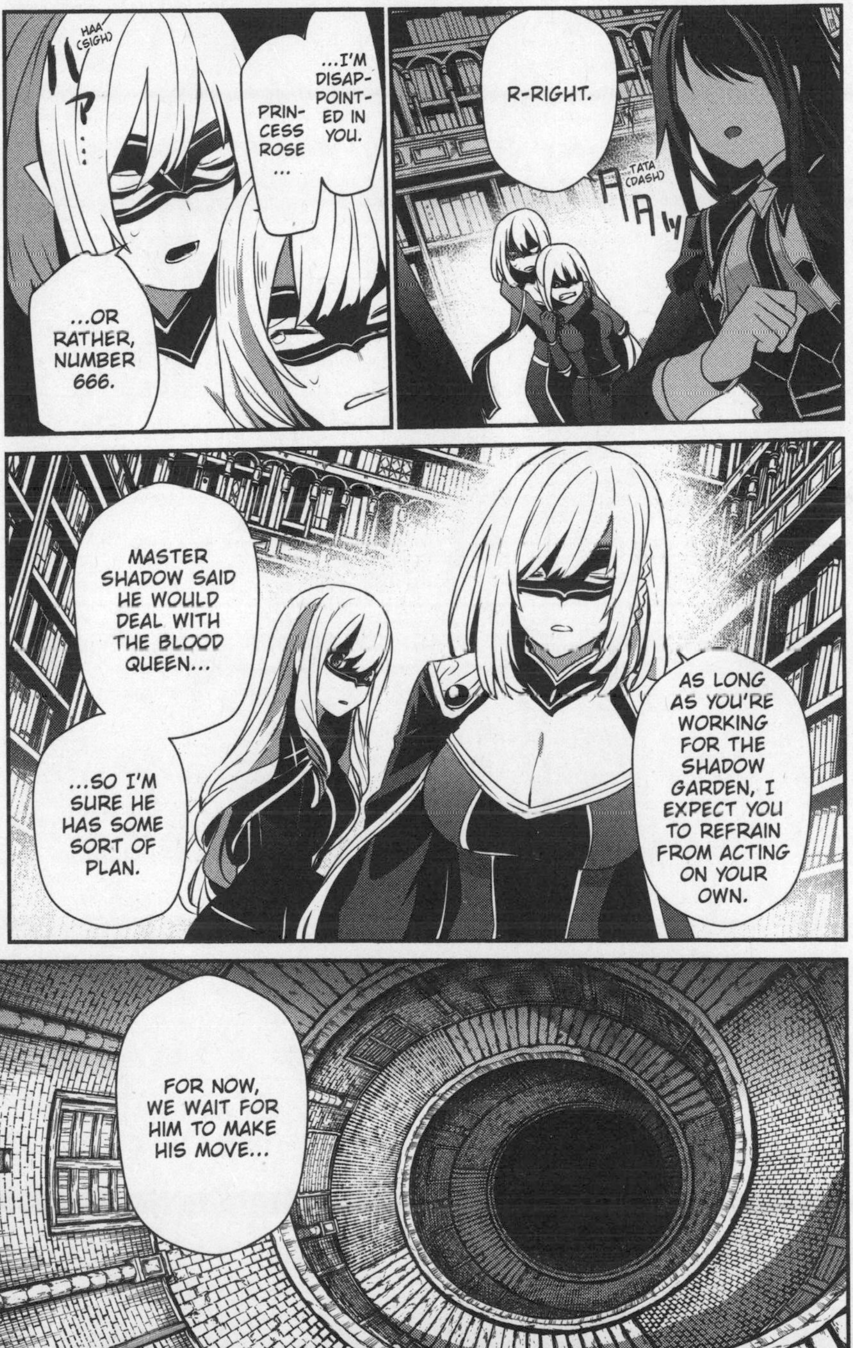
R-RIGHT.
TATA (DASH)
...I'M DISAPPOINTED IN YOU.
PRINCESS ROSE...
HAA (SIGH)
...OR RATHER, NUMBER 666.
AS LONG AS YOU'RE WORKING FOR THE SHADOW GARDEN, I EXPECT YOU TO REFRAIN FROM ACTING ON YOUR OWN.
MASTER SHADOW SAID HE WOULD DEAL WITH THE BLOOD QUEEN...
...SO I'M SURE HE HAS SOME SORT OF PLAN.
FOR NOW, WE WAIT FOR HIM TO MAKE HIS MOVE...

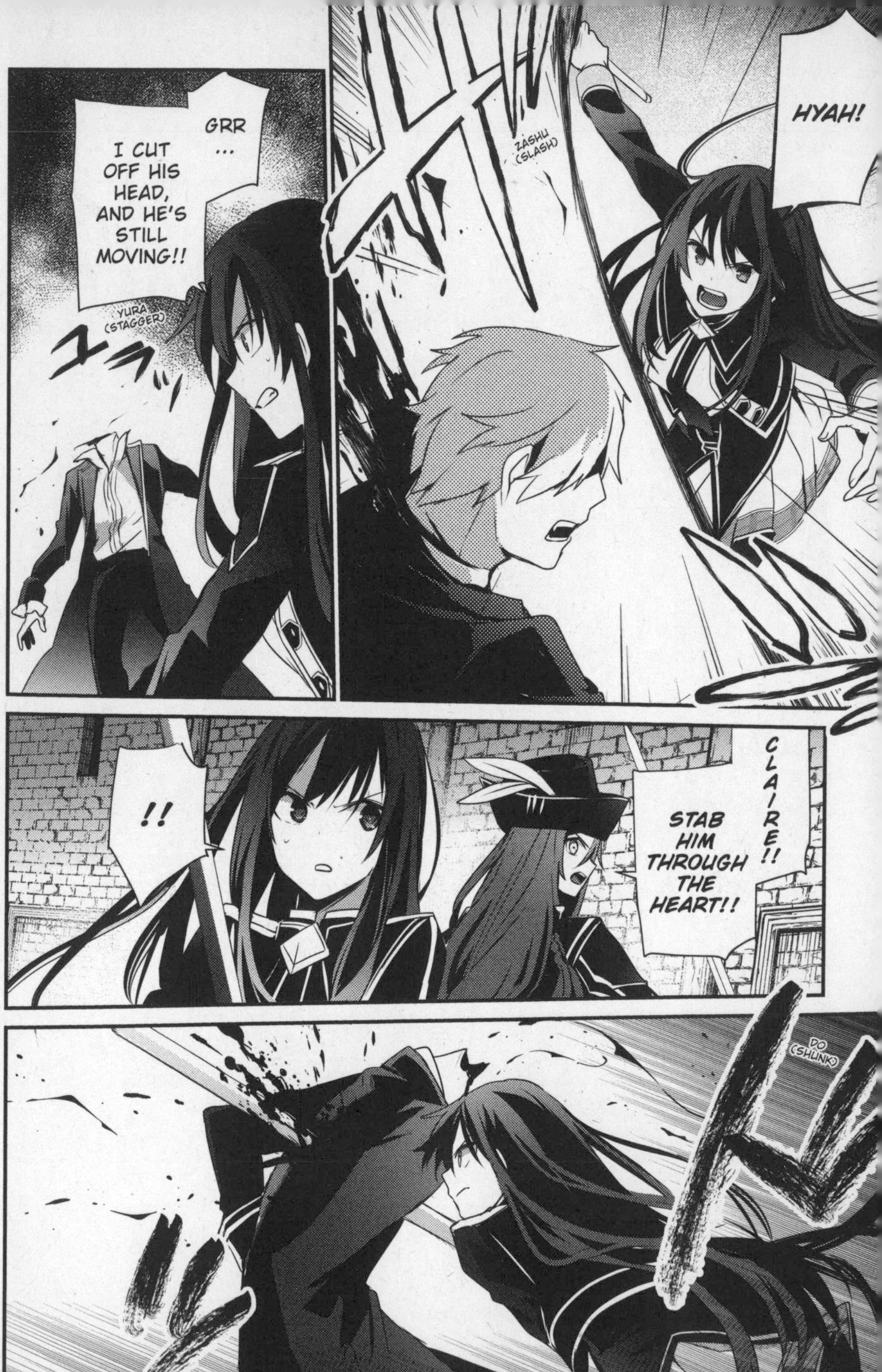
HYAH!
ZASHU (SLASH)
GRR ...
I CUT OFF HIS HEAD, AND HE'S STILL MOVING!!
YURA (STAGGER)
CLAIRE!!
STAB HIM THROUGH THE HEART!!
!!
DO (SHUNK)

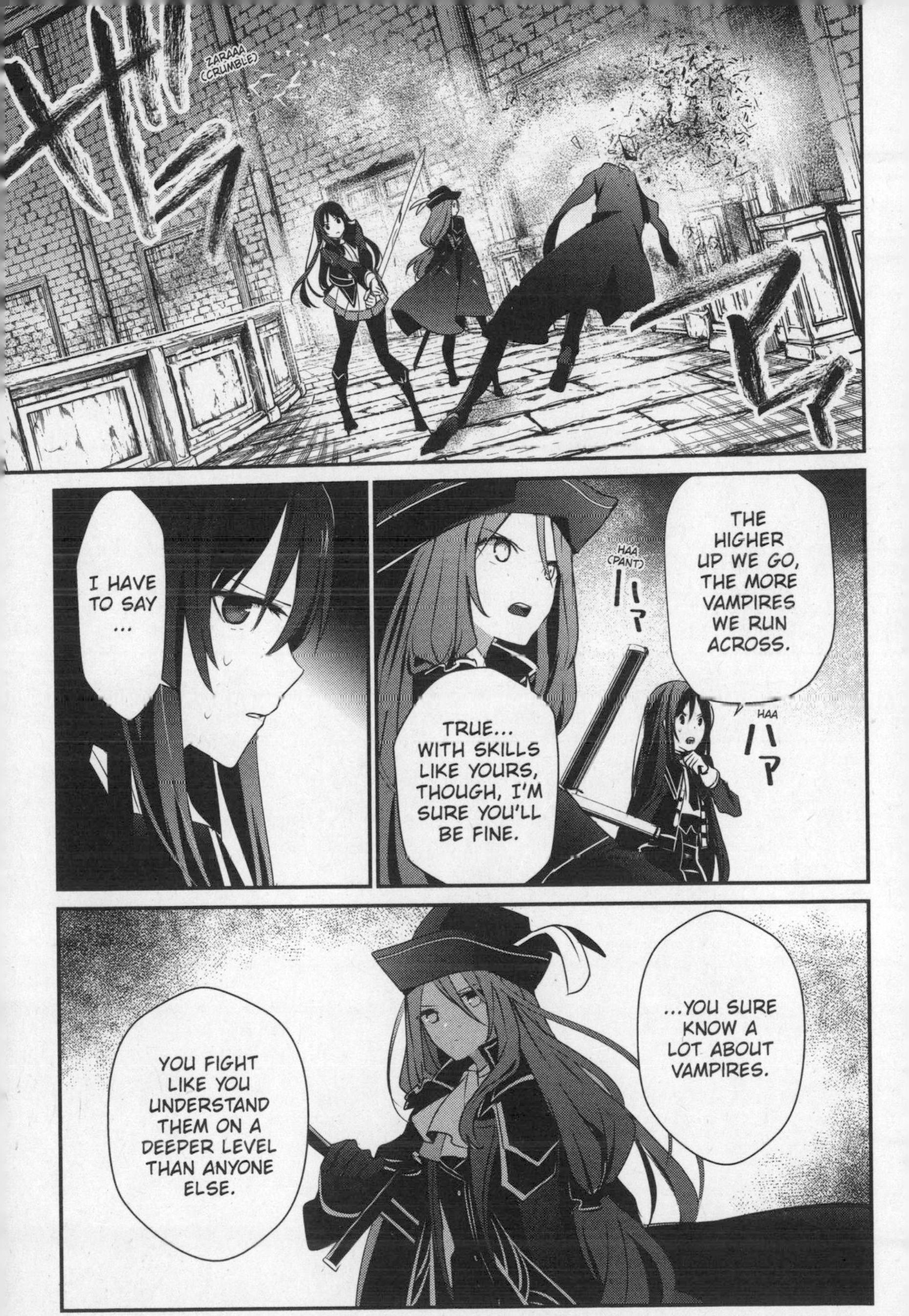
ZARAAA (CRUMBLE)
HAA (PANT)
ハア
THE HIGHER UP WE GO, THE MORE VAMPIRES WE RUN ACROSS.
HAA
ハア
TRUE... WITH SKILLS LIKE YOURS, THOUGH, I'M SURE YOU'LL BE FINE.
I HAVE TO SAY...
...YOU SURE KNOW A LOT ABOUT VAMPIRES.
YOU FIGHT LIKE YOU UNDERSTAND THEM ON A DEEPER LEVEL THAN ANYONE ELSE.

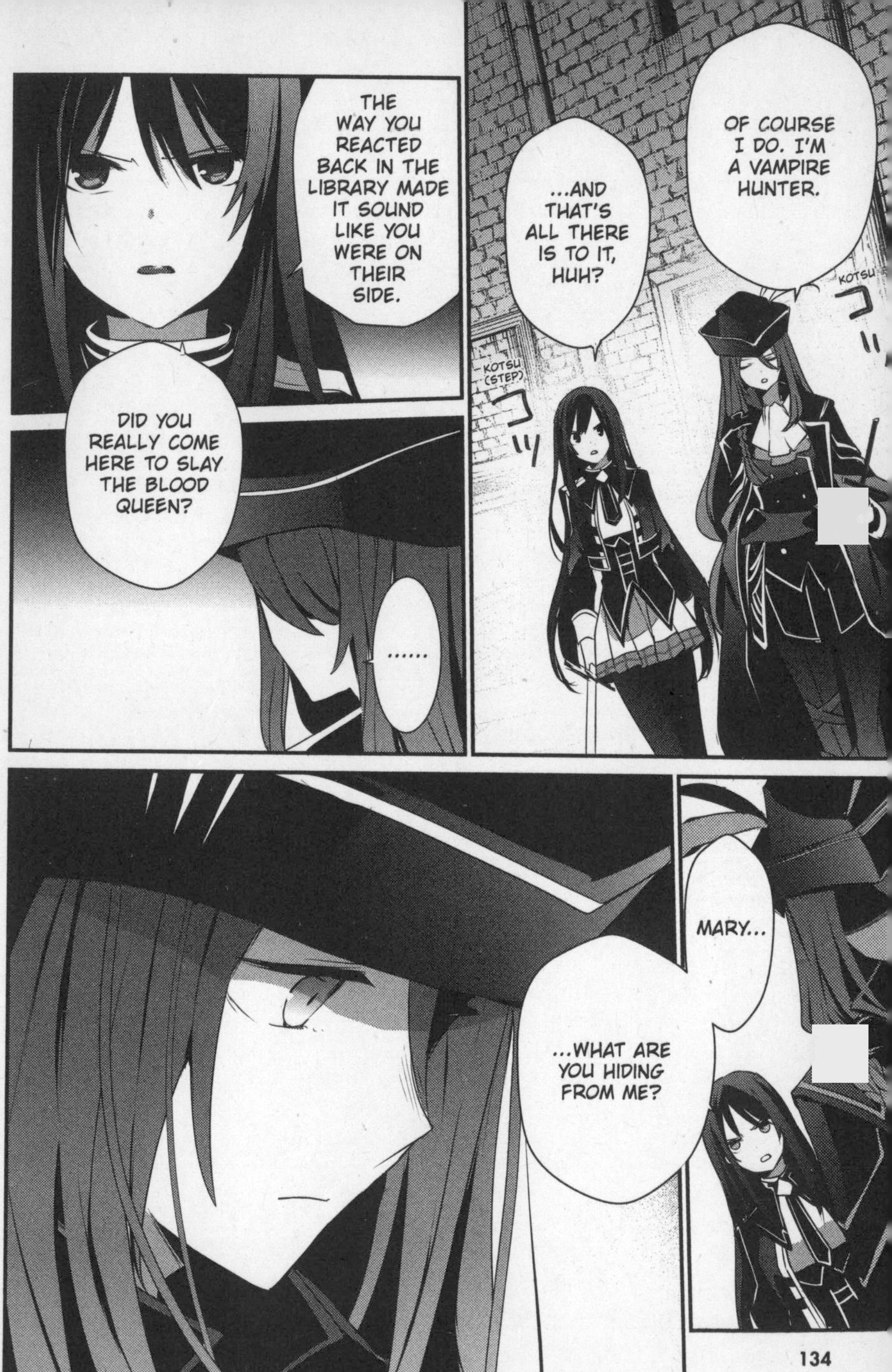
OF COURSE I DO. I'M A VAMPIRE HUNTER.
KOTSU
...AND THAT'S ALL THERE IS TO IT, HUH?
KOTSU (STEP)
THE WAY YOU REACTED BACK IN THE LIBRARY MADE IT SOUND LIKE YOU WERE ON THEIR SIDE.
DID YOU REALLY COME HERE TO SLAY THE BLOOD QUEEN?
......
MARY...
...WHAT ARE YOU HIDING FROM ME?

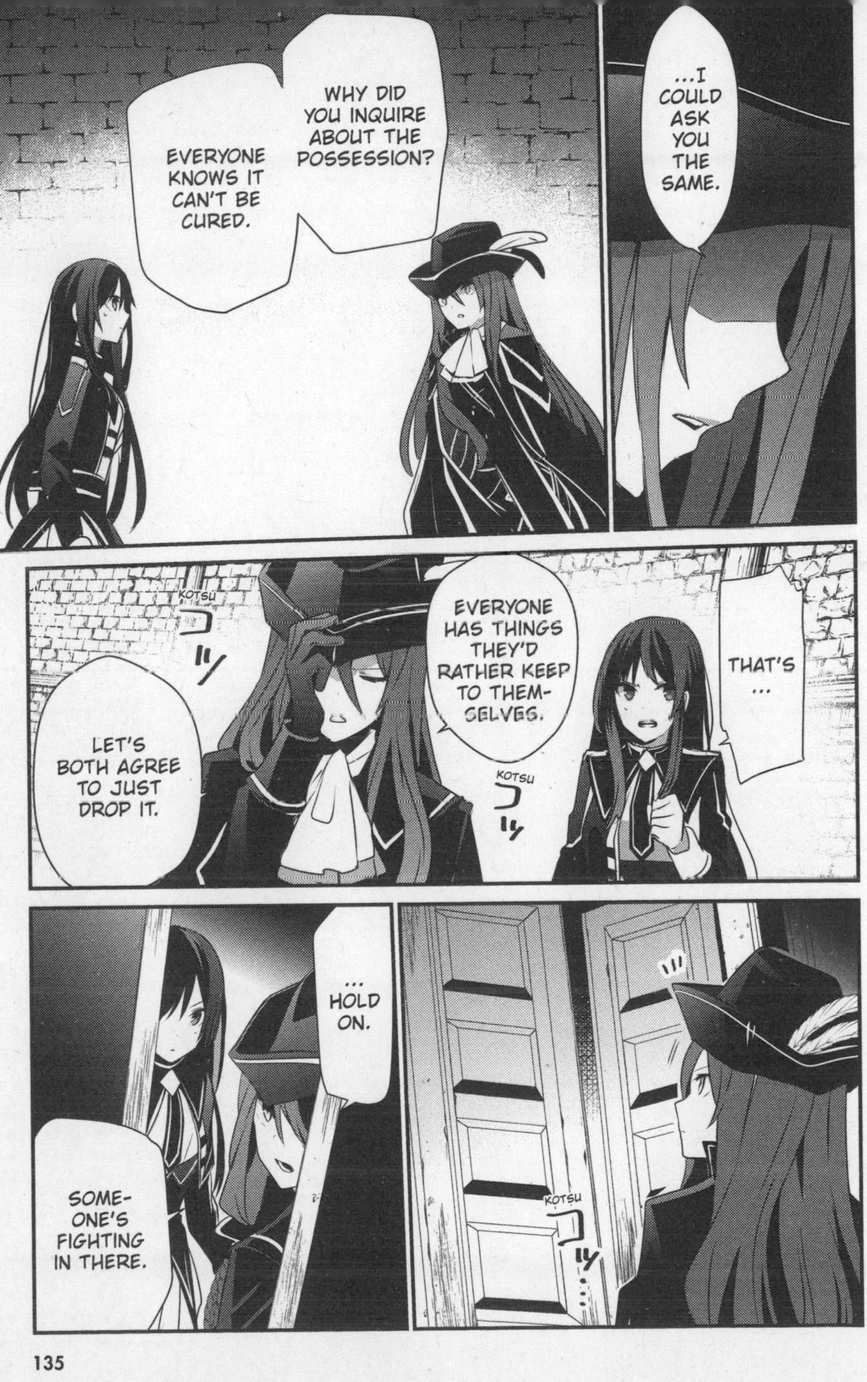
...I COULD ASK YOU THE SAME.
WHY DID YOU INQUIRE ABOUT THE POSSESSION?
EVERYONE KNOWS IT CAN'T BE CURED.
THAT'S ...
EVERYONE HAS THINGS THEY'D RATHER KEEP TO THEM-SELVES.
KOTSU
LET'S BOTH AGREE TO JUST DROP IT.
KOTSU
KOTSU
... HOLD ON.
SOME-ONE'S FIGHTING IN THERE.

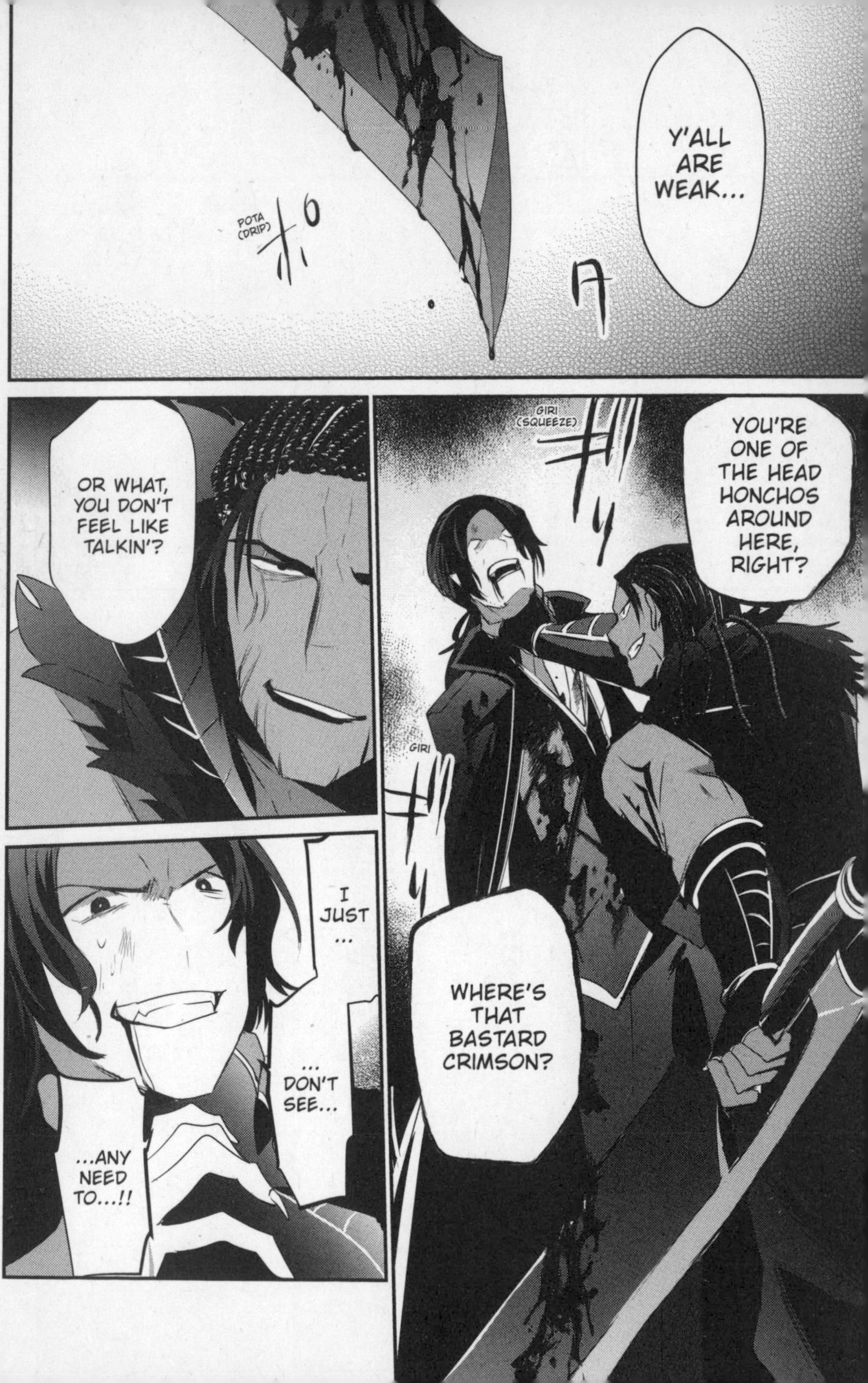
Y'ALL ARE WEAK...
POTA (DRIP)
GIRI (SQUEEZE)
YOU'RE ONE OF THE HEAD HONCHOS AROUND HERE, RIGHT?
GIRI
WHERE'S THAT BASTARD CRIMSON?
OR WHAT, YOU DON'T FEEL LIKE TALKIN'?
I JUST ...
... DON'T SEE...
...ANY NEED TO...!!

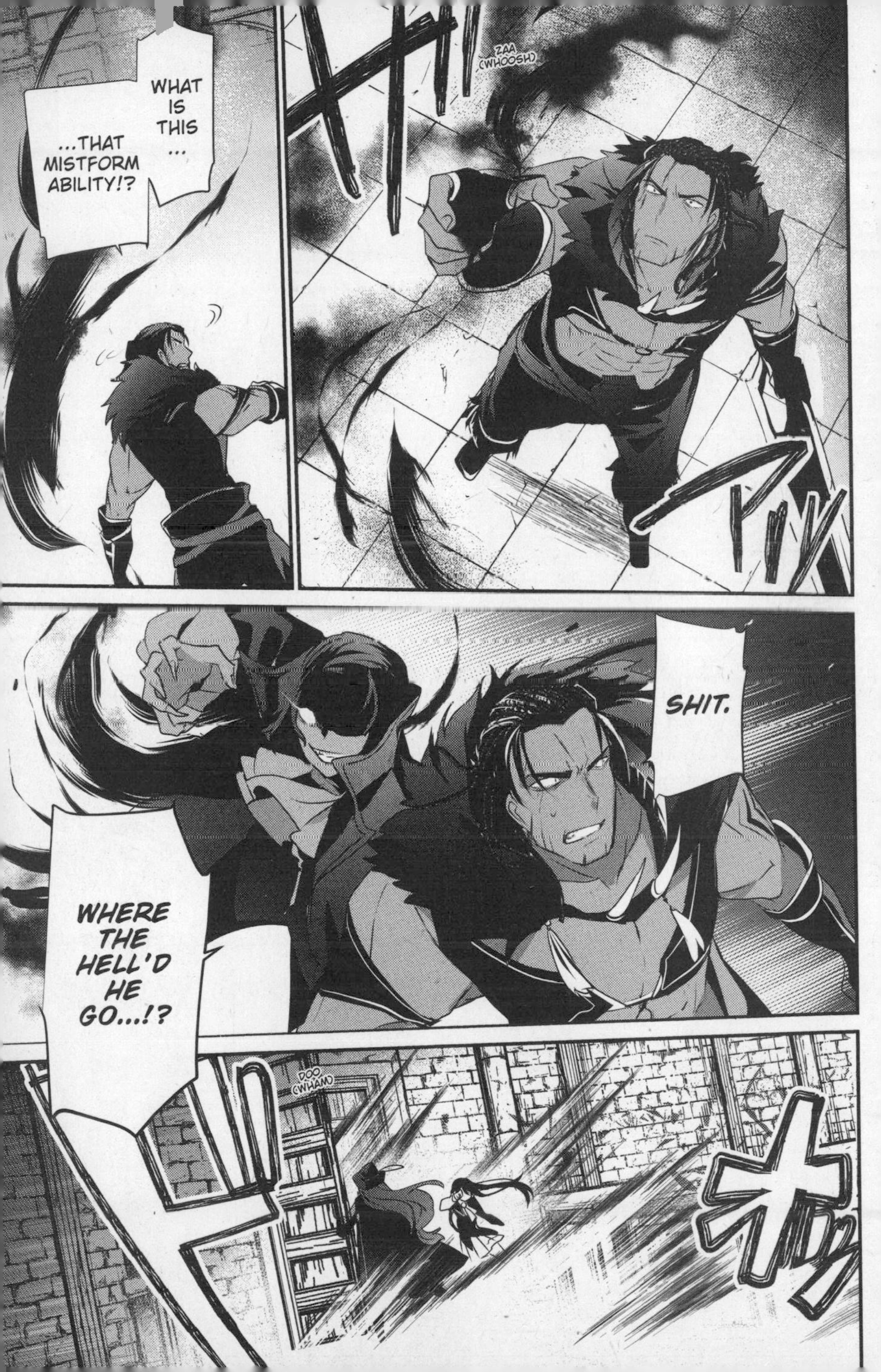
ZAA (WHOOSH)
WHAT IS THIS ... ...THAT MISTFORM ABILITY!?
SHIT.
WHERE THE HELL'D HE GO...!?
DOO (WHAM)

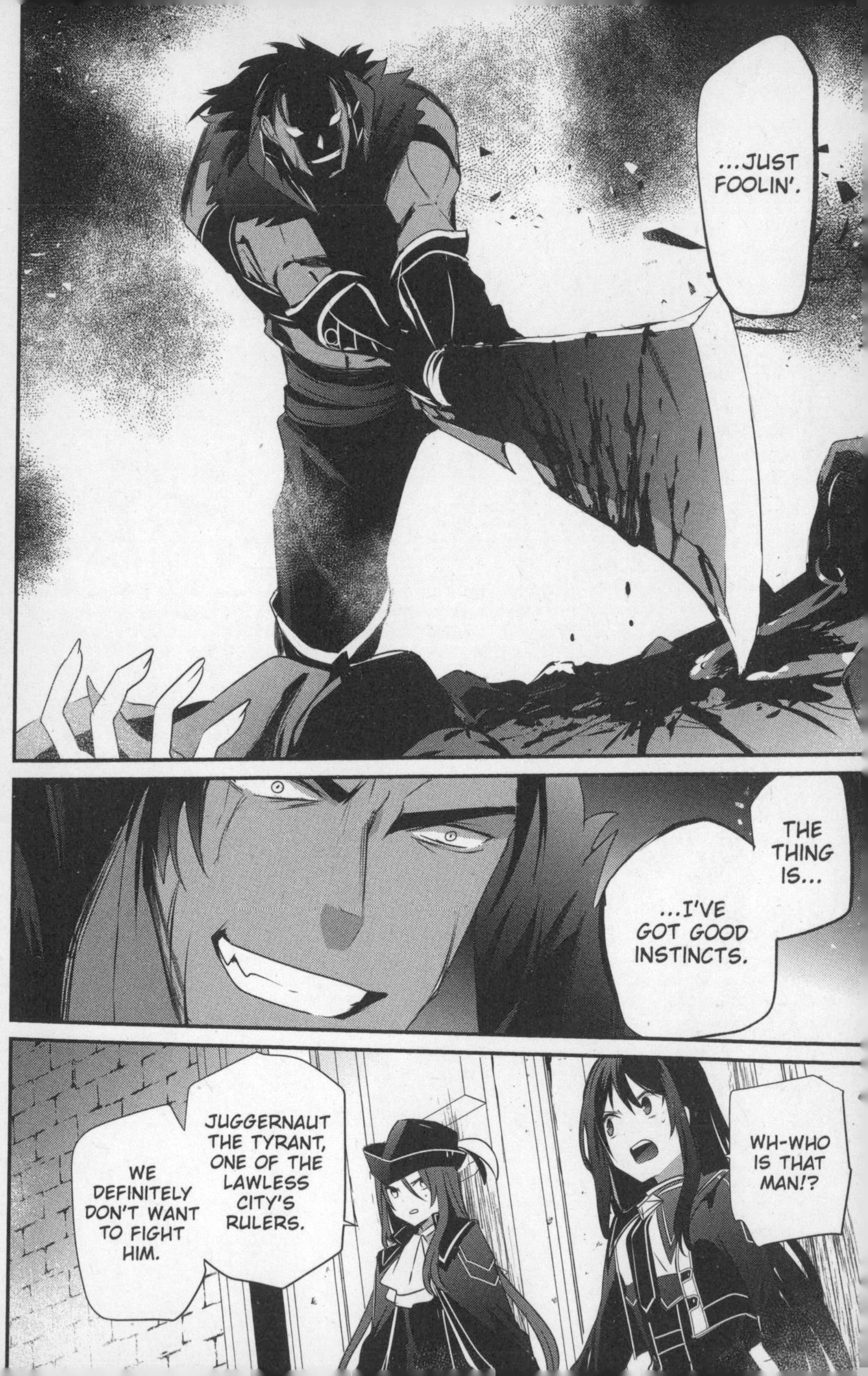
...JUST FOOLIN'.
THE THING IS...
...I'VE GOT GOOD INSTINCTS.
WH-WHO IS THAT MAN!?
JUGGERNAUT THE TYRANT, ONE OF THE LAWLESS CITY'S RULERS.
WE DEFINITELY DON'T WANT TO FIGHT HIM.

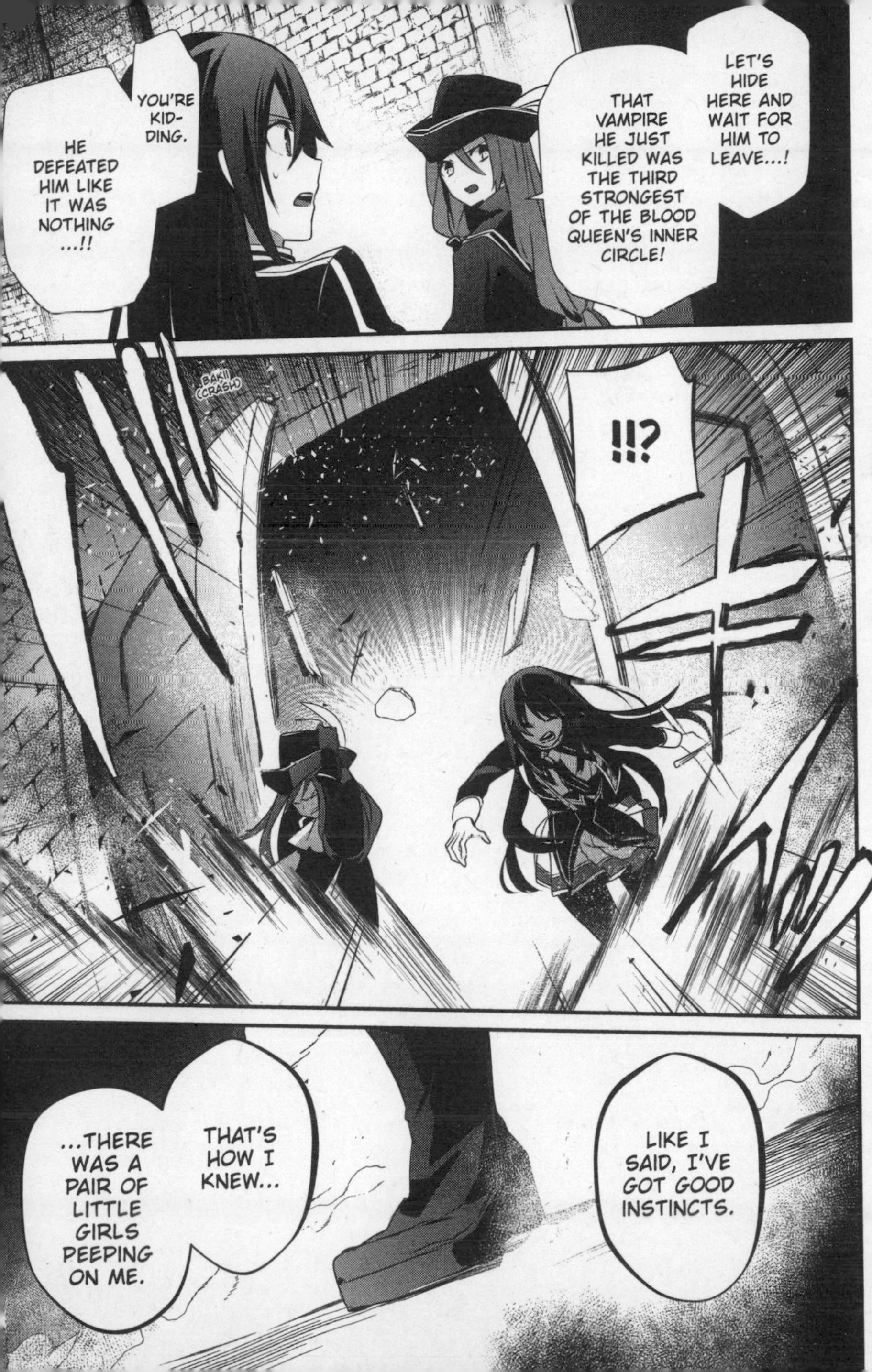
LET'S HIDE HERE AND WAIT FOR HIM TO LEAVE...!
THAT VAMPIRE HE JUST KILLED WAS THE THIRD STRONGEST OF THE BLOOD QUEEN'S INNER CIRCLE!
YOU'RE KID-DING.
HE DEFEATED HIM LIKE IT WAS NOTHING...!!
!!?
BAKI! (CRASH)
LIKE I SAID, I'VE GOT GOOD INSTINCTS.
THAT'S HOW I KNEW...
...THERE WAS A PAIR OF LITTLE GIRLS PEEPING ON ME.

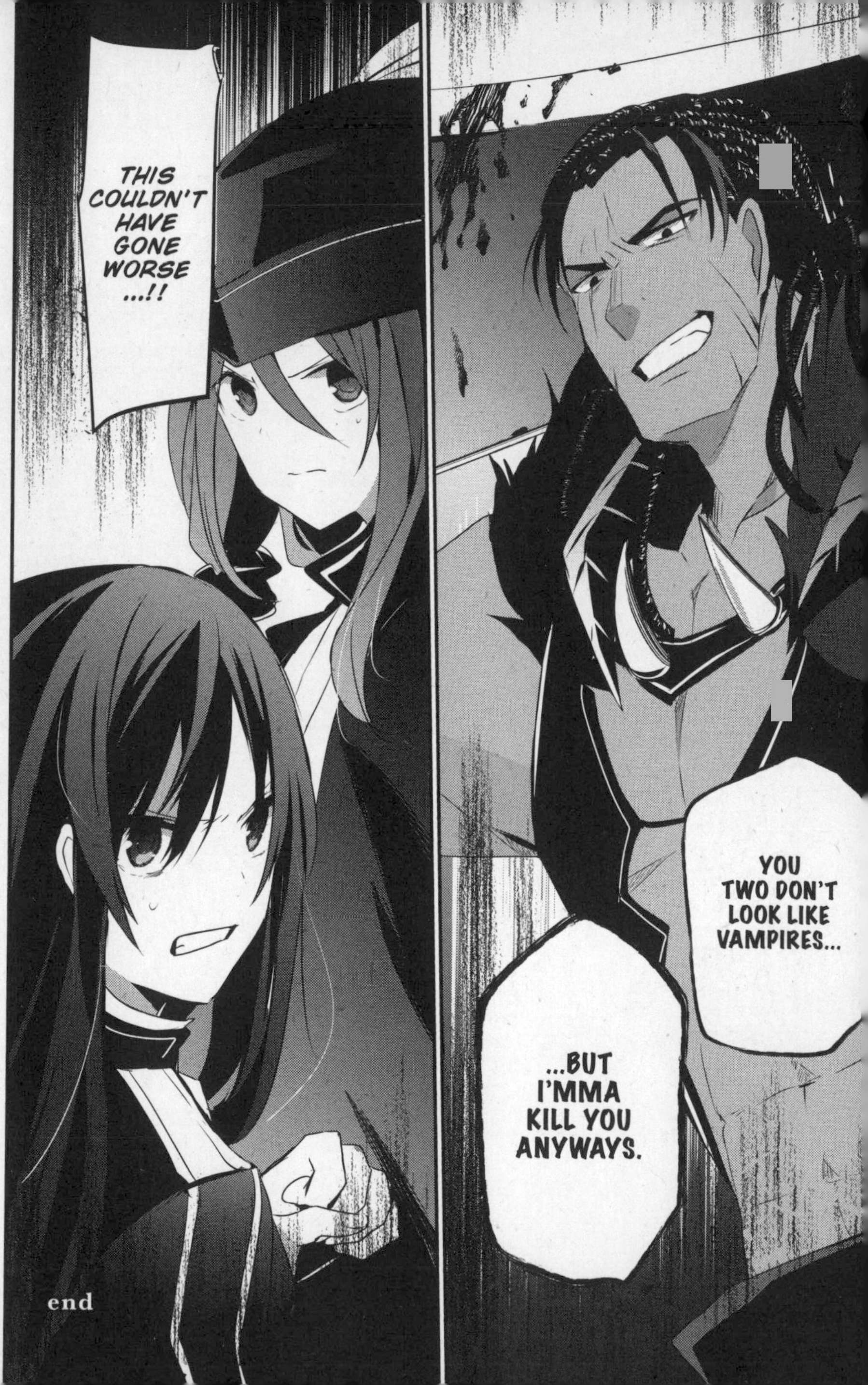
YOU TWO DON'T LOOK LIKE VAMPIRES...
...BUT I'MMA KILL YOU ANYWAYS.
THIS COULDN'T HAVE GONE WORSE ...!!
end

To be continued in *The Eminence in Shadow*, Vol. 8

Art
Anri Sakano

Original Story
Daisuke Aizawa

Character Design
Touzai

The Eminence in Shadow 7

LETTERING: Phil Christie

TRANSLATION: Nathaniel Hiroshi Thrasher

KAGE NO JITSURYOKUSHA
NI NARITAKUTE! Volume 7
©Anri Sakano 2022
©Daisuke Aizawa 2022
©Touzai 2022
First published in Japan in 2022 by
KADOKAWA CORPORATION, Tokyo.
English translation rights arranged
with KADOKAWA CORPORATION, Tokyo
through Tuttle-Mori Agency, Inc., Tokyo.

English translation © 2023 by
Yen Press, LLC

Yen Press
150 West 30th Street
19th Floor
New York, NY 10001

Visit us at yenpress.com
facebook.com/yenpress
twitter.com/yenpress
yenpress.tumblr.com
instagram.com/yenpress

First Yen Press Edition: July 2023
Edited by Yen Press Editorial:
Thomas McAlister, Carl Li
Designed by Yen Press Design:
Madelaine Norman, Wendy Chan

Yen Press is an imprint of
Yen Press, LLC.
The Yen Press name and logo are
trademarks of Yen Press, LLC.

Library of Congress Control Number:
2021935892

ISBNs: 978-1-9753-6295-9 (paperback)
        978-1-9753-6296-6 (ebook)

10 9 8 7 6 5 4 3 2 1

LSC-C

Printed in the United States of America

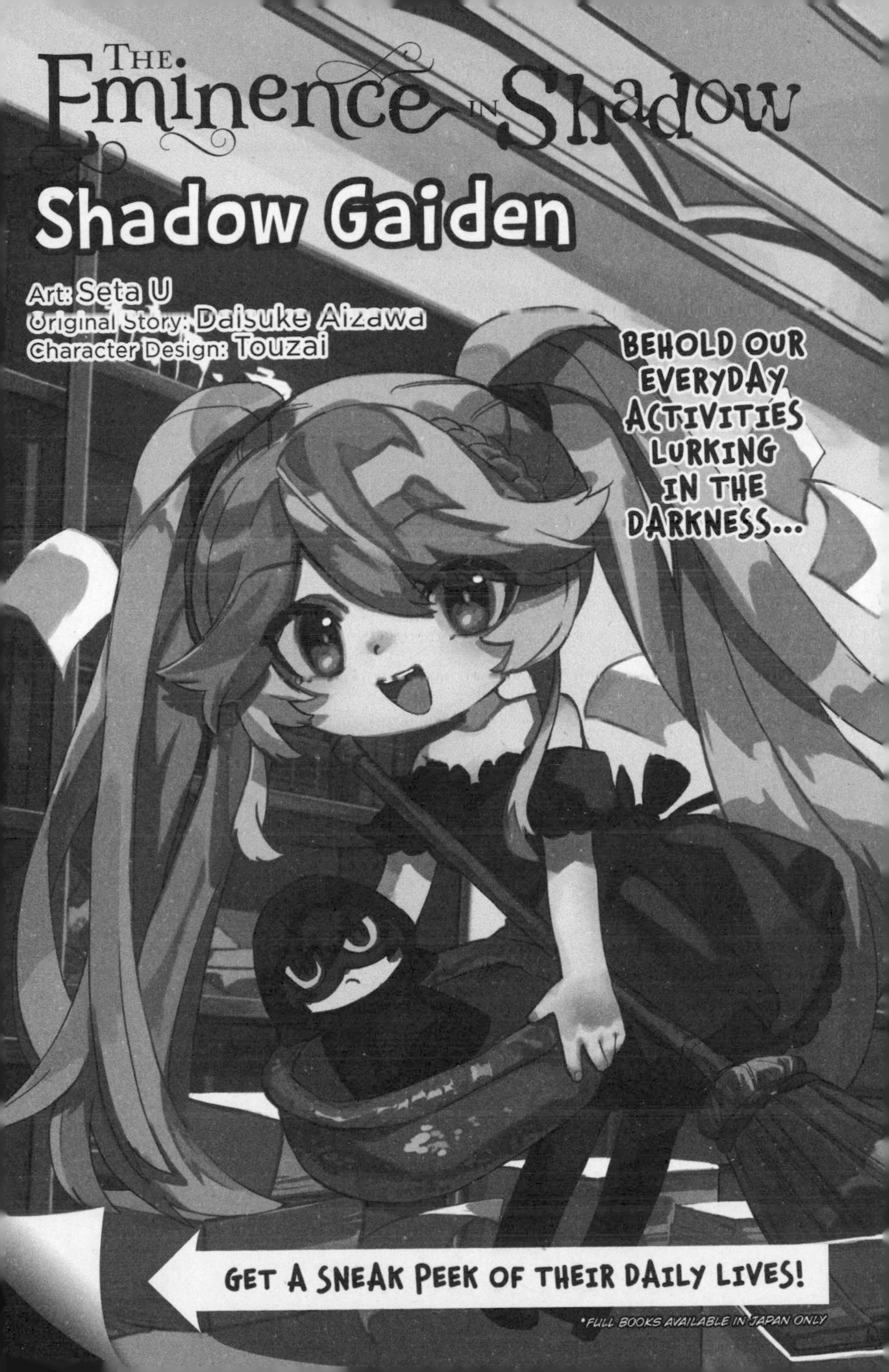
THE Eminence IN Shadow
Shadow Gaiden
Art: Seta U
Original Story: Daisuke Aizawa
Character Design: Touzai
BEHOLD OUR EVERYDAY ACTIVITIES LURKING IN THE DARKNESS...
GET A SNEAK PEEK OF THEIR DAILY LIVES!
*FULL BOOKS AVAILABLE IN JAPAN ONLY

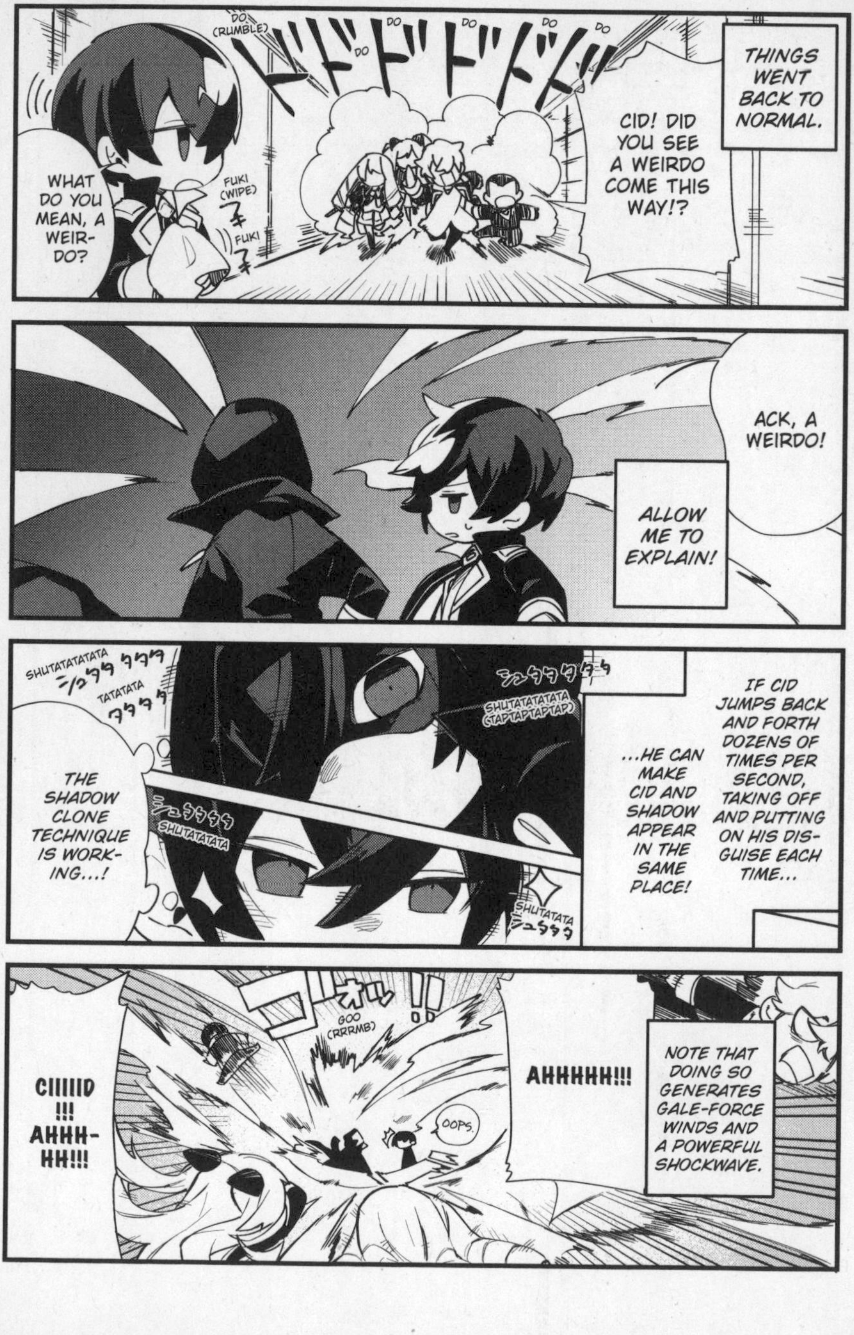
THINGS WENT BACK TO NORMAL.
DO (RUMBLE) DO DO DO DO DO
CID! DID YOU SEE A WEIRDO COME THIS WAY!?
FUKI (WIPE)
FUKI
WHAT DO YOU MEAN, A WEIR-DO?
ACK, A WEIRDO!
ALLOW ME TO EXPLAIN!
IF CID JUMPS BACK AND FORTH DOZENS OF TIMES PER SECOND, TAKING OFF AND PUTTING ON HIS DIS-GUISE EACH TIME...
...HE CAN MAKE CID AND SHADOW APPEAR IN THE SAME PLACE!
SHUTATATATATA (TAPTAPTAPTAP)
SHUTATATATATA
TATATATA
SHUTATATATA
SHUTATATA
THE SHADOW CLONE TECHNIQUE IS WORK-ING...!
NOTE THAT DOING SO GENERATES GALE-FORCE WINDS AND A POWERFUL SHOCKWAVE.
AHHHHH!!!
GOO (RRRMB)
OOPS.
CIIIIID!!! AHHH-HH!!!

HE HAS A FUN TIME EVERY DAY LIKE THIS.